DAILY LIFE IN

Immigrant America, 1870–1920

Recent Titles in
The Greenwood Press "Daily Life Through History" Series

DAILY LIFE IN

Immigrant America, 1870–1920

JUNE GRANATIR ALEXANDER

The Greenwood Press "Daily Life Through History" Series

Daily Life in the United States
Randall Miller, Series Editor

GREENWOOD PRESS
Westport, Connecticut • London

Library of Congress Cataloging-in-Publication Data

Alexander, June Granatir, 1948–
   Daily life in immigrant America, 1870–1920 / June Granatir Alexander.
      p. cm. — (The Greenwood Press "Daily life through history" series, ISSN
1080–4749. Daily life in the United States)
   Includes bibliographical references and index.
   ISBN-13: 978–0–313–33562–4 (alk. paper)
  1. United States—Emigration and immigration—History—19th century.
  2. United States—Emigration and immigration—History—20th century.
  3. Immigrants—United States—Social life and customs—19th century.
  4. Immigrants—United States—Social life and customs—20th century.   I. Title.
  JV6453.A55   2007
  305.9'06912097309034—dc22   2007026800

British Library Cataloguing in Publication Data is available.

Library of Congress Catalog Card Number: 2007026800
ISBN-13: 978–0–313–33562–4
ISSN: 1080–4749

First published in 2007

Greenwood Press, 88 Post Road West, Westport, CT 06881
An imprint of Greenwood Publishing Group, Inc.
www.greenwood.com

Printed in the United States of America

The paper used in this book complies with the
Permanent Paper Standard issued by the National
Information Standards Organization (Z39.48–1984).

10 9 8 7 6 5 4 3 2 1

For John
as always
with love and gratitude

Contents

Series Foreword

The books in the *Daily Life in the United States* series form a subset of Green-wood Press's acclaimed, ongoing *Daily Life Through History* series. They fit its basic framework and follow its format. This series focuses on the United States from the colonial period through the present day, with each book in the series devoted to a particular time period, place, or people. Collectively, the books promise the fullest description and analysis of "American" daily life in print. They do so, and will do so, by tracking closely the contours, character, and content of people's daily life, always with an eye to the sources of people's interests, identities, and institutions. The books in the series assume the perspective and use the approaches of the "new social history" by looking at people "from the bottom up" as well as the top-down. Indian peoples and European colonists, blacks and whites, immigrants and the native-born, farmers and shopkeepers, factory owners and factory hands, movers and shakers and those moved and shaken—all get their due. The books emphasize the habits, rhythms, and dynamics of daily life, from work, to family matters, to religious prac-tices, to socializing, to civic engagement, and more. The books show that the seemingly mundane—such as the ways any people hunt, gather, or grow food and then prepare and eat it—as much as the more profound reflections on life reveal how and why people ordered their world and gave meaning to their lives. The books treat the external factors shaping people's lives--war, migration, disease, drought, flood, pest infestations, fires, earthquakes, hurricanes and tornados, and other natural and man-made disasters that disrupted and even shattered daily lives—but they understand that the everyday concerns and routines of life also power-fully defined any people. The books therefore go inside homes, work-places, schools, churches, meeting halls, stores, and other gathering places to find people on their own terms.

Capturing the daily life of Americans poses unique problems. Americans have been, and are, a people in motion, constantly changing as they move across the land, build new communities, invent new products and pro-cesses, and experiment with everything from making new recipes to mak-ing new governments. A people always in the process of becoming does not stand still for examination of their most private lives. Then, too, dis-covering the daily life of the diverse American peoples requires expertise in many disciplines, for few people have left full-bodied written accounts of their prosaic but necessary daily activities and habits and many people have left no written record at all. Thus, the scholars writing the books in the series necessarily borrow from such fields and resources as archae-ology, anthropology, art, folklore, language, music, and material culture. Getting hold of the daily life in the United States demands no less.

Each book at once provides a narrative history and analysis of daily life, set in the context of broad historical patterns. Each book includes illustra-tions, documents, a chronology, and a bibliography. Thereby, each book invites many uses as a resource, a touchstone for discussion, a reference, and an encouragement to further reading and research. The titles in the series also promise a long shelf life because the authors draw on the latest and best scholarship and because the books are included in Greenwood's Daily Life Online, which allows for enhanced searching, updated content, more illustrative material, teacher lesson plans, and other Web features. In sum, the *Daily Life in the United States* series seeks to bring the American people to life.

Randall Miller

Acknowledgments

Writing this volume was at once an exhilarating and humbling experience. As I sought and drew together material for the book, I could not help but be thrilled by the rich literature on immigrant-related topics. The immense outpouring of published works that has occurred during the past half century is especially gratifying to scholars committed to the study of migration and the immigrant experience. I am greatly indebted to the hundreds of scholars who have used their language skills, innovative methodologies, and analytical prowess not only to document the history of individual groups but also to add new dimensions to our understanding of the immigrant experience. The historical synthesis that I have produced here is beholden to their efforts. And it is with humility and gratitude that I acknowledge that this volume in the *Daily Life Through History* series is grounded in the fine research of so many others. It is to the community of immigration scholars, therefore, that I owe a tremendous intellectual debt.

Although several individuals offered encouragement and advice, I wish to acknowledge a special few who assisted with the writing and actual production of this book. I want to thank Randall Miller, who, as editor for the *Daily Life in the United States* series, invited me to write this particular volume. Randall carefully read the manuscript and offered helpful comments and suggestions. The people at Greenwood Press have been wonderful. As history editor, Michael Hermann oversaw the initial stages of this project. His enthusiasm and positive assessment of early chapters were heartening. Both Mariah Gumpert, who subsequently became the in-house editorial contact for the Daily Life in the United States series, and Bridget Austiguy-Preschel, who supervised the production of the book for Greenwood, demonstrated remarkable patience, support, and professionalism as we worked through the sometimes difficult aspects of producing this volume. It was a pleasure to work with them.

I am pleased with the illustrations in this work, but I can take credit neither for their quality nor for procuring most of them. As he did for another book project, with painstaking care, Jay Yocis, production manager of University Relations at the University of Cincinnati, skillfully produced digital images from original newspapers, magazines, and posters supplied by the author. Using Adobe Photoshop, Ashley Kempher, photography assistant at the University of Cincinnati Photo Services, downloaded images from Web sites and made digital image corrections and restorations at the author's request. As he has done for past projects, John K. Alexander enthusiastically served as my technical advisor and "production manager." He was indefatigable in the search for appropriate illustrations. With amazing tenacity, he efficiently handled the meticulous details of actually obtaining pictorial materials for inclusion. But while this volume benefited from John's sharp eye and tenacity as "production manager," it benefited far more from his willingness to serve as my first reader. Once again, I relied heavily on the perceptive criticism and valuable advice of this extraordinarily knowledgeable historian. John was extremely generous with his time, even when critiquing drafts of my manuscript plainly intruded on his own scholarly work. His backing of my scholarly endeavors, though, goes well beyond this single undertaking. For more than three decades, John's selflessness and support have greatly enhanced the life we share together. Thus, to John, who has given me so much, I dedicate this book.

Chronology

1875	First federal law restricting immigration: banned coolie labor; denied entry to convicts and prostitutes
	Refrigerated freight cars patented
1876	Telephone patented Hay loader invented
1877	Widespread railroad strike paralyzes major transportation networks
1878	New York opens first elevated train
	Anti-Chinese riots in San Francisco
	Twine binder introduced
1879	Incandescent lighting for home use perfected
1880s	Minnesota's Mesabi Range opened to iron-ore mining
	Threshing machines improved by steam power and addition of blowers
1880	All-purpose house paint manufactured by Sherwin-Williams Company
1882	Chinese Exclusion Act restricts entry of laborers for 10 years
	Immigration law excludes convicts, lunatics, idiots, and paupers
	Steam turbine patented
	Standard Oil Trust created
1882–1883	Transcontinental railroad routes of Santa Fe, Southern Pacific, and Northern Pacific completed
1885	Alien Contract Labor Act bars employers from importing alien laborers
1885–1887	Drought and severe winters on the Great Plains
1886	Chinese driven from homes in anti-Chinese riots in Seattle, Washington
	Statue of Liberty dedicated
	Bombing in Haymarket Square (Chicago) blamed on anarchists
	American Federation of Labor formed
1887	American Protective Association organized
	Trolley cars developed
	Agricultural prices fall drastically
1889	Land in Oklahoma (previously "Indian Territory") opened to settlement

1890	Jacob Riis's exposé *How the Other Half Lives* published
	United Mine Workers of America founded
1891	Legislation expands the list of inadmissible immigrants
	New York's Castle Garden closed; immigrants processed at Barge Office at the Battery
	Position of superintendent of immigration created
	Eleven Italian immigrants lynched in New Orleans
1892	Ellis Island opened
	Chinese Exclusion Act extended for 10 years
	Violent strike at Carnegie steelworks in Homestead, Pennsylvania
1893–1897	Severe economic depression
1893	Great Northern Railroad completed
	Anti-Chinese riots in California
1894	Riots break out during miners' strike in Pennsylvania's anthracite coal region
	Bureau of Immigration established
	Pullman strike in Chicago ignites nationwide boycott of railroads
	Immigration Restriction League formed
1895	First subway opened in Boston
	U.S. superintendent of immigration changed to commissioner general of immigration
1896	Wireless telegraph patented
	Plessy v. Ferguson upholds "separate but equal" principle for racial segregation
	"New immigrant" arrivals surpass number of "old immigrant" arrivals
1897	President Grover Cleveland vetoes legislation requiring literacy test for entering adult immigrants
	Ellis Island main building destroyed by fire; site closed as receiving station and immigrants entering through New York again processed at Barge Office
	"Lattimer Massacre" in northeastern Pennsylvania
1898	Spanish-American War
	Annexation of Hawaiian Islands
1899	Senate approves treaty transferring Philippines, Puerto Rico, and Guam to the United States

Philippine revolt against U.S. annexation gets under way

Hull House opens in Chicago

1900   Carnegie Steel Company incorporated

Ellis Island reopens

International Ladies Garment Workers Union formed

1901   President William McKinley assassinated by Leon Czolgosz, a Polish anarchist

Vice-President Theodore Roosevelt assumes the presidency

Sale of Carnegie Steel Companies results in creation of U.S. Steel Corporation

1902   Massive strike in anthracite coal industry

United States finally squelches revolt in the Philippines

Chinese Exclusion Act made permanent

1903   Congress passes law making anarchism grounds for deportation

Anarchists, polygamists, and radicals added to list of inadmissible immigrants

Ford Motor Company founded

1904   Strikes in Massachusetts's textile mills

National Child Labor Committee created to counter child labor abuses

Robert Hunter's *Poverty* published

1905   Industrial Workers of the World (IWW) formed

1906   San Francisco earthquake

Ability to speak English made requirement for naturalization

Bureau of Immigration and Naturalization established

Upton Sinclair's exposé *The Jungle* published

John Spargo's exposé *The Bitter Cry of the Children* published

Meat Inspection Act passed

Pure Food and Drug Act passed

1907   List of inadmissible immigrants expanded; stricter provisions for administration of immigration and deportation

Law enacted to revoke the U.S. citizenship of women who marry noncitizens

	Immigration peaks with more than 1.2 million arrivals
	Congressional commission on immigration established
	Gentlemen's Agreement with Japan to reduce emigration
1907–1910	Financial panic followed by three-year recession
	Congressional commission surveys immigration and immigrant life
1908	*Muller v. Oregon* upholds ten-hour day for female workers
	Congressional legislation passes to regulate child labor in District of Columbia
	Henry Ford introduces the Model T
1910	Angel Island immigrant depot opened
1911	Triangle Shirtwaist Company fire
	Commission on Immigration report published (known as Dillingham Report)
1912	Strikes in textile mills of Lawrence, Massachusetts
	Progressive (Bull Moose) Party launched; Theodore Roosevelt runs for president on its social reform platform
	Woodrow Wilson elected president
1913	California law passed preventing Japanese from owning land
	Assembly lines introduced into Ford automobile factories
1914	War breaks out in Europe
1915	Five Dollar Day Plan introduced by Henry Ford
	First nationwide Americanization Day
	National Americanization Committee organized
	Beginning of German submarine warfare
	German U-boat sinks British passenger ship *Lusitania*; 128 Americans killed
	Assembly line introduced at Ford's Highland Park, Michigan, plant
	President Woodrow Wilson vetoes legislation requiring literacy test for entering adult immigrants
1916	Keating-Owen Act bars items made by child labor from interstate commerce
1917	United States enters World War I
	Committee on Public Information created

Selective Service Act passed

First Liberty Loan drive launched

Espionage Act enacted

Law requiring literacy test for entering immigrants passed over Wilson's veto

Asian Barred Zone established

Bolshevik Revolution in Russia

Residents of Puerto Rico granted U.S. citizenship

1918 Wilson's "fourteen point" war aims; espouses principle of self-determination

Sedition Act enacted

Influenza epidemic kills millions worldwide

Armistice (November 11) ends World War I

1919 Peace Conference opens at Versailles (France)

Treaty of Versailles ending World War I negotiated

U.S. Senate rejects Treaty of Versailles

Labor strikes in industries nationwide

Boston police strike

Great Steel strike

Bomb attempts directed at prominent figures

Suspected so-called foreign radicals rounded up

Buford sets sail with 249 aliens deported to Russia

1920 Red Scare ends

Economic recession

Nineteenth Amendment ratified (women's suffrage)

1921 Congress establishes nationality-based quotas and imposes numerical restrictions on European immigration

Introduction: Getting a Perspective on Immigrant Daily Life

In 1870, Gustaf and Ida Lindgren took their five children and left Sweden. After several years of bad crops, these tenant farmers joined a small group of family and friends who had decided America offered a better chance to continue their rural way of life. A couple of years afterward, Angelus Viebrock and his wife migrated from northwestern Germany to Illinois. Their rented farm became the first destination for his in-laws, the Wittens, who departed a decade later. Young Johann and Rebecka, who were expecting their first child, stayed in Illinois before moving on to take up farming in Nebraska. At about the same time the Wittens were planning to leave Germany, Lee Chew and five other males from a village in Canton were booking passage on a ship bound from Hong Kong to San Francisco. Seeing a once-poor man return to China with "unlimited wealth" inspired young Chew and "filled" his "mind with the idea" that he, too, could make good by going to America. He worked two years as a house servant before opening a laundry. Even as he saved to start his own business in the United States, he sent money to his parents back home. In 1892, when Annie Moore chose to leave her homeland, this young Irish woman had no way of knowing that she would become the first immigrant to pass through Ellis Island. Her goal was to improve her future, not attain a symbolic place in history.

In the decades that followed, the promise of America attracted millions from lands outside its borders. Offering a description of what was happening in her area in the early 1900s, a schoolteacher in Croatia reported, "The talk is all of America." She heard tell, "Fifteen are going from our village tomorrow—men, women and young girls are on their way to America." News had also spread, however, that a woman who had gone years earlier and married would return that day with her husband and six children. With the $6,000 they had saved, the returning couple planned to purchase "a large meadow" near the village and raise their children there. Over the years, emigration had had a strong impact on the area. In the 1880s, two men had departed for the United States, and "now nearly half the village is there," the schoolteacher guessed. It appeared that "whoever has the strength and youth is at work in America." On a stroll through her village, which could have been any one of thousands of places throughout the world, a person could see the impact of what contemporaries called "America fever." There were heartbreaking ramifications. One encountered women who had not recently heard from husbands who had gone away to work. They were being accused of having forgotten about wives and children who were waiting for money the men had pledged to send. There were the mixed emotions of the parents whose younger son had returned from America but whose elder brother, so far, had not come back to his family. Had these people forgotten their families or had some tragedy befallen them? There were also people paying off debts and purchasing goods with money that loved ones in America had sent. There were untold instances of happiness replacing loneliness. The joy that one young migrant in America felt when he received a picture of his wife and child was surpassed only by the joy of having them join him two months later. Such personal ties shed light on thoughts that lurked in the minds and influenced the lifestyles of many who departed for the United States. In fundamental ways, responsibilities to those left behind or a desire to return to their lands of birth not only affected decisions migrants made but also how they fashioned their lives in America.

Taken together, the Lindgrens, Viebrocks, Wittens, Lee Chew, Annie Moore, and the many people leaving the teacher's village add flesh and emotions to often bare-bones statistics of immigration. They reflected the "migration mentality" that throughout human history emboldened people to go to lands outside their own. It was a mentality characterized by people's willingness to take decisive measures to achieve practical goals. If demographers' estimates are correct, more people made that decision in the late nineteenth and early twentieth centuries than during any previous era of human history. Although millions of migrants went to other destinations, this book focuses on those who chose the United States. Similar to the people whose stories introduced this volume, rarely did individuals make their decisions in desperation and seldom did they simply get caught up in an epidemic of "America fever." Migration was typically the result of a levelheaded choice selected from among several options. It is worth noting that far more people opted to stay at home than to emigrate. Whether individuals realized it—and most probably did—setting out for the United States was just the first of many major decisions they would wrestle with. For, regardless of where they came from, migrants were joining millions of others who, like them, would have to deal with the realities of American society while weighing how best to achieve their objectives.

This volume makes no pretense of offering bold new interpretations; it aims, instead, to take readers back to one of the most dynamic periods of migration history. It attempts to illuminate the reality of the immigrant experience by examining what life was like for the millions who believed that, in one way or another, America held the promise of a better life. In chapter 1, readers will encounter the raw data of immigration in the period spanning 1870 to 1920. The chapter does not include every single immigrant group that came during the period, for that is the stuff of a lengthy volume dedicated to migration. This study is less about the origins and number of immigrants who set out for America than about their experience once in the country. Still, readers need an appreciation of the volume, diversity, and basic characteristics of the migratory waves that brought millions of people to the United States. The chapter strives to convey the dynamic nature of the immigration of that era. Readers who watch closely will be impressed by how new migratory streams kept starting up and flowing into or redirecting the countless crosscurrents in the flood of people coming into and going out of the United States. Chapters 2 through 6 are devoted to trying to re-create what day-to-day life was like for ordinary immigrants. One must bear in mind throughout that, as immigrants went about their daily lives, the migratory streams continued and kept bringing more and more people into their midst.

The scope of this work is limited by what can reasonably be treated in a single volume. Because this book deals primarily with the period from 1870 to 1920, when the overwhelming majority of migrants hailed from Europe, it will unavoidably dwell on migrations from that continent. It also tries to incorporate Chinese and Japanese immigrants, whose movement into the United States occurred during this time. Although the initial stages of what would be a large influx from Mexico and a smaller one from the Caribbean region also started in this period, their movements merit a separate volume that can sensitively explore the intricate dimensions of their experiences in America.

Before investigating the complexities of immigrant life, it is necessary first to address some general misconceptions and oversimplifications about the " immigrant experience." Individuals approaching the subject of immigration and immigrant life need to be aware of preconceived notions they might bring to the undertaking. While particularly momentous events and eras seemingly have an uncanny power to cast some sort of spell that distorts the past, the history of immigration has been especially bewitching. Indeed, scholars often refer to "myths" that perpetuate a false understanding of America's immigrant past and undermine the ability to come to grips with the immigrant experience. History at its best, though, not only illuminates the past, it also helps later generations better understand their present society and serves as a guide to help them grapple with nettlesome issues. Although this book explores the lives of ordinary people who came to the United States a century ago and longer, it can help put current immigration issues in historical perspective. As Americans of the early twenty-first century engage in heated, often divisive debates over immigration and its impact on their society, acquiring a deeper, more accurate knowledge of immigrant life in times gone by can help them gain a more realistic understanding of immigration in the present.

Many, although not all, of the mythical aspects of immigration history arise from America's much touted image as a "nation of immigrants." Scholars are particularly fond of pointing out that the United States was neither the sole destination nor the only country to accept large numbers of foreign-born peoples. In the Western Hemisphere alone, Argentina, Canada, and Brazil attracted multitudes from distant lands. Yet Americans seem unique in the way they embrace immigration not only as part of their history but also of their national identity. The country's image also obscures the fact that the United States did not always welcome immigrants. Earlier immigrants and their descendants were routinely hostile to groups that came later. Although they encountered hostility in different ways and to different degrees, no ethnic group escaped the sting of prejudice, contempt, and discrimination. Often referring to the "immigration problem," settled Americans typically accused newcomers of taking jobs from those already here, depressing wages, and draining the country of its resources. They further alleged that later nationalities were ruining the quality of life in America by, for example, destroying neighborhoods and causing social disorder. Immigrants who had distinguishing physical characteristics—specifically, people of color—encountered particularly fierce animosity. Besides harsh treatment at the hands of local residents, hatred toward Asians—especially the Chinese—led to the enactment of discriminatory laws.

Americans considered immigrants from southern and eastern Europe, who dominated the movement into the United States from the 1890s onward, as especially "undesirable." Rather than seeing these "new immigrants" as benefiting and enriching American society, contemporaries accused these newer groups of harming and detracting from it. Yes, immigrants had their sympathizers and even advocates; nevertheless, the immigrant or immigration "problem" was a catchphrase of the day. Ironically, the contempt for newcomers as well as the tendency to treat contemporary immigration as a problem rested on the ill-founded assertions that previous immigrants were both superior to and different from those now arriving. When people at the turn of the twentieth century cast approving glances back to earlier migrations and their ancestors' experience, they did so through eyes that shaded out what President Grover Cleveland knew to be a fact. "It is said," he observed in 1897, "that the quality of recent immigration is undesirable. The time is quite within recent memory when the same thing was said of immigrants who, with their descendants, are now numbered among our best citizens."

This, then, is a history about people living in an often hostile environment. It is not, however, the story of helpless victims. The picture of daily life that emerges is a complicated one of people assessing situations, making decisions, and maintaining control over their lives. While hostility toward them was a reality of life for immigrants, it is not one that should be unduly dwelled upon. In the story that unfolds here, animosity toward the foreign born serves as a backdrop as well as a constant undercurrent that surfaced at times and intruded harshly on peoples' lives. Readers will confront immigrants not as "foreigners," as members of an ethnic group, as heroic individuals, as the "downtrodden," or as "problems" but rather as ordinary people living complex lives.

Popular accounts of the "immigrant saga," as it is sometimes called, have traditionally portrayed immigrants as coming, settling down, working hard, and staying in the United States. Indeed, in oft-romanticized versions, immigrants are portrayed as individuals and families that set down roots and proceeded to struggle against huge odds to lift themselves out of poverty. The mobile aspects of their lives are often overlooked or altogether lost. In recent decades, historians have demonstrated that like modern-day migrations, the turn-of-the-twentieth-century waves carried highly mobile people. As this investigation of day-to-day life from year to year reveals, mobility took different forms. First, many permanent immigrants made one or more successive moves within the United States; second, the initial decision to remain in America was not irreversible. After 11 years, the Lindgrens and four of their five children returned to Sweden. Others came with no intention of staying. Indeed, countless numbers arriving from places like the schoolteacher's Croatian village were not permanent immigrants but, instead, migrant laborers seeking temporary employment. For many immigrants, America was simply a place to work and make money so they could have a better life somewhere else.

To grasp the many-sided dimensions of immigrant life, one must pay close attention to what life was like for temporary migrants, married men on their own, and individuals who moved about the country. The story was often as much about "migrant life" as about people who put down permanent roots. The fact that many individuals viewed their situation as temporary influenced where and how they chose to live. Readers will see that, in important ways, temporary migrants differed from those who had decided they had a definite future in America; yet, as will become apparent in the following pages, the lives of temporary and permanent migrants were closely intertwined.

In recent decades, historians have delved into the past and provided a much fuller understanding of the permanent immigrants, transients, and migrant labors who made up the massive migratory waves of the pre–World War I era. Indeed, the years since the 1960s have witnessed an unprecedented outpouring of scholarly studies. By taking fresh approaches to the study of immigration history, scholars have shifted from timeworn themes that highlighted illustrious personages or "contributions" to ones that emphasize ordinary people. Fueled in large measure by the idea that each group has a right to its own history, the scholarship on immigration has increased by leaps and bounds. These scholarly studies offer a complex, sometimes confusing, and even contradictory picture of immigrant and ethnic life in America. But what they make clear is that not all immigrants were alike. In fact, the diversity of America's immigrant population has historically been more striking than its numerical size. And it is this diversity that presents a particularly tricky challenge to anyone seeking to portray the experience of ordinary immigrants.

Immigrants and ethnic groups differed in dramatic ways. Besides obviously distinctive languages and histories, each immigrant group had its own set of values, cultural traditions, and ways of life. In terms of lifestyles, these characteristics might be manifested in the groups' distinctive marital relationships, occupational choices, child-rearing practices, educational patterns, foods, festive traditions, and other folkways. For some nationalities, religion was a distinguishing feature and an essential aspect of their ethnic identity. There were also wide variations within the same nationality. Religion, gender, social class, and conflicting ideologies represented some of the major internal differences. Each immigrant group also contained a broad range of ages and included persons at different stages in their family cycle. There were people who had completed their families, those with young children or adolescents, and those just starting their families.

Because culture played such an influential role, scholars caution against making generalizations about immigrants in America. They warn that fusing the experiences of such divergent groups distorts history and, furthermore, demeans the richly diverse nature of the immigrant experience. In undertaking the study of immigrant daily life, neither historians nor readers should take these cautions lightly. At the same time, because immigrants faced similar circumstances, there is a common story to be told. So this work will necessarily make generalizations. Its portrayal of everyday life, though, strives to highlight the common elements of their experiences while not ignoring the unique. Differences will be emphasized when they shed light that will provide a more complete picture; however, in drawing together material for this volume, the goal was to present representative illustrations that would convey the reality of everyday life for the broadest range of immigrants. For their part, readers must be ever mindful that profound differences existed among America's immigrants and that individual experiences varied. Moreover, one must bear in mind that even members of the same ethnic group deviated from what was considered the common pattern for their group. In short, many people simply did not fit into any pattern. Readers interested in delving into the history of specific groups should consult the bibliography that accompanies this volume. It contains a selected list of readings that the author hopes will satisfy readers' initial curiosity while whetting their intellectual appetites for more and directing them to a remarkably rich trove of historical literature on immigration and ethnic groups.

Despite the tremendous diversity of the peoples whose lives are portrayed in this volume, a basic theme united their experience. Immigrants adjusted to American society, but it was an ongoing adjustment that blended past traditions, present realities, and future goals. This was a central theme of immigrant life and the underlying point of this book. While ongoing adjustment is a principal theme, it is nevertheless an enormously complicated one. It is grounded in the fact that immigrants' own cultures were significant factors influencing life in America. Instead of shedding their cultures, immigrants drew on them in their struggle to adjust to new circumstances in a foreign land.

By examining how immigrants lived their lives, it becomes evident that when they left their native lands they did not intend to abandon their languages, values, customs, and traditional ways of doing things. Contrary to conventional views and mythical versions of the "saga," by and large immigrants of the past were not quick to "Americanize." Many were not even eager to learn English, adopt American lifestyles, and become U.S. citizens. In the chapters of this book, readers will discover how immigrants sought to preserve their cultures by building their own ethnic communities, which included a wide range of social, religious, educational, self-help, and commercial institutions. At the same, immigrants did not remain unaffected by America's dominant culture. The pressure to Americanize, the country's educational system, popular entertainment, and consumer products all had an impact on ethnic communities. The point deserves emphasis. A mixture of cultural values and traditions, together with personal goals and the need to cope with the changing realities of life in America, significantly influenced how immigrants shaped their lives.

Appreciating the daily life of ordinary immigrants requires looking at their world through their eyes. This work, therefore, attempts to let readers view daily life from the immigrants' perspective. Among other things, it avoids traditional topics such as social settlements, urban political machines, and politics. Settlement houses such as Chicago's Hull House provided important social services and for some first- and second-generation immigrants were oases amid terrible slums. These social agencies as well as political machines, however, actually touched the lives of only a small fraction of the millions of foreign-born individuals who migrated to America. The author has tried to re-create the lives of ordinary immigrants by examining budgets, wages, income, rent, diet, health, and folk customs. The aim is to take readers into the fields and gardens, the mills, slaughterhouses, coal mines, labor camps, factories, and shops where they worked. This approach is designed to let people see the type of jobs immigrants did, commercial endeavors they engaged in, businesses they operated, and leisure-time activities they liked. It also invites "outsiders" into the sod houses and crude dwellings in the West, tenements in urban areas, boardinghouses seemingly everywhere, and an array of makeshift housing in remote areas that, for immigrants, represented "home" in America. While being made aware of squalid conditions in the "foreign districts," readers will also get a look at the rich institutional and social life in these neighborhoods. Similarly, they will catch a glimpse of what life was like for women and children as well as for men. In both rural and urban areas, one could always find women and children hard at work and youngsters at play. And readers will see the kind of hostility the foreign born of all ages encountered. By taking such an intimate look at mundane aspects of their lives, one can see the strategies immigrants developed in order to survive and achieve the goals that brought them to America.

To grasp the complexities of the everyday lives of immigrant men, women, and children, it is also necessary to keep in mind the different levels of their existence. The home, the workplace, neighborhoods, and rural settlement areas provided the physical setting, but their lives consisted of a range of personal matters and public activities. Each day people made private decisions and took part in happenings that affected only them or their families. Even as personal issues absorbed their attention, immigrants moved beyond private concerns to participate in activities important to community life. They established places of worship and schools, formed ethnic organizations, and attended various ethnically based affairs. They became embroiled in bitter disputes as differences or disagreements in their communities caused harmony to give way to conflict. Finally, some immigrants interacted with the broader society, while others kept their day-to-day lives within the parameters of their own ethnic communities.

Regardless of their origins or where they went in the United States, the millions of people who arrived between 1870 and 1920 entered a country undergoing tremendous change. This book tries to place immigrants in the broader context of major developments that took place during the half century after 1870. The chronology that supplements the volume highlights significant national events of the period and blends them with events important to immigration history. A basic point is that, as immigrants went about their daily lives, they played a crucial role in the quest to people the nation and put the country's vast natural resources to use. They were vital to the demographic, economic, social, and cultural changes that characterized the period. But above all, by clinging to their pasts while at the same time adjusting to a strange land, immigrants not only benefited America, they also changed it.

NOTE

Immigrant life stories and quotations included in this introduction were derived from Emily Greene Balch, *Our Slavic Fellow Citizens* (1910; repr., New York: Arno, 1969); H. Arnold Barton, ed., *Letters from the Promised Land: Swedes in America, 1840–1914* (Minneapolis: University of Minnesota Press, 1975); Walter D. Kamphoefner, Wolfgang Helbich, and Ulrike Sommer, eds., *News from the Land of Freedom: German Immigrants Write Home,* trans. Susan Carter Vogel (Ithaca, NY: Cornell University Press, 1991).

1

Immigration 1870 to 1920: A Historical Overview

During the half century between 1870 and 1920, millions of people throughout the world left their homes and migrated to other countries. Since ancient times, people around the globe had been moving from one region to another, so migration was not a new phenomenon. In the final decades of the nineteenth century and the early years of the twentieth century, however, worldwide migration reached unparalleled heights. During the 50 years between 1870 and 1920, at least 26 million men, women, and children entered the United States as "immigrants." This massive immigration brought diverse peoples from different origins. Bound for America, Europeans set sail on a westward journey across the Atlantic Ocean, while Asians voyaged eastward across the Pacific. People already living in the Western Hemisphere went northward and southward, but they traveled mainly by land. For many turn-of-the-twentieth-century immigrants, the journey was round-trip as individuals went back and forth between the United States and their homelands. Migration thus created a constant coming and going of different peoples to America's shores and across its borders. All told, during this period at least 20 million immigrants finally stayed in the United States. Although they came from various countries and continents, they shared the common objective of wanting somehow to improve their lives. Migrating to America held out the possibility of achieving that goal.

THE "OLD" VERSUS "NEW" IMMIGRATION

In the nineteenth century, European immigrants came to the United States in two great waves. The first wave, which included people primarily from countries in northern and western Europe, began in the pre–Civil War era, declined during the war, and regained strength in the immediate postwar years. As this first influx continued full force, a second surge of European emigration got under way. This wave, which originated in eastern and southern Europe, started slowly in the 1880s, picked up momentum in the 1890s, and reached high tide in the early 1900s. Although people from first-wave countries continued migrating to the United States after the 1890s, the emergence of the second wave marked a fundamental shift in the geographic origins of immigrants. Americans of the day responded to this shift by distinguishing between people who had come from different regions of the European continent. Individuals who emigrated from northern and western Europe were seen as part of what was called the "old immigration," while people from eastern and southern Europe made up the "new immigration." Thus, regardless of when they actually arrived in the United States, former inhabitants of Germany, Ireland, Great Britain, Sweden, and other countries in northern and western Europe were considered "old immigrants." People from Italy, Greece, Russia, the Austro-Hungarian Empire, and other countries in southern and eastern Europe were designated as "new immigrants." Although in their simplest meaning, the terms "old" and "new" referred to geographic origins, Americans of the day ascribed distinct characteristics to old immigrants and new immigrants.

In the scholarly and popular literature on immigration, the "old" and "new" labels have endured, but latter-day critics have argued that these designations present a distorted picture of nineteenth- and early twentieth-century immigration. They point out that these categories completely ignore non-Europeans, especially Asians and people from countries in the Western Hemisphere who migrated to the United States. Critics further complain that the "old" and "new" divisions imply a sharp break in the migration flow from Europe that, in fact, did not occur; instead, individuals from old immigration countries continued coming throughout the pre–World War I era. Furthermore, analysts protest that such clear-cut labels overshadow basic similarities between old and new immigrants who came to the United States. Finally, critics argue that the separate categories overlook the fundamental differences that existed among the "old" immigrants groups and among "new" immigrant groups.

On one hand, standard criticisms of the old-new classifications are justifiable. The complaint that this dual division ignores migrations from non-European countries is particularly valid. On the other hand, when put in the context of how contemporary Americans viewed their world, the designations have validity. Characterizing immigration by European waves reflects the fact that in the nineteenth and early twentieth centuries the vast majority of immigrants did, in fact, come from Europe. During the nearly fifty years between the end of the U.S. Civil War and the onset of World War I, which contemporaries called the Great War, Europeans accounted for at least 90 percent of immigrants recorded entering the country. At the same time, Asians represented only 2.6 percent and peoples from the Western Hemisphere claimed about 7 percent of the documented migration into the United States. In the single decade from 1901 to 1910, Europeans made up nearly 93 percent of foreign-born arrivals.

The old-new paradigm also calls attention to the fact that, in the final decade of the nineteenth century, the chief sending countries changed from northern and western Europe to the continent's southern and eastern regions. With this change came a fresh wave of European immigrants that not only increased the country's foreign-born population but also added to its ethnic diversity. In addition, despite similarities between the old and new immigrations, there were vital differences between the two. The southern and eastern European migrations had characteristics and followed patterns that differed markedly from the earlier movements from other parts of the continent. Moreover, the terms "old immigrant" and "new immigrant" had real meaning to turn-of-the-twentieth-century Americans and significantly influenced their views of foreign-born peoples. Scholars can try to refute the accuracy of what Americans believed, but they cannot negate the force of those convictions. And, in seemingly countless ways, popular beliefs about the different immigrations—the old, the new, and the non-European—affected the lives of immigrants. Before exploring the intricacy of immigrant daily life in the era spanning the years from 1870 to 1920, it is necessary to put this immigration in a comparative historical context and highlight the patterns, the diversity, and the complexity of the massive influx of foreign-born peoples into the United States during that half century.

THE OLD IMMIGRATION: SOURCES AND MIGRATION PATTERNS

The national census in 1870 reflected the extensive pre–Civil War migration into the United States. Nearly 4.7 million of the country's more than 5.5 million foreign-born residents listed Great Britain, Ireland, Germany (which until 1871 was not a nation but rather a loose confederation of about three dozen states), France, and Scandinavian countries as their birthplaces. Although immigration from northern and western Europe temporarily declined during the war, the movement resumed in the late 1860s. This migration continued at a high rate for another quarter century and brought nearly 7.5 million more Europeans from the continent's northwestern regions between 1870 and 1900.

After the Civil War, there were shifts in the ongoing wave of immigrants. In the prewar era, Ireland had **German Empire** been the leading source of America's immigrants, but, by 1872, Germany had taken over the lead and held it until 1896. Dur-

"Immigrants Landing at Castle Garden," ca. 1880. *Harper's Weekly*, May 29, 1880, p. 341.

ing the 1880s alone, more than 1.4 million individuals from Germany set foot on American soil. Despite some fluctuations, the number of German immigrants remained consistently high until the early 1890s, when the annual migration began a steady, progressive decline. All told, between 1870 and 1900, overpopulation and deteriorating economic conditions in their homeland helped convince nearly 2.7 million Germans to depart for America. In the latter third of the nineteenth century, settlement patterns established in the pre–Civil War era continued influencing where Germans lived. Many German immigrants settled in sections of rural New York, but because a large segment of those who arrived during the early stages of this mass migration were seeking land, they also moved to rural states in the Midwest. By the 1880s, over 86 percent of foreign-born Germans lived in Middle Atlantic and north-central states. Until the mid-1890s, the German emigration remained predominantly a family movement, with parents leaving together and taking their children with them.

Ireland As the nineteenth century gave way to the twentieth century, people from Ireland continued migrating to the United States. The volume was not quite as large as the earlier exodus; nevertheless, between 1870 and 1900, about 1.5 million more Irish natives sought to improve their lives by leaving their homeland and going to America. This second phase of the Irish immigration peaked in the 1880s, when the total number of arrivals surpassed 650,000. The Irish also continued to follow their pre–Civil War settlement patterns. Some Irish immigrants traveled to the country's inland states and to the West, but the bulk favored the northeastern United States. They differed from other old immigrants because, despite their rural backgrounds, from the onset of mass immigration the Irish overwhelmingly chose to settle in cities and towns. The preference for urban areas remained so strong that by 1920 nearly 9 out of 10 foreign-born Irish men and women made their homes in urban America.

After 1870, people from elsewhere in the United Kingdom also continued settling in the United States. In fact, **Great Britain** in the 1870s and 1880s, Great Britain—which includes England, Scotland, and Wales—temporarily edged out Ireland as the chief source of emigration from the British Isles. Between 1870 and 1900, more than 2.4 million natives of Great Britain entered the United States, and another 836,000 came in the opening decade of the twentieth century. The English represented the largest number of emigrants from Great Britain, Scots were the second largest, and the Welsh were a distant third.

The heaviest English migration took place between 1879 and 1893, when more than 840,000 English men, women, and children arrived in the United States. Late nineteenth-century English immigrants who wanted to farm deviated from settlement patterns established by families who had come before them. Later English migrants chose areas west of the Mississippi River instead of settling in eastern and north-central states. During the 1880s, the annual Scottish migration ranged from 9,000 to 24,000, but, after peaking in 1888, it dipped dramatically in the 1890s and surged again in the early 1900s. The traditionally small Welsh migration remained relatively tiny in the final decades of the nineteenth century. The 1890 census counted 100,079 foreign-born Welsh living in the United States. Both Scottish and Welsh immigrants followed traditional settlement patterns. Scots tended to favor the northeastern and Middle Atlantic states, but they also moved into the Midwest and even farther into California. The Welsh typically preferred states where there were mining industries and quarries. This preference took them to Vermont, Maine, Pennsylvania, Ohio, Illinois, and a few states farther west.

People from countries in Scandinavia also belonged to the great immigration wave that spanned the pre– and **Scandinavia** post–Civil War eras. The 1870 census counted 241,685 former inhabitants of Sweden, Norway, and Denmark living in the United States; over the next three decades, another 1.2 million Scandinavians passed through U.S. ports. The movement crested during the 1880s, when more than 656,000 Swedes, Norwegians, and Danes arrived. The population pressures and worsening economic conditions that had touched off the earlier emigration from this northwestern corner of Europe continued fueling emigration from Scandinavia in the last quarter of the nineteenth century.

Swedes made up more than half of the Scandinavian migration. In just two decades stretching from 1870 to 1890, at least 600,000 of Sweden's natives made the overseas voyage to America. Into the 1880s, Swedish immigrants typically came as families and were primarily agricultural people hoping to obtain farmland. As a result, large numbers of Swedes settled in the land-rich areas of the upper Midwest, especially in Minnesota, but many also made their way to the Dakotas and Nebraska. While land hunger nurtured the early stages of the Swedish migration, some Swedes found urban areas attractive; consequently, between 1868 and 1893, they contributed to the rapidly growing foreign-born populations of Chicago and Minneapolis.

Most of the nearly 272,000 Norwegians who came between 1870 and 1890 wanted to become farmers. They also tended to migrate as families and concentrated heavily in rural parts of the upper Midwest, especially in Wisconsin, Minnesota, and North Dakota. Danes emigrated in much smaller numbers than other Scandinavians, but their post–Civil War movement resembled that of Swedes and Norwegians. The slightly less than 120,000 Danes who came to the United States between 1870 and 1890 chose agricultural states. In addition to the upper Midwest, a sizable number of them settled in Iowa, where most became farmers.

Holland, Switzerland, and Belgium Other peoples from northern and western Europe who had been part of the pre–Civil War immigration also continued trickling into the United States during the second half of the nineteenth century. Resembling larger migrations in this continuing wave, these smaller movements fluctuated but typically reached their high points sometime in the 1880s. Dutch migration reflected this pattern when it peaked in the 1880s, subsided during the 1890s, and surged again in the early 1900s. During the late 1800s, the Dutch headed for the several northern states that stretched from New York to the Rocky Mountains. The ongoing emigration from Switzerland crested in the 1880s, when some 82,000 Swiss entered the United States. Probably 60 percent of the 136,460 Swiss who arrived between 1870 and 1900 settled in rural areas, and a large number of them made their homes in one of several midwestern states or California. Belgians also continued immigrating to the United States, and, similar to the Swiss, their numbers were relatively small. Although some Belgians went to Iowa, Pennsylvania, New York, and Massachusetts, most chose to set down roots in states bordering Lake Michigan.

Basque Country and Portugal Basques, who originated from a region that stretches from northeastern Spain into the northwestern tip of France, made their way to California in the 1850s. Although they did not have an independent homeland, the Basques constituted a separate ethnic group. Having first migrated to South America, these Europeans subsequently went north in search of gold. Once the early arrivals had established a foothold, emigration directly from Basque country got under way and continued for several more decades. Instead of mining gold, however, Basques took up sheepherding. By the 1870s, Basques dominated the sheepherding operations throughout California and were setting out for nearby states. They concentrated in California, Nevada, and Idaho, but Basque sheepherders moved into the other coastal and far western states. Because immigration statistics for this group were incorporated into figures for both France and Spain, it is impossible to determine how many Basques came to the United States.

The Portuguese migration contributed a unique diversity to the influx into the United States. Although immigration officials recorded more than 217,400 arrivals from Portugal between 1870 and 1920, these individuals had come both from the country's mainland and from islands Portugal controlled in the North Atlantic Ocean. In addition to the Azores and Madeiras to the west, these island clusters also included Cape Verde, located south of Portugal and near the western coast of Africa. Officials did not identify specific origins; therefore, it is impossible to determine how many Portuguese came from the continent and how many originated from the islands. The migratory streams from these separate places, though, were different. Because upward of 70 percent of the inhabitants of Cape Verde had a combined African and European ancestry, the migration from these islands was made up of "racially mixed" individuals. Once in the United States, Cape Verdeans were viewed as blacks and not only encountered prejudice but also were forced to live in segregated areas. A few Portuguese ended up in California, but, regardless of their origins, the vast majority settled in towns in southeastern New England and especially in eastern Massachusetts.

People continued emigrating from northern and western Europe until the outbreak of World War I in 1914 abruptly interrupted mass departures from the continent. By the late 1880s, however, important changes were taking place in what had been the nineteenth century's first great immigration wave into the United States. As the century came to a close, more men and women were leaving with different goals in mind, and they were typically going to America's metropolitan areas rather than to rural, agricultural regions. Irish immigrants had always preferred urban destinations, and, even in the pre–Civil War years, large numbers of Germans had settled in New York, Philadelphia, Baltimore, Saint Louis, New Orleans, Milwaukee, and Cincinnati, while Swedes went to Chicago and Minneapolis. Still, until the late nineteenth century, the old immigration characteristically was made up of "land seekers." Although the patterns and pace of change varied among the immigrant groups, by the 1890s more and more people from the old immigration countries came wanting jobs not farmland. As "labor seekers," these northern and western Europeans went directly to America's industrial cities and towns. The shift from seeking land to finding work also affected the makeup of the various immigration streams

Changing Settlement Patterns

flowing into the country. By the mid-1890s, married couples with children stopped dominating the transatlantic migration from northwestern Europe, and there was an increased tendency for young men, both single and married, to set out on their own.

At the same time that a search for jobs was reshaping emigration from first-wave countries, an identical quest was giving rise to a second great wave of immigration. The hope of getting work in America's burgeoning industries inspired millions from eastern and southern Europe to make the transatlantic voyage to the United States and find their way to cities, industrial towns, and mining fields.

THE NEW IMMIGRATION: SOURCES AND
MIGRATION PATTERNS

The geographic shift that caused southern and eastern Europe to replace the continent's northwestern region as the chief source of American immigration began slowly. It started as a minor stream in the 1880s, when less than one-fifth of the Europeans who came to the United States were new immigrants. As early as 1896, however, people coming from eastern and southern Europe surpassed the total arriving from first-wave countries. And, once they gained the lead, the new immigrants did not relinquish it until U.S. legislation curtailed immigration in the early 1920s. Indeed, in the first decade of the twentieth century, the gap widened as new immigrants outnumbered old immigrants by a ratio of more than three to one. All told, between 1891 and 1920, the number of immigrants recorded entering the United States from new immigration countries was more than double that from the old immigration sources. Migrants from countries chiefly in the Western Hemisphere but also from Japan accounted for the remaining foreign-born people passing through immigrant receiving stations.

Austro-Hungarian Empire

The second great wave of immigration had its beginnings in Austria-Hungary. Governed by the Habsburg dynasty, this huge empire historically contained a motley population of Slavic and non-Slavic peoples. Czechs, Slovaks, Carpatho-Rusyns, Ukrainians, Slovenes, Croatians, and Poles represented the major Slavic groups living in Habsburg domains. In the late 1870s, this ethnic diversity was further magnified when the Habsburgs were allowed to occupy Bosnia-Herzegovina, provinces to the empire's south inhabited primarily by Orthodox Serbs and Muslim Bosnians. Austrians, Germans, and Magyars (Hungarians) were the chief non-Slavs in Austria-Hungary. The individual national minorities typically dwelled in distinct sections of the empire, and, therefore, regional migrations were, in essence, nationality movements. Over time, as the migration impulse spread through each geographic region and beyond, it touched off additional ethnic movements that brought a continuous, ever-increasing flow of diverse peoples into the United States. As a result, what began as a trickle in the 1870s, when fewer than 73,000 natives of Austria-Hungary made their way to America, expanded into an enormous multiethnic migration. The number of immigrants arriving from Austria-Hungary increased over sevenfold to 593,000 in the 1890s and skyrocketed to more than 2.1 million in the first decade of the twentieth century. All told, between 1880 and 1918, more than 3.9 million Austro-Hungarian subjects landed on American shores.

Bohemians and Moravians—known by World War I as Czechs—were the first of Austria-Hungary's Slavs to emigrate overseas. Although Czechs followed a pattern almost identical to that of northern and western Europeans of the old immigration, because their homeland was located in the Austro-Hungarian Empire, they are typically considered new immigrants. In 1870, more than 40,000 Czechs were living in the United States. Once immigration resumed after the Civil War, a steady stream of Czechs continued flowing into the United States. Families dominated the early stages of the Czech movement, and, like the old immigrants, Czechs were land seekers. Thus in the 1870s and 1880s, these Slavs gravitated to rural areas of the country, especially to the farmlands of Texas, Wisconsin, Minnesota, Iowa, Nebraska, the Dakotas, and Oklahoma. Some Czechs preferred cities, and those who did typically stayed in New York or went to Chicago, Cleveland, or Saint Louis.

The next wave of Slavic overseas migration from Austria-Hungary probably began in the 1870s with a handful of Slovaks in northeastern Hungary, an agricultural and poor section of the kingdom. The number of Slovak emigrants increased in the 1880s, intensified during the next decade, and reached full force after 1900. By the time World War I brought the outflow of people from Hungary to a near standstill, roughly a half-million Slovak men, women, and children had traveled to the United States. At about the same time that Slovaks were starting to leave for America, Carpatho-Rusyns, who also lived in poor districts along the eastern borders of northern Hungary, were doing the same. Ukrainians added to the mix of ethnic minorities departing from the eastern fringes of the Habsburg Empire. From the 1880s, when their migration started, until 1914, an estimated 250,000 Ukrainians passed through the receiving depots. The majority of these Slavs came from Austria-Hungary, but some originated from the Russian Empire as well. In the 1890s, Slovenes from Carniola joined the emigration, and, after 1900, Croatians, from the semiautonomous province of Croatia-Slavonia, also made their way to America. Because immigration officials lumped these two peoples together, it is impossible to determine how many Slovenes and Croatians entered the United States. Estimates place the number of Slovenes at roughly 250,000 to 350,000 and the total number of Croatians at perhaps 400,000. Although a small movement, the emigration of Dalmatians, Bosnians, and Herzegovinians intensified the already diverse migration from the Austro-Hungarian Empire. For the twenty-year period covering 1899 to 1920, approximately 50,000 of these peoples from the empire's southwestern Adriatic region set sail for the United States.

The migration impulse also eventually spread to Austria-Hungary's non-Slavic peoples. A few Magyars went overseas in the 1890s, but these ethnic Hungarians did not leave for America in sizable numbers until after 1900. Once under way, however, the Magyar migration gained momentum, and in first two decades of the twentieth century up to 460,000 Hungarians departed for the United States.

Poles Austria-Hungary was home to the majority of Slavs who sailed to America, but Polish Christians were the single largest Slavic group to make the transatlantic voyage. The Polish migration, however, was complicated by the fact that Poland was not an independent nation. The country had been partitioned three times in the eighteenth century; consequently, regions of Poland fell under Austrian, Russian, or German control. Poles from the German sector were the first to go overseas. They traveled to the United States before the Civil War, but most came during the 1870s and especially in the 1880s. Following settlement patterns comparable to those of Czechs, these early Polish immigrants from the German Empire headed primarily to the rural sections of the Midwest and Texas. In the early 1890s, as the current that had brought an estimated 434,000 German Poles to the United States was subsiding, new currents of Polish immigration were starting up elsewhere. One originated in Galicia, which was part of the Austro-Hungarian Empire; the other came out of Congress Poland, which was controlled by Russia. These new migratory streams brought another 570,000 or more Poles in the 1890s, but the heyday of Polish immigration occurred between 1900 and 1914, when more than a million Poles arrived at U.S. ports.

Russian Empire Very few ethnic Russians migrated to the United States. Indeed, from the 1880s onward, Jews represented the largest single group departing the Russian Empire. At the turn of twentieth century, however, several nationalities living under Russian control joined the transatlantic movement. This ethnically diverse outflow of peoples included Germans, Finns, Ukrainians, Lithuanians, Christian Poles, and Belorussians.

Jews

Economic motives prompted Austria-Hungary's subjects to migrate overseas, but it was different for Jews who lived in several eastern European lands. Although some Jews did leave to seek better economic opportunities, many were escaping repression of one form or another. In addition, the eastern European Jewish migration, which represented the second largest component of the new immigrant wave, consisted of several distinct migratory streams. Perhaps three-fourths of the estimated 2 million Jews who immigrated to the United States came from the Russian Empire, especially from Lithuania and Congress Poland; the remaining one-fourth departed from the Austro-Hungarian Empire and Romania. Regardless of where they had lived, most Jews endured persecution or entrenched discrimination. In Russia, where conditions were particularly harsh, laws forced Jews to live in confined areas and restricted what occupations they could engage in. In 1881–1882 and again

in 1905, thousands of Jews were massacred in pogroms. These sporadic out-
breaks of vigilante violence, coupled with persistent oppression and dire economic conditions, caused many Jews in Russia to take flight to America.

Germans and Finns

In the 1870s, German Mennonites from the Black Sea region in modern-day
Ukraine as well as Germans from rural villages along the southeastern banks
of the Volga River began setting out for America. The revocation of special
privileges that Germans had long enjoyed in Russia sparked these particular
migrations. Mennonites, who were pacifists, particularly disliked the introduction of compulsory military service; they also resented other newly initiated mandates that went against their religious beliefs. Bound together by
religion, the Mennonite exodus was a group migration in which people left
together for the same destination and established tightly knit communities
in America. Because it was not a group movement, the German migration
from the Volga River region differed from the Mennonite migration; nevertheless, Volga Germans went to the same locations in the United States.
Expert farmers, the vast majority of Germans from both the Black Sea and
Volga River areas settled in the Great Plains and Midwest, where they took
up farming. How many Germans emigrated from Russia to America will
never be known for certain, but the number probably exceeded 120,000.

In the 1880s, people from Finland joined the stream of immigrants leaving Russian-controlled lands. A few Finns had departed for America in the
1860s, and approximately another 3,000 came in the 1870s; however, mass
Finnish migration did not get under way until the 1880s, and the largest
number entered the United States after 1900. The Finnish movement com-
prised mostly landless people from rural Finland, but, although most Finns
initially found wage-paying jobs, many dreamed of becoming farmers. Consequently, the approximately 98,000 Finns who migrated in the closing two
decades of the nineteenth century settled in the same geographic areas as
Swedes, Norwegians, and Danes. In 1900, nearly half of all Finnish immigrants lived in Michigan and Minnesota, while more than one-fourth resided
in northern states stretching from New Jersey to Oregon and Washington. The
Finnish migration differed from Scandinavian movements into the middle
and upper western parts of the country because families did not dominate
the early phase of the Finnish influx. Two-thirds of the Finns who entered
the United States between 1899 and 1910 were male, and, moreover, single,
young men represented the largest component of this migratory flow.

Balkans

Small migrations from southern and eastern Europe
further enriched the diverse nature of the massive flood   **Southern Europe**
of peoples into the United States. In addition to the   **and the Balkan**
Serbs who joined Croatians and Dalmatians departing   **States**
Habsburg provinces in the Adriatic region, more than

150,000 Serbs, Montenegrins, and Bulgarians from independent countries in the Balkan Peninsula added more currents to the wave of Slavic immigrants. The majority of the estimated 50,000 Bulgarians originated from Macedonia, an area southwest of independent Bulgaria and under Turkish control. People from Romania contributed to the non-Slavic influx. The first people to leave were Jews, but in the mid-1890s ethnic Romanians also began exiting the country. By 1920, perhaps 85,000 Romanians had made their way to America. Greece, located in the extreme southern part of the Balkan Peninsula, was another source of the second great immigration wave. Resembling other migrations, the Greek movement progressively spread from one part of the country to the other, and it went on to include Greeks living in Asian Turkey. The Greek emigration did not begin in earnest until after 1900, but during the twentieth century's first two decades more than 450,000 Greeks traveled to the United States.

Italy

At the same time that people in the Balkan Peninsula, Austria-Hungary, and the Russian Empire were packing their bags to leave for America, Italians were doing the same. With more than 4.2 million making the transatlantic voyage between 1870 and 1920, Italians made up the largest single group of new immigrants. Although a few Italians from Italy's northern region had made their way earlier, the vast majority of migrants came from the country's southern provinces and arrived after 1900. More than 3 million Italians landed in the United States during the first decade and a half of the twentieth century. Annual tallies show that from 1901 to 1914, the number of Italian arrivals never dipped below 130,000; in seven of those years, the total exceeded 200,000.

Destinations   The vast majority of southern and eastern European immigrants who arrived in the United States disembarked in New York. Once admitted, these foreign-born individuals were free to travel anywhere in the country. Second-wave immigrants set out in several directions and could be found in nearly every state; nevertheless, they did not spread out as widely as most land-seeking groups did. Southern and eastern Europeans overwhelmingly chose the northeastern and Middle Atlantic regions of the country, especially New York, New Jersey, Pennsylvania, Ohio, and Illinois. In addition, unlike European immigrants of an earlier era, arrivals from the 1890s onward gravitated to America's cities and industrial areas.

Similar to first-wave immigrants, nationality groups from southern and eastern Europe migrated to different—yet specific—locations. Large numbers of Italians went to New York, New Jersey, Pennsylvania, and a few northeastern states. Poles preferred the Middle Atlantic states and industrial sections of the Midwest. People from Austria-Hungary displayed a tendency to make their way to the same places. Slovaks most often chose the mill and mining towns in industrial states, particularly Pennsylvania,

New Jersey, New York, Illinois, and eastern Ohio. Ukrainians clustered in the Northeast, especially in New York, Pennsylvania, and New Jersey. Croatians gravitated to several places in the East and Midwest but preferred Pennsylvania to all other states. Carpatho-Rusyns also favored the mining and steel regions of Pennsylvania. Slovenes opted for southwestern Pennsylvania and West Virginia, but large numbers went to northeastern Ohio and the Chicago area. Lithuanians streamed into the mining districts of western Pennsylvania and southern Illinois. Eastern European Jews stayed primarily in cities in the eastern United States, especially in New York. Although a portion went to California, Greeks typically moved to cities and small towns in the Northeast.

From the onset of mass migration in the early nineteenth century, large numbers of newcomers settled in urban areas. The near-constant flow of new immigrants turned the already rising populations of America's cities and towns into rich conglomerations of diverse peoples. As the major port of entry, New York City was a tremendously popular destination; however, southern and eastern Europeans also flocked to Chicago and other inland cities, including Detroit, Cleveland, Buffalo, and Pittsburgh. In addition, new immigrants helped swell the populations of small mill towns and coal-mining hamlets.

NON-EUROPEAN ORIGINS

Most immigrants who came during the two great waves prior to World War I sailed across the Atlantic Ocean, but there **Chinese** were those who crossed the Pacific Ocean to get to America.

At the same time that Irish, British, and German people were landing on America's eastern shores in the 1850s, Chinese migrants were passing through West Coast ports. Social and economic problems that made life increasingly difficult, coupled with political chaos in the mid-nineteenth century, caused inhabitants of southeastern China to emigrate. In addition, news about the discovery of gold in California prompted Chinese to set out for the United States. In 1860, there were more than 35,000 foreign-born Chinese in the United States; some twenty years later, the Chinese population had risen to slightly more than 105,000. All told, during the nearly thirty-year period stretching from 1850 to 1880, approximately 326,000 Chinese immigrants arrived at American ports. In 1882, however, the U.S. Congress passed legislation temporarily barring Chinese laborers from entering the country. Merchants, professional people, and tourists could still gain admittance. In 1892, Congress extended the ban on Chinese laborers for another 10 years and in 1902 made it permanent. After passage of the exclusion law, Chinese immigration came to an almost complete stop. During the 20 years between 1884 and 1914, fewer than 38,000 Chinese legally entered the United States.

Chinese immigrants followed settlement patterns not unlike those of other nationality groups. They could be found in nearly every state but concentrated in particular sections and, in general, preferred the western United States. In the 1850s and 1860s, the Chinese lived and worked in mining regions of the West; they also found jobs laying railroad tracks. By the 1880s, sizable numbers of Chinese were residing in California's agricultural regions and were also concentrating in the San Francisco area.

Japanese
The Japanese represented the only other major group to migrate from Asia to America during the pre–World War I era. Laborers began traveling directly from Japan to the United States in the early 1890s; however, later in the decade another stream got under way from nearby Hawaii, which had been the primary destination of earlier Japanese migrants. Following the annexation of the islands by the United States in 1898, some foreign-born Japanese residing there decided to go to the American mainland, where they hoped to find better jobs. In the quarter century after 1891, more than 240,000 Japanese made their way to North American shores. Entering the United States through Pacific Coast ports, the Japanese favored the far western states and especially California. Like the Chinese movement, government action ultimately curtailed Japanese immigration. Instead of the U.S. Congress imposing restrictions, however, the United States pressured the Japanese government to limit the number of people who could emigrate from its territory. To achieve this end, in 1907 President Theodore Roosevelt negotiated the Gentlemen's Agreement whereby the Japanese government promised to curb emigration by denying passports to laborers.

Syrians and Armenians
In the final quarter of the nineteenth century, a few people from the Middle East were migrating to the United States. Although most immigrants from the region were Christians from Lebanon, U.S. officials listed them as "Syrians." What was an annual migration of just a few hundred in the late 1880s grew to more than 4,000 by 1898. The influx continued into the early 1900s and crested in 1913, when more than 9,000 Syrians entered the country. New York was the most popular destination for Syrians, but they also moved into Boston, and a few went on to Detroit and even Birmingham, Alabama.

The migration of Armenians, who came primarily from lands controlled by the Ottoman Turks, resembled the emigration of eastern European Jews. Similar to the Jews, Armenians fled economic and political discrimination as well as outright persecution at the hands of their Turkish rulers. More than 100,000 Armenians perished in a bloody massacre in 1895; perhaps another 20,000 were slain in 1909. Ongoing repression, coupled with continual economic pressures, prompted an estimated 70,000 Armenians to flee to America between 1890 and 1920. The largest pre–World War I migration occurred in 1913 when upward of 9,000 Armenians came. After braking during the war, the Armenian immigration gained momentum in the immediate postwar era and continued until stopped by U.S. immigration laws in the early 1920s.

WESTERN HEMISPHERE

During the half century spanning 1870 to 1920, more than 2.4 million individuals from the Western Hemisphere traveled overland or made a short journey by boat to reach destinations in the United States. Because U.S. officials only erratically recorded information on people coming across land borders and from the Caribbean, the number of migrants from the Western Hemisphere will never be known. In addition, long, porous borders allowed individuals to come and go easily at places where there were no officials to document entries or departures.

The largest influx of migrants came from Canada. The movement from that country, however, included both English- and **Canadians** French-speaking peoples, and each came in its own distinct streams. The French, who were mainly natives of Quebec, had a history of migrating to the United States, but in the late nineteenth century what had been traditionally a migration of temporary seasonal workers turned into a family movement. The 1890 census counted more than 302,000 French Canadians, and within 10 years the total jumped to nearly 395,000. Typically making the journey by rail, the majority of French Canadians settled in the manufacturing and mill towns of New England.

At approximately the same time that the French of Quebec were boarding trains for New England, large numbers of Canada's English-speaking citizens were crossing into New York and the central states stretching along the countries' shared borders. In 1900, the U.S. census counted more than 800,000 English-speaking Canadians living in the country. A few English Canadians preferred coastal cities, especially Gloucester, Massachusetts, with its well-established fishing industry. The character of this English influx changed in the 1870s and 1880s, when families and older individuals joined the migration, which historically had been dominated by young, unmarried men seeking temporary employment. This shift meant that more people were planning to stay permanently in the United States. Nevertheless, proximity to their homeland allowed both English and French Canadians to maintain close ties with their families and to travel regularly back and forth between their former homes and their new residences in the United States.

People from Mexico as well as Central and South America made their way north into the United States. Although the **Mexicans,** heaviest influx occurred after 1900, the migration from south- **South and** ern regions of the Western Hemisphere was under way in the **Central** 1890s. The largest migratory wave originated in Mexico, where **Americans** economic and political pressures nurtured a gradually escalating migration movement. As large estate owners gobbled up more land, there were fewer opportunities for Mexico's other classes to get ahead. To improve their lot and supplement their families' incomes, small landowners and farm laborers decided to seek employment in the United States. Political turmoil in the early twentieth century further contributed to this out-migration. In part because immigration officials did not consistently record entrants from North American countries, the statistics on Mexicans are incomplete. Also, like Canadians, Mexicans routinely went back and forth across the border, and, similarly, their movements were not officially recorded. In 1890, census takers counted 78,000 foreign-born Mexicans in the United States, and by 1900 the number had risen to just slightly more than 103,000.

The available figures show that the Mexican migration gained momentum in the second decade of the twentieth century. Between 1911 and 1920, at least 219,000 Mexicans crossed the border into the United States. The U.S. Congress contributed to this upsurge during World War I by relaxing immigration laws so Mexicans workers could easily enter the country and help resolve the labor shortage created by the war. During World War I, Mexicans went to northern states to work in heavy industry, but during the early decades of the twentieth century the majority continued moving primarily into the country's southwestern region, where they worked in agriculture and construction. In the 1890s, peoples from South and Central America also started trickling into the United States. By 1920, perhaps 87,000 people from several countries south of Mexico had made the journey northward. Preferring urban destinations, immigrants from these countries settled in the Northeast as well as along the Pacific and Gulf Coasts.

Caribbean   While peoples from the Western Hemisphere were traveling northward and southward to get to the United States, residents of the hemisphere's Caribbean islands were making a short journey northward and westward. The Caribbean migration from these regions differed from other contemporary movements in part because blacks made up a significant portion of the migration from the islands. Cuban laborers came as early as the 1870s to work in cigar factories built by Cuban manufacturers, and over the next several decades small numbers of Cuba's natives continued moving into the country. People from the West Indies migrated later. How many individuals from Cuba and other islands in the Caribbean entered the United States cannot be ascertained, but aggregate figures place the total influx for the period covering 1891 to 1920 at approximately 264,000. Similar to contemporary migrations from Europe, people from these islands preferred cities. They chose to settle mainly in urban areas along the East and Gulf Coasts.

THE MIGRATION PROCESS

Motivations   Statistics reveal the volume of immigration, but they do not explain what motivated so many people to set out for the United States during the half century between 1870 and 1920. There is no simple explanation. Individual reasons were infinite. Difficulties in their native lands—coupled with knowledge about opportunities in America—prompted people to weigh their options and finally choose to migrate. In essence, migration reflected a pragmatic assessment of one's present situation and future possibilities. Thus, by and large, what has been traditionally described as the "push" from the homeland and the "pull" of America combined to fuel the massive immigration of the late nineteenth and early twentieth centuries.

Despite fundamental differences among nations of the world, conditions common to most countries convinced individuals to make their way by land or sea to the United States. All over nineteenth-century Europe, countries experienced substantial population growth that reduced economic opportunities. In northern and western countries, this population increase meant less available land for a growing number of aspiring farmers. Improved farming techniques lessened the need for agricultural laborers at a time when the pool of working-age individuals was getting larger. A desire to maintain their social status caused land-hungry northern and western Europeans to look to America, which had an abundance of fertile land and needed people to cultivate it. A combination of population pressures and declining opportunities also caused the peoples of southern and eastern Europe to look overseas. At the turn of the twentieth century, nations in this region of the continent did not have sufficient industry to absorb the increasing supply of young laborers. While opportunities were shrinking in Europe, industrialization in the United States was creating a voracious demand for unskilled laborers. Comparing the limited possibilities in their countries with those available elsewhere also prompted people in North America to migrate to the United States.

Although the quest for land and the desire for good-paying jobs were important underlying forces stimulating mass emigration, other factors weighed into people's decision. Young men left to avoid military conscription. Discrimination and religious or political persecution also led some men and women to abandon their homeland. It must, nevertheless, be emphasized that, for most immigrants, coming to America was a voluntary choice. Whether they went alone or as part of a family, men and women were looking for a chance to change their lives for the better.

Economic motives prompted many individuals to migrate, but it was the development of steam-powered transportation that allowed transoceanic and international travel to reach unprecedented heights. Before the 1870s, when overseas travelers went by sailing ship, the transatlantic voyage took two months or more. After 1873, when steamships replaced sailing vessels and depending on where they originated, transoceanic trips were typically reduced to two weeks or less. While steamships made journeys across the ocean quicker, cheaper, and safer, steam-powered trains improved overland trips. Efficient railroad systems facilitated travel to and from port cities and made crossing international borders by land much easier. Realizing the economic potential of the "immigrant trade," steamship companies fiercely competed for passengers. To accommodate would-be travelers, passenger lines either established offices or engaged local individuals to serve as sales representatives in towns and cities throughout Europe. They distributed pamphlets and guidebooks that advertised America's abundant land and publicized the "high wages" industries paid unskilled workers. All this positive publicity did not cause emigration to get under way; instead, steamship companies exploited the growing migration mentality and reinforced popular beliefs that the United States offered opportunities that would allow people to secure a better future for themselves and their families.

Chain Migration
Personal ties were the most potent forces stimulating mass migration. In 1907, the U.S. commissioner general of immigration claimed that personal letters were encouraging "endless chains" of immigration into the United States. He was complaining, but he was not wrong. There were definite links between homeland origins and American destinations. Reports on the international mail service confirmed that there was a constant transoceanic flow of materials. Between 1900 and 1906, an estimated 514,568,230 letters were mailed overseas from the United States. Personal letters might include a steamship ticket or money to buy passage so loved ones could join an immigrant already in the United States. When they answered officials' questions at any of the several American receiving stations, immigrants themselves revealed the power of personal relationships. For instance, from the fall of 1907 into midsummer 1910, nearly 94 percent of individuals entering the United States said they were joining family or friends. Regardless of when or where they entered the country, most people knew exactly where they were going, and most were headed for locales where kith and kin already lived and worked. Thus "chain migration," the process whereby immigrants followed family and friends to the same locales in America, played a crucial role in shaping the settlement patterns of specific nationalities. Once emigration from a particular region got under way, the movement typically spread from place to neighboring place and had the practical effect of encouraging further migration and reinforcing links between Old World origins and New World destinations.

Remittances and Return Migration
Beside remittances for tickets and travel fare, immigrants sent money to provide financial assistance to their families. In the period spanning 1900 to 1906, the New York post office, which handled most overseas transactions, reported sending 12,304,485 money orders amounting to $239,367,047.56. Approximately half of this sum went to Austria-Hungary, Russia, and Italy; the remaining half went to several other countries. Immigrants also relied on banks to forward money. In 1903, Hungarian banks reported receiving $17 million, while a reliable estimate for Croatia-Slavonia put the amount coming from the United States at probably $10

million. With money earned in America, families paid off debts and purchased goods they could not have otherwise afforded.

Many immigrants sent money back home because they planned eventually to return to their native land. New immigrants differed from early arrivals of the old immigration wave because, from the outset, countless numbers of southern and eastern Europeans intended to remain only temporarily in the United States. In fact, a large segment of these new immigrants were actually migrant workers desiring short-term employment in America's rapidly expanding industrial economy. Some new immigrants planned their stays around the agricultural growing cycle in Europe. Their strategy was to labor in the United States during the winter, return home in the spring to plant, and then come back to America in the fall. Others preferred to pass the cold months in southern Europe's warmer climate and again make their way to America in the spring. Most migrants, however, did not establish rigid routines and probably set out intending to remain a few years before returning to their homelands. How many immigrants traveled back and forth or went home permanently will never be known. Beginning in the mid-1880s, even people from northern and western Europe returned home more often than had been the case during early stages of the old immigration wave.

It was not until 1908 that officials recorded the number of aliens departing the country. In that year alone, approximately 783,000 foreign-born individuals entered the United States and nearly 400,000 left. From the fall of 1907 to the summer of 1910, slightly over 2.5 million immigrants passed through America's receiving stations; at the same time, more than 823,000 departed. Immigrant groups had different return rates: Italians, Hungarians, Croatians, Slovenes, and Slovaks had the highest, while eastern European Jews had the lowest. Historians calculate that, overall, 30 percent to 40 percent of the people who came to the United States between 1880 and 1920 did not stay permanently. Referring to these temporary immigrants as "birds of passage," many contemporary Americans viewed returnees and repeat migrants with disdain. They accused these "birds of passage" of exploiting America by coming in good economic times and draining money from the country. It was true that, when the American economy took a downturn and laborers were thrown out of work, some immigrants left and then returned when working conditions improved.

In general, regardless of where they originated, temporary migrants—often called "sojourners"—merely wanted the opportunity to enjoy a better life, but they wanted that better life to be in their homelands. With money earned in America, people bought land, invested in businesses, or built homes; thus, becoming a migrant laborer held out the possibility of improving individuals' social and economic status in their native countries. Over time, however, many sojourners who had planned to stay only temporarily or had made several repeat journeys did finally remain in the United States.

America's growing demand for industrial laborers
Gender and Age   affected the makeup of immigration into the country.
Immigrants were typically young adults. More than
four-fifths of the people who arrived in the late nineteenth and early twentieth centuries were between fourteen and forty-four years old, and the majority of them were probably in their twenties and thirties. Although the migratory streams included families as well as married men who came on their own, single men predominated in the new immigration. The ratio of males to females fluctuated from year to year, but, during the first decade of the twentieth century, males represented nearly 70 percent of all new arrivals. A gradual shift, however, began to take place. After 1911, the proportion of females increased to one-third of arriving immigrants, and in 1915 it jumped to nearly 43 percent. The ratio of men to women also differed among the various groups. For example, in the pre–World War I era, more than 90 percent of Greeks, Croatians, Slovenes, and Serbs were men. Nine out of 10 Romanians were also male. Men constituted slightly more than 78 percent of Italian immigrants and made up 70 percent of the Polish, Slovak, and Lithuanian migratory streams.

Two old immigrant groups—the Irish and the Swedes—were marked exceptions to the general male-dominated pattern that characterized immigration at the dawn of the twentieth century. Twice in the late 1890s and again in 1902, more Swedish females than males entered the United States. It was the Irish movement, however, that diverged dramatically from the typical male-to-female ratio. For each of the last five years of the 1870s, more Irish women than men migrated to America. And at least 13 times from the 1880s to 1920, the annual influx of Irish females exceeded that of Irish men. Young, unmarried women hoping to get jobs in domestic service or in the textile industry were largely responsible for the higher proportion of females in these migrations. Eastern European Jews also deviated from the general trend. They differed because the Jewish migration was overwhelmingly a family movement and thus had a more balanced male-to-female ratio.

The fact that so many immigrants were job seekers largely accounts for the gender imbalance that characterized immigration into the United States. Then again, immigrants' personal intentions and strategies also influenced the composition and, especially, the changes over time. More men arrived during the early stages of migration, in part because some married couples planned a two-step process with the husband going ahead and the wife following later with the couple's children. When sojourners changed their minds and chose to remain in the United States, their families joined them. Young women moved to America to meet up with their fiancés. Some female immigrants were party to prearranged marriages and did not know—or barely knew—their future husbands. Not all immigrant women, however, came as wives or fiancées. Similar to young, unskilled men, some single women in particular left their homelands in the hope of finding more opportunities and securing a better future.

Overland Travel

For people who decided to go to America, their life as immigrants began with a trip across land and often across national borders to reach a port city. Depending on where migrants lived, getting to a seaport could take a few days, a week, or even longer. People departing rural areas probably combined travel by carriage and by railway; some—men, in particular— walked part of the distance. In the latter decades of the nineteenth century, the overland journey became easier and cheaper as expanded railroad systems linked more remote districts with hubs where people could transfer to connecting lines. Crossing some international borders could be complicated. In the 1890s, German law required all individuals entering German territory to submit to medical inspections at control stations along the border. Eastern Europeans headed to German, British, French, Dutch, or Belgian ports and planning to continue to America were denied permission to cross German lands if examiners believed they did not meet health requirements and thus would be barred from the United States. Beginning in the early 1890s, once migrants arrived in port cities, they had to undergo a medical examination and provide personal information to a shipping agent before they could board ships. Individual shipping lines conducted the inspections because U.S. law mandated that passengers who were denied entry had to be returned to their ports of departure at the shipping companies' expense.

The Transoceanic Journey

Steerage

The majority of immigrants made the transoceanic voyage in steerage, which at a cost of about $20 was the most economical way to get from Europe to America. Steerage was profitable for the steamship companies because it allowed them to pack between 900 and 1,400 passengers into the lower decks of their ships. Passenger lines could thus handle the massive volume of migrants desiring to sail to the United States. The overseas trip from northwestern Europe usually took 9 to 12 days, while the crossing from Adriatic ports could last up to 21 days. During the time they were on the high seas, daily life for steerage passengers was typically an unpleasant ordeal.

Located in the lower depths of a vessel, steerage levels could extend the full length of a ship. Sleeping quarters were divided into compartments specifically designated for men, women, and families; married women traveling with children but without their husbands were housed in the family sections. The compartments, where 200 to 400 people slept, were huge dormitories furnished with bunk beds "one above the other, with little light and no comforts," one man recalled. In addition, there was a complete lack of privacy because people were "housed together in such larger numbers and must spend every hour of the twenty-four . . . in the presence of so many others." Protecting one's modesty was difficult. Even at night, "It was practically impossible to undress properly for retiring."

Once they went to bed, immigrants slept on bunk beds with mattresses "filled with straw and covered with a slip made of coarse white canvas." Instead of pillows, sometimes there were only life preservers at the head of each bed; one shipping line provided a pillow made of sea grass covered with cloth. Passengers usually got a lightweight blanket they could take with them when they left the ship. By the end of the trip, these covers were so dirty that it was apparently easier for the shipping companies to give them away than to collect and clean them.

After a poor night's sleep, immigrants coped with the hardships of daily life in steerage. Although passenger lines provided meals, in the words of one immigrant, the food was "miserable" and "meals are anything but orderly procedures." Immigrants began their day with a breakfast probably consisting of cooked cereal, bread, and jam. It was the other meals, however, that caused immigrants to judge the food "miserable." At the beginning of the voyage on one line, each passenger was provided with utensils and an ingenious multipurpose food pail to be used for meals throughout the trip. The pail was for soup. A lid that fit onto the pail was meant for meat and potatoes, a rounded dimple in the cap was designed for vegetables or stewed fruits, and a beverage cup fit over the lid's

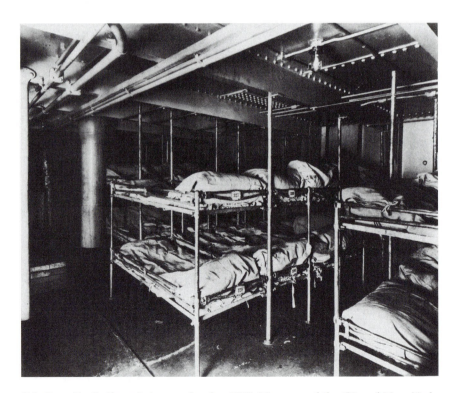

S.S. Duca Degli Abruzzi steerage bunks, 1908. Museum of the City of New York. The Byron Collection.

rounded dimple. Describing mealtime on one liner, a traveler reported that "The food was brought in . . . in large galvanized tin cans. The meat and vegetables were placed on the tables in tins resembling smaller-sized dishpans." Because on this particular voyage there were no serving plates, knives, or spoons, passengers had to use their own utensils or dip their dinner pails into the kettles to get the food. Immigrants also described soup and other fare being slopped into passengers' dinner pails. By and large, companies adhered to regulations requiring ships to provide tables for steerage passengers, but some dining areas were so stuffy that, when possible, immigrants took their food out on deck to eat.

Maintaining personal hygiene was a daily challenge. Each compartment ordinarily had a men's and a women's washroom with several basins in which passengers could wash their hands and faces with cold salt water. Travelers washed their hair, clothes, and dirty dinner pails in the washrooms' tubs, which also were the only receptacles people could use when they suffered from seasickness, a common illness in steerage. There were no facilities for full body cleansing and no place where passengers could take warm baths.

There was little escape from steerage. On some liners, immigrants could go on deck, but the promenade allotted to steerage travelers was normally small. Graphically describing conditions below deck, one passenger related that the 900 steerage passengers "are positively packed like cattle,

"Dinner in the steerage," ca. 1877. *Scribner's Monthly,* September 1877, p. 580.

making a walk on deck when the weather is good, absolutely impossible." In bad weather when the hatches are down, "the stenches" become so "unbearable" that "many of the emigrants" go outside, "for they prefer the bitterness and danger of the storm to the pestilential air below." From the moment they boarded the ship until they arrived in America, immigrants' daily life in steerage was one of enduring cramped quarters, unappetizing food, "sickening odors," "crying children," and unsanitary conditions. Critics and immigrants alike condemned steerage as a "dismal, damp, dirty, and most unwholesome place" where "the air was heavy, foul, and deadening to the spirit." Although the food and environment in steerage could be abominable, shipping lines still took precautions to ensure that conditions on their ships did not spawn diseases, epidemics, or ordinary illnesses. Company owners and captains knew that, before passengers could disembark in the United States, health officials would board and inspect the vessels.

Third Class

Competition for the immigrant trade led steamship companies to introduce improvements. At the start of the twentieth century, some lines abolished steerage and replaced it with "third class" or offered both types of accommodations on their vessels. Third class, which was often referred to as "new steerage," provided much better accommodations. Passengers paid more, though. In 1908, one line charged an additional $7.50 for third-class passage between Hamburg, Germany, and New York. Travelers who could come up with the fare, which increased costs by a third or more, slept in small cabins with, on average, four to six sleeping berths. On some ships, the rooms had hooks and a chest of drawers for clothes. Besides containing more—as well as more conveniently located—washing and toilet facilities than was the case in "old steerage," third-class levels had a dining room and maybe a "general room" for socializing. The food, although sometimes monotonous, was usually wholesome. And even on lines that provided long bench-style slabs instead of tables with cloths, the dining rooms in third class were superior to what steerage passengers had traditionally coped with. Exposed pipes and steel beams created an unsightly decor throughout the section, but immigrants enjoyed more privacy and generally good sanitary conditions. With rare exception, however, there were no showers or bathtubs in third class. On ships that had these facilities, passengers paid a fee to use them. So, despite less crowded circumstances, foul air typically permeated the crowded third-class levels.

Despite the addition of third class, neither this changeover nor other improvements in ship accommodations were universal. As late as 1921, old steerage was still common on transoceanic ships. Although it is impossible to determine how many immigrants traveled in the separate categories, historians who have studied travel patterns conclude that a substantial majority of them made the voyage in old steerage.

Immigrants on steerage deck (1907). Courtesy of Library of Congress.

Ports of Entry

Between 1870 and 1920, New York reigned as the most popular port of entry for both old and new immigrants. While New York's dominance was never challenged, several other port cities served as gateways for newcomers. During the half century after 1870, migrants from several countries continued to follow paths blazed in the pre–Civil War era. Boston remained a common point of entry for Irish migrants. Germans kept arriving in Baltimore while both British and German migrants went to Philadelphia. Once the second wave got under way, some new immigrants also chose these other ports. Italians booked passage on ships to Boston, Philadelphia, and New Orleans. Poles and Russians opted for Philadelphia as well. Greeks, Portuguese, eastern European Jews, and Armenians also came ashore in Boston. New Orleans, which earlier in the nineteenth century had been a favorite destination for French, German, and Irish immigrants, later drew Italians and Greeks.

Immigrants who opted to go to one of America's other ports were usually following established migration patterns. Often these migrations were the result of trade routes between specific shipping lines and particular U.S. destinations. For example, German companies had links to Baltimore, and thus ships regularly sailed between harbors in northern Germany and this Maryland city. Immigrants stayed and enhanced the ethnic diversity of port cities, but these landing sites also served as important launching points to move farther into the country. Railroad systems and water routes connected the ports of entry to inland areas. Germans and, later, Poles who arrived in Baltimore were on their way to purchase land in the Midwest. Cheap fares and a good transportation system let immigrants go by steamboat from the Port of New Orleans into the midwestern and western regions of the United States.

As Europeans sailed into northeastern harbors and New Orleans, Asian immigrants disembarked at western ports. The Chinese typically got off in San Francisco but also came through Seattle to the north. Initially, most Japanese entered through San Francisco; however, as the Japanese migration picked up in the early years of the twentieth century, Los Angeles became the favored point of entry. Reflecting patterns similar to Europeans, many Asians who arrived in California moved on to somewhere else. Following enactment of the 1882 statute restricting Chinese immigration, laborers discovered they had a good chance of getting into the country through New Orleans because officials there only haphazardly enforced the law.

The number of immigrants choosing other ports declined precipitously in the last quarter of the nineteenth century. Arrivals at New Orleans, for example, plummeted from a high of 350,000 in one ten-year period before the Civil War to linger at about 3,000 per year afterward. Even ports that saw their totals keep pace with earlier years could not match the phenomenal number of immigrants passing through New York. At least two-thirds of the immigrants recorded entering the United States after 1891 disembarked in New York.

ENTERING THE UNITED STATES

The "Ellis Island" Experience

Immigrants who arrived in the 1870s and 1880s were quickly registered and allowed to proceed to their destinations. Those who came ashore in New York City passed through Castle Garden, a processing station established to help immigrants upon their arrival and protect them from swindlers. At this state-operated depot, immigrants could claim their luggage, exchange

money, purchase tickets for overland travel, and obtain reliable information. After 1882, when the U.S. Congress passed a law excluding convicts,
lunatics, idiots, and paupers from entering the country, state officials continued to oversee the admission of aliens. In 1891, Congress enacted legislation
that expanded the list of persons ineligible for entry into the United States.
It classified individuals "with a loathsome or contagious disease," polygamists, and persons likely to become public charges as inadmissible aliens.
In addition, the law required each foreign-born individual seeking admittance to provide personal information. Finally, it transferred responsibility
for processing immigrants from state to federal officials. To conduct the
more elaborate screenings mandated by the new law and, simultaneously,
to process the skyrocketing number of immigrants who were landing in
New York City, the U.S. government opened Ellis Island in 1892. Although
immigrants who came through other ports were subjected to examinations,
"Ellis Island" became the catchphrase for the ordeal associated with entering the United States at the turn of the twentieth century.

Arriving at an American port ended an often unpleasant journey, but
immigrants landing from the early 1890s onward faced a process that
for some people was more traumatic than traveling in steerage. Whether
ships docked on the East Coast, West Coast, or a Gulf port, each passenger was supposed to be checked. Immigration officials, however, merely

"The Labor Exchange—Emigrants on the Battery in front of Castle Garden, New
York." *Harper's Weekly*, August 15, 1868, p. 516.

asked first- and second-class passengers a few cursory questions and then allowed them to leave the ship. People traveling in steerage and in third class were subjected to more thorough inspections. The examination procedures were meant to keep out inadmissible immigrants, but the receiving stations were also intended to assist newcomers.

When authorities established Angel Island in San Francisco Bay, however, they had a far less accommodating goal in mind. The facility, which was opened in 1910, was supposedly a receiving depot for all immigrants disembarking at this West Coast port. In reality, it was an interrogation and detention center primarily to enforce America's tough restrictions on Chinese immigration. Besides confining immigrants of all nationalities who were suspected of carrying contagious diseases or were awaiting deportation, this escape-proof island station was designed to detain as well as prevent Chinese newcomers from communicating with family or friends on the mainland. After a three-week journey across the Pacific Ocean, Chinese passengers were ferried to the island for rigorous questioning and follow-up investigations to determine whether they were eligible to enter the country. Depending on how long it took to determine an applicant's eligibility, stays on the island could last a couple of weeks to several months. Detention periods of three to six months were not unusual, and some new arrivals reportedly remained on Angel Island for one to two years. During the entire period, people were housed in prison-style conditions. Although other nationalities spent time on Angel Island, more than 90 percent of the detainees were Chinese.

Medical Inspections

For immigrants of diverse nationalities who had boarded the same ship and had endured steerage together, the shared experience continued as they went through Ellis Island. After ships put down anchor and the initial inspections were completed, immigrants crowded onto barges and were ferried to Ellis Island, where each new arrival was examined to determine whether he or she qualified for admission to the United States. Although immigrants probably spent on average two to three hours on Ellis Island, for many newcomers going through the admission process was an agonizing ordeal filled with apprehension. That ordeal began almost as soon as immigrants stepped off the barge. Officials pinned an identification tag on each person, who then proceeded to the baggage room to claim his or her luggage. With tags attached to their hats, coats, or dresses, individuals carried their bags up long stairs while doctors waited at the top and checked to see whether climbers breathed heavily. Labored breathing might signal a heart or lung disorder. The physicians were also on the lookout for limps or other obvious physical problems. As immigrants filed by, doctors inspected their hands, arms, throats, scalps, and skin for signs of any type of malady. They looked for lumps, unusual growths, and skin abrasions. Anyone with apparent problems or suspected of being sick, having a contagious disease, or suffering a physical or mental defect was, literally, marked for further examination. Using chalk, doctors placed an identifying letter on the upper-right shoulder of their clothes. For example, "Sc" suggested a scalp problem, possibly lice or ringworm; seemingly "inattentive or stupid-looking" persons were marked with an "X," which signified a possible mental disorder.

Following this preliminary inspection, people moved on to the "eye man," who checked them for vision ailments. Using a buttonhook, the doctor lifted people's upper eyelids to search for any sign of conjunctivitis or of trachoma, which was a highly contagious disease. Immigrants who went through Ellis Island without any difficulties almost universally considered the eye exam the worst part of the entire physical inspection. Aliens who got a chalk mark during the initial general inspection, however, probably felt differently. After the "eye man" finished probing, these marked individuals were pulled aside and detained for more meticulous examinations. Depending on the specific problem, the detention might last a few hours, a few days, a few weeks, or much longer. Sick immigrants were transferred to the Ellis Island infirmary for treatment; however, individuals with medical conditions that rendered them legally inadmissible were denied entry to the United States and forced to return home.

Immigrants crossing bridge from barge to Ellis Island, 1902. Courtesy of Library of Congress.

Using a buttonhook to check for eye disease among immigrants arriving at Ellis Island, 1907. National Archives and Record Administration 90-G-125-12.

Registration

Persons who successfully passed the medical inspections pressed forward to registration in the Great Hall. In this massive room, divided into what one immigrant scornfully described as "passageways made by iron railings," families and individuals slowly filed through one of the many pipe-railed lanes toward immigration officials. One by one, inspectors recorded vital information for each arrival: name, age, gender, marital status, nationality, and place of origin. Officials also asked people how much money they had brought with them, where they were headed in the United States, and if they already had a job. In addition, questioners tried to discover whether the new arrival had a criminal record or was a polygamist or a prostitute. They also inquired about individuals' political beliefs and whether they were anarchists. To comply with newly enacted literacy laws, after 1917 examiners tested adults to evaluate their ability to read a language. Giving the wrong answer to some questions could result in an immigrant being detained or being sent back home.

Admissions and Exclusions

Heartrending accounts about families facing painful decisions when a parent or child was deemed inadmissible, coupled with reports of other

Immigrants being processed at Ellis Island, ca. 1904. Courtesy Library of Congress.

agonizing experiences at Ellis Island, caused many to dub it the "Isle of Tears" or "Heartbreak Island." The stories were probably mostly true, and immigrants' fears about "Ellis Island" were real. The overwhelming majority of foreign-born men, women, and children who made their way through the long, intimidating lines, however, had little cause for worry. Despite poignant stories about exclusion, when compared to how many immigrants were admitted to the United States, the number of people excluded was actually small. Official immigration figures reveal that between 1892 and 1920, nearly 18.6 million foreign-born individuals arrived at America's several receiving stations, and only 308,835 of them—less than 1.7 percent—were denied entry. Whether they came through New York's Ellis Island or a checkpoint at one of the several other port cities, the overwhelming majority of immigrants were permitted to move on.

After officials finished registering them, immigrants perhaps used the stations' facilities to exchange money, purchase tickets to inland destinations, or send telegraph messages. Some new arrivals went outside to greet family or friends eagerly awaiting their appearance. Diverse people whose daily lives during previous weeks had been similarly shaped by their decision to migrate to the United States thus finally went their own ways as they spread out in different directions and continued their journey to an often-predetermined destination.

**The End
of Mass of
Immigration**   As immigrants seeking to better their prospects came by
water and by land in the late nineteenth and early twentieth centuries, the U.S. Congress continued to expand the
list of people ineligible for entry into the United States. The
1891 law, which barred persons for medical reasons, also
made "idiots, paupers," or "persons likely to become a public charge"
inadmissible. In 1903, Congress banned epileptics, prostitutes, and polygamists. The 1903 law was significant, however, because it established the
precedent that individuals' political beliefs or ideologies justified denying
them admission. "Anarchists or persons who believe in or advocate" the
violent overthrow of governments were henceforth to be turned away at
America's borders. The idea that individuals who might burden society or
who held controversial political beliefs should not be permitted into the
country continued to influence immigration legislation in the twentieth
century. By creating the Asiatic Barred Zone in 1917, federal legislators
also furthered the discriminatory practice of trying to keep out Asians.
Most natives of the zone, which was a triangular region in the Far East that
included India, Burma, Siam, the Malay states, the East Indian islands,
Polynesian Islands, and parts of Arabia, Afghanistan, and eastern Russia,
now belonged to the inadmissible category.

Establishing the Asiatic Barred Zone was a secondary aim of the 1917
law. Popularly known as the Literacy Act, the statute stipulated that pro-
spective immigrants sixteen years old or older had to demonstrate they
could read in any language. Married women whose husbands were literate were exempt, as were certain close relatives of legally admitted
immigrants. Enacting a literacy requirement reflected a long-standing
animosity toward new immigrants. Since the end of the nineteenth century, Americans opposed to the rising level of immigration from eastern
and southern Europe had been advocating a literacy qualification. Critics of the new immigrants deemed them biologically and culturally inferior peoples who would not easily assimilate but, instead, would debase
American society. They believed stipulating that persons must be able to
read and write would significantly reduce the number of southern and
eastern Europeans coming into the United States.

The desire to keep out new immigrants, together with fears that the
end of the Great War would bring a flood of people to America, finally
led to a fundamental change in U.S. immigration policy. For the first time
in American history, limiting the total number of immigrants who could
enter the country became official U.S. policy. The Quota Act passed in 1921
capped immigration at 358,000 and established individual country quotas
based on nationalities. The annual quotas for nationality groups—and,
hence, for each country—was set at 3 percent of the foreign-born individuals of that nationality recorded in the 1910 U.S. census. Three years
later, Congress replaced the 1921 quota legislation with a more stringent
measure. The Immigration Act of 1924 lowered the annual limit to slightly

less than 165,000 immigrants per year and stipulated that within a few years it be limited to 150,000.

Besides changing the census year to 1890, the 1924 legislation modified the formula for determining country quotas by reducing allocations to 2 percent of totals recorded in that census. Because the new immigration did not get really under way until after 1890, this formula substantially reduced the number of southern and eastern European immigrants permitted into the United States. These quotas, however, were only temporary. The Immigration Act of 1924, which is often referred to as the National Origins Act, mandated that new quotas based on each nationality's contribution to the ethnic composition of the United States in 1920 be established. In a conscious effort to restrict the new immigration, policy makers devised a complicated "national origins" formula to ensure that old immigrant countries would receive the lion's share of the annual quotas. Finally, because it excluded persons ineligible for citizenship, the law essentially banned all immigration from Asia, except for Filipinos, who were U.S. nationals. With the quota laws of the 1920s, the mass immigration that had flowed from the nineteenth into the early twentieth century finally came to an end.

The influx of millions of people during the decades stretching between 1870 and 1920 had significantly altered American society. The 1920 census reinforced the reality that 50 years of near continuous immigration had transformed America into a much more richly diverse country than it had earlier been. Not even official tabulations, which listed immigrants as coming from 40 "countries of origin" and representing 31 "mother tongues," could accurately depict the true diversity that characterized the nearly 14 million people that made up the country's foreign-born population in 1920. By exploring the mundane as well as the complex aspects of immigrants' lives, the following chapters attempt to turn the statistics and data encountered here into the real human experiences that they were.

NOTE

Immigrant life stories and quotations included in this chapter were derived from Edward A. Steiner, *On the Trail of the Immigrant* (New York: Revell, 1906); U.S. Congress, Immigration Commission, *Reports of the Immigration Commission,* vol. 37, *Steerage Conditions—Importation and Harboring of women for Immoral Purposes—Immigrant Homes and Aid Societies—Immigrant Banks* (61st Cong., 3d sess., 1911, S.Doc. 753).

2

Life on the Land: Immigrants in the American West

Many foreign-born people who migrated to the United States during the last quarter of the nineteenth century came with a modest goal. They aspired to maintain their traditional agricultural way of life by becoming independent farmers in America. In pursuing this conservative quest, however, immigrants discovered that making a living from the land required continually adjusting to different, often difficult circumstances. So, to achieve their objective, immigrants learned new farming methods while, at the same time, they used knowledge and applied techniques acquired in their homelands. Even as farm families adapted to new situations and struggled to overcome seemingly formidable obstacles, they preserved important aspects of their "old lives." Moreover, despite their rather ordinary objectives, immigrant farmers played a mighty role in transforming the upper Midwest and the vast territory stretching westward from the Mississippi River. They helped turn the region not only into an ethnically diverse area but also into an agricultural region capable of supporting the country's rapidly growing population.

EARLY YEARS ON THE LAND

Lure of the Land
By 1870, westward settlement had expanded beyond the Mississippi River. The California gold rush of the late 1840s had drawn fortune hunters to the Pacific Coast, but it was an abundance of land that attracted most people to the Midwest and western United States. In the mid-nineteenth century, the U.S.

Congress tried to make the West even more attractive by passing the Homestead Act. Enacted in 1862, this law essentially gave away land in the vast region stretching from the Mississippi River to the Pacific Coast. For a small filing fee, U.S. citizens or individuals who declared their intention to become citizens could obtain 160 acres of uncleared land. To retain possession, homesteaders had to erect a dwelling, clear five acres, and live on the land for five years. What the government seemed to be promising was that, with minimal money but a great deal of hard work, people could become independent landowners.

To encourage railroads to build tracks and establish western routes that would further development of the western United States, the federal government gave companies huge land grants. By 1871, railroads had received more than 131 million acres of free land, which they, in turn, could sell for a profit. Railroad moguls, however, had an incentive to sell cheaply. Their major objective was to increase traffic along their western routes; to achieve this, they needed people to settle in sparsely populated regions. Therefore, railroad companies used cheap land to lure both native and foreign-born migrants to the Midwest, Great Plains, Southwest, and Pacific Coast. State and territorial governments shared a goal similar to the railroads: they wanted people to settle within their borders. For states, additional residents meant more congressional representatives and thus enhanced political clout; for territories, increased populations led to statehood. In addition, states and territories wanted to promote economic development within their boundaries. State and territorial governments, therefore, established "emigration bureaus" to recruit new residents. In an almost cutthroat competition for immigrants, these bureaus dispatched agents to America's port cities as well as overseas to help route immigration to their respective regions. Emigration bureaus also published foreign-language guidebooks and pamphlets, which contained information about America and were distributed in European countries. Reflecting the fierce rivalry for immigrants, the various publications extolled the advantages of a particular state or territory while, at times, drawing attention to the alleged shortcomings of a rival area. One characteristic that all the government, railroad, and emigration bureaus shared in common, however, was an emphasis on the ready availability of fertile, inexpensive land.

The desire of railroads, states, and territories to boost the population of the western United States meshed perfectly with the objectives of steamship companies. Realizing that their profits depended on expanding the immigrant trade—not on leisure travel—passenger lines developed strategies to keep the migration flow going. Competing for passengers, steamship lines highlighted short travel times and claimed their ships were superior. "Go to America with . . . the biggest ships, the lowest prices, the best food," one passenger line advertised. To facilitate the journey for people desiring to go directly to a western destination, passenger lines cooperated with railroads by offering package deals that, as one ad publicized, included steamship passage as well as tickets to "all cities of the West." Steamship companies also exploited the land theme to recruit business. Their publications containing practical information about the United States underscored the country's cheap farmland and agricultural riches. European newspapers printed ads for overseas tickets, travel schedules, and stories about opportunities awaiting immigrants. Thus, during the 1870s and 1880s, an array of materials touting America's land-rich frontier was widely disseminated and shared among inhabitants throughout northern and western Europe. All this promotional literature sparked the imagination of people weighing what the future held for them.

Letters from relatives and friends confirmed what the publications were claiming: the United States contained an abundance of cheap land. Correspondence from pioneers—those emigrants who had ventured forth earlier—became the single most important factor steering people to the American West. In the spring of 1870, a woman informed people back home that, although one could still find 160-acre plots "free of charge" in some states, in Texas, where she lived, most of the free government land had been claimed long ago. Be that as it may, "good land may be bought for $2 an acre," she assured them. "Your finest plowlands at home cannot compare with the rich dark prairies here [Nebraska], where golden harvests grow from year to year," a Swede enthusiastically wrote. "My traveling companion has bought eighty acres . . . of land for around fifty dollars," he reported in early 1880. A countryman informed people that in Michigan in 1883, "Everyone can get railroad land for five dollars per acre covered with virgin forest." Trees meant an easy supply of building materials and maybe ready income from lumber sales. While immigrants might exaggerate their own accomplishments and paint an overly positive picture of conditions in the United States, they were still right when they claimed that America offered possibilities inconceivable in rural areas of European countries. For landowners in Europe who realized that their holdings were too small or overworked to provide their children with secure futures, for farmers who endured misfortunes and now risked falling into the landless ranks, and for landless people who aspired to become independent landowners, immigrating to America was a sensible option.

Almost as soon as they stepped ashore, immigrants who were headed west began the second phase of their journey. To reach their final destinations, some people would travel partway by train and then finish their trip by boat or wagon **The Journey West** and sometimes a combination of both. After spending perhaps two weeks—or more than two months before 1873—crammed into steerage, immigrants arriving in New York pressed their way through crowds in Castle Garden. If they had prepaid railroad tickets, new arrivals passed quickly by ticket offices at the receiving station and went to wait for their westbound trains. In 1881, contemporary observers estimated that three-fourths of the immigrants arriving in New York came with prepurchased train tickets. As immigrants stood or sat in the waiting areas, railroad agents walked through, checked their tickets, wrote their destinations on tags, and pinned them somewhere on the traveler's outer clothes. This ensured that immigrants who did not speak English would board and, when necessary, transfer to the correct train. Travelers need only show their tag to a conductor or agent at the train stations.

The journey west in the 1870s and 1880s was long, tiresome, and rarely pleasant. People often crowded into designated "emigrant cars," which were usually old freight cars converted for passenger traffic. With compartments filled to capacity, men, women, and children squeezed together as they sat, ate, and slept on hard wooden benches. There were no separate sleeping berths, and because cars also lacked dining facilities immigrants usually had to bring enough provisions to last the entire trip. They could buy some food at stations located in cities or towns along the way. In the 1870s and 1880s, emigrant cars were often attached to freight trains that chugged along at a slow pace. Apart from enduring an agonizingly slow ride, immigrants faced another potential inconvenience. While en route, emigrant cars might be "switched off" to a side track so that additional freight cars could be added to the train. If passengers were switched off, they then had to wait several hours or longer until another train came along. When switch offs occurred at small way stations in remote areas, travelers had no access to food, water, shelter, or other human comforts. Graphically highlighting the abuses of this practice, a contemporary reporter documented one instance in which "an emigrant party" that included "old people, delicate women and children" was forced to wait all night in "a cold drenching rain" for another train.

Regardless of whether their trip was direct or temporarily interrupted, in the 1870s and 1880s, many immigrants were headed to isolated settlement areas with no direct connections to the main railroad lines. Because the nearest train station could be a substantial distance from their final destination, immigrants had no choice but to proceed by wagon or boat. If family or friends met them at the depot, however, getting off the train turned into an immediate reunion, and the remainder of the journey was in the company of people more solicitous of their comfort than the railroad companies had been.

Immigrant Settlements   As land-hungry immigrants streamed into the upper Midwest and the western United States, ethnic groups concentrated in the same locations. Consequently, although individual states and territories became home to several nationalities, immigrant groups carved out their own geographic niches and dominated the local landscapes where they settled. For example, by the early 1900s, Swedes accounted for nearly 90 percent of the foreign residents of Issanti County in eastern Minnesota, and in rural western sections of the state Norwegians made up 75 to 100 percent of the population. Germans concentrated in well-defined areas of Wisconsin, Missouri,

"In the emigrant train." *Harper's Weekly,* January 24, 1874, p. 76.

Minnesota, and Texas. But even in states that did not attract them in large numbers, Germans tended to cluster together. According to one calculation, three-fifths of the adults residing in a small township in southeastern Nebraska were German. At the turn of century, ethnic bunching also occurred in the Dakotas, Nebraska, and other western states.

Newcomers added to the ethnic homogeneity of a region by purchasing available land and, hence, filling vacant areas. Prosperous earlier arrivals contributed to ethnic clustering when they bought additional land and

"Switched Off" the immigrant train. *Harper's Weekly*, January 24, 1874, p. 76.

further reduced the amount that speculators had to sell to "outsiders." Even when they could not afford to expand, older residents tried to make sure that neighboring landowners were fellow countrymen and country-women. Ole Nielsen "often wished" that a 160-acre tract near his Iowa farm belonged to one of his relatives, but since "this was not possible," he revealed that he had "done everything" possible to persuade one of his "acquaintances to buy it." He was also happy that a Norwegian he knew purchased another nearby parcel.

The continual influx of aspiring farmers resulted in hundreds of small immigrant-run farms dotting the landscape of the Midwest and western United States. Indeed, by the 1880s, foreign-born families owned much of the arable land in some local areas. True, the individual settlements might comprise hundreds of farms spread over a large area; nevertheless, they represented ethnic concentrations. Thus, although people might live several miles apart, a person who hailed from the same place likely owned the neighboring farm, and, no matter in which direction they went, immigrant settlers could find people who spoke their language and shared their geographic and cultural roots. A Swedish immigrant inadvertently confirmed how chain migration patterns were shaping the ethnic makeup of rural America when he related that "West of us there live nothing but Swedes for a distance of about sixteen miles. East and south and north of us there lives a mixed population of Americans, Germans and Bohemians, Negroes, and Mexicans, so it is certainly a strange mixture."

New arrivals on the frontier first of all needed a place to live. Migrating to regions where people from their homelands resided meant immigrants could expect that relatives or friends would provide temporary lodging. **Arriving and Acquiring Land** One Swedish minister recalled that in 1877 after he and a friend met a group of "sixty or seventy Swedish immigrants" who had made their way to Nebraska, the newcomers "packed themselves into a house they had rented for the time being." In Kansas, German Mennonites from Russia built a barracks to house newcomers until they could construct their own dwellings. Individual families opened their homes to the recently arrived. The welcoming hand that pioneers extended to later immigrants helped make their first days on the frontier a little easier; nevertheless, goodwill and assistance often did not lessen the initial disappointment that overwhelmed many people when they arrived in the American West. Already distraught by how "desolate the country seemed" without hills and only a few trees instead of forests, one woman's distress worsened when the family reached its destination in Kansas. Describing the attic where they were put up as "divided into three rooms but with no doors," she "hung a sheet in front of our 'door.'" Surveying their lodgings, she lamented that "there was no table, no chair, no bed, *nothing*, and there we were to stay?" Her despair was evident as she told family back home, "I set the candle on the floor, sat down beside it, took the children in my lap and burst into tears."

For would-be farmers, acquiring land was their first real order of business. Although "government land" went almost free to immigrants who declared their intention to become citizens, as early as the 1870s, settlers found that homestead land was in short supply. Railroads and speculators had managed to gobble up the best ground in some regions, and so immigrants who wanted to remain in a particular settlement area had no choice but to purchase or rent parcels from them. Depending on its location, railroad land typically cost as little as $2 to $5 per acre, while speculators demanded more for the prime parcels they owned. Immigrants who leased land generally negotiated agreements whereby, in return for farming the rented sector, they worked for the owners or gave them a portion of their annual crops.

Whether buying or renting, immigrants had to be especially wary lest they fall victim to unscrupulous agents or crooks eager to bilk unwitting "foreigners." Some immigrants were swindled, but many had safeguards working in their favor. The widely circulated guidebooks and pamphlets they read before leaving their homelands provided basic information about farming regions and how to obtain land in the United States. Also, rather than take the word of a stranger, experienced farmers preferred to rely on their own expertise. They knew rich soil and favorable agricultural conditions when they encountered them; hence, many immigrants naturally wanted to inspect the terrain before making a purchase. Most important, since new arrivals were likely going to places where family and friends already lived, they could rely on the knowledge and experience of people they trusted. These seasoned residents advised newcomers about the location of good land and helped ensure that tricksters did not defraud or gouge them. Some new arrivals were particularly fortunate because already settled relatives or friends had bought them a parcel while the pickings were still good.

First Houses   Finding good farmland was the first challenge immigrants faced; constructing a dwelling to live in was the second. Most immigrants wisely timed their departures to arrive in the spring when the weather was suitable for building as well as planting. Settlers who did not reach their destinations until the fall had only a few months to put together something fit for human habitation before winter set in. Many immigrants quickly discovered that being quartered in stark attics or a barracks was pleasant compared to where they might live during their first few years as aspiring farmers. The type of housing they built depended on materials available. In prairie regions of the Great Plains, where timber was in short supply, people constructed sod houses composed of tough squares of turf (grass, tangled roots, and soil) layered on top of one another. They also created "dugouts," which were essentially caves burrowed into the side of a bank or hill. The front facades could be sod or wood. Sod houses and dugouts were reasonably cool in the summer and warm in the winter, but they had dirt floors and sod roofs, moreover, leaked when it rained.

In forested areas, some newcomers made dugouts, but people also built wood or log dwellings. These primitive structures more closely resembled sheds than solid, comfortable houses. Quickly constructed wood buildings were typically drafty despite the tar paper that some owners put around the exterior or the mud or sod they stuffed into the cracks. Tar-paper shacks

Ole Myrvik's sod house, Milton, North Dakota, 1896. Fred Hultstrand History In Pictures Collection, NDIRS-NDSU, Fargo, ND.

were probably the least comfortable of the hurriedly put-together shelters; they were flimsy and afforded little protection against harsh weather. Regardless of what materials went into producing the immigrants' first frontier homes, these dwellings were usually very small. They might be only 10 feet by 12 feet, the minimum size required for houses on parcels claimed under the Homestead Act. Some first homes were, in comparison, a relatively roomy 20 feet by 12 feet. Dugouts also varied in size, but they could be as big as 14 feet by 14 feet.

Besides being cramped, the various quickly constructed residences were unpleasant places to live. Houses and dugouts usually had chimneys; however, on cold days when doors had to remain closed, interiors could become smoky. In both winter and summer, the indoors were typically bleak. Many dwellings, including those in lumber-rich areas, had hard-packed dirt floors. Even wood-planked floors were often wobbly, squeaky, and uneven, with huge gaps where dropped items easily fell through and were lost. Because windows were crude, sunshine could not easily enter the immigrants' abodes. One dismayed immigrant described the structures inhabited by fellow Swedes as "wretched wooden sheds." Their sod houses and dugouts were "hovels," he declared. Makeshift furnishings matched the stark living quarters. Beds, tables, chairs, and cabinets were rudimentary and put together from readily available materials. "During the first years," the immigrant "is deprived of many comforts previously enjoyed," one woman later admitted to her family. Compared to dwellings in their homelands, immigrants' initial quarters were dismal.

Finnish homesteaders near Kypo, Michigan, 1900. Courtesy Immigration History Research Center, University of Minnesota.

Some immigrants were so ashamed of their houses that they were thankful their family and friends in Europe would never see their first home in America.

As they hurriedly constructed some sort of shelter, immigrants on the frontier needed to lay in a supply of food for winter. Even for those settlers who had money to spend on provisions, the nearest town could be miles away and not an easy trip during winter months over roads that were no more than rutted paths. Immigrants who arrived in the spring had little time to waste before seeds had to go into the ground. In timber-rich areas, they quickly fenced garden areas with wood railings that would keep out animals and prevent humans from inadvertently trampling tender plants. Latecomers who did not reach their destinations until late summer or fall, when it was too late to plant food for the family table, faced a precarious and potentially disastrous future. Without the assistance of more established settlers who either gave or sold them food, many newcomers might not have survived their first winter. When spring came, families could begin a planting and harvesting regime that fit the normal growing cycle.

Setting Up Farms
After making it through the first winter, immigrant settlers had no time to waste when spring came. As soon as the weather permitted, they started clearing the land so they could plant gardens and grain crops. This two-part process—clearing before planting—was a new experience that required even the most skilled farmers to readjust their work habits. One foreign-born farmer underscored the differences between immigrants' homelands and

America when he reflected that in Europe sons could "work the turf" that their fathers had long ago "broke," but in America "one must clear one's own way on ground where not only strength and an unbending willpower are needed, but also courage and self-denial. This at least during the early period." In forested areas, huge trees had to be felled and massive stumps completely dug out; in prairie regions, thick brush with deep, tangled roots had to be ripped out; nearly everywhere, stones and rocks had to be removed. Throughout the 1870s and 1880s, as thousands of immigrants poured into the farmlands of the American Midwest, the ordeal of initially settling in and getting their farms started was repeated over and over. Swedish immigrants even had a special word for the harsh early years: *hundår*, which translated as "dog years."

Although clustering together in the same geographic areas meant that relatives and acquaintances could offer advice or lend a helping hand, each immigrant family had its own farm to get into working order. As a result, the arduous job of clearing the land became a family activity, with husbands working alongside wives and children of all ages performing whatever tasks they physically could. From early spring until the final fall harvest, immigrant families passed their days rolling stones or logs—sometimes both—pulling up roots, hoeing, planting, and weeding. In addition to the grueling field labor that devoured large amounts of people's daily lives, settlers spent time improving their houses and making furniture. Women also cooked, sewed, washed clothes, and tried to keep their humble abodes clean.

Clearing a field near Waino, Wisconsin, ca. 1911. Courtesy Immigration History Research Center, University of Minnesota.

Family labor was crucial to transforming uncultivated soil into fertile cropland, but setting up a farm required equipment and animals. Immigrants might have brought a few small implements—perhaps some carpenter's tools—but it was impossible to pack all the equipment necessary for the various tasks that awaited them. They required sturdy axes to chop down trees, grubbing hoes to pull out stumps, and scythes to cut high grasses and weeds. Farmers needed plows to turn the soil and harrows to break up the clods and even the plowed earth. In addition to finding a wagon and the necessary implements for clearing and cultivating, new settlers had to acquire animals to pull the various equipment. Although nationalities differed in the type of beast of burden they preferred, obtaining either a team of horses or oxen was a high priority. Depending on the soil and how well the land was cleared, with a team of horses pulling a 16-inch plow a farmer could cultivate 50 to 80 acres of land in a month. Plowing with oxen took longer. Prices varied by place and over time, but a team of oxen could be purchased for as little as $50 or as much as $200, and a team of horses cost $200 to $400.

Setting up farms and acquiring the minimal necessities required an immediate outlay of cash. Immigrants who had been landed farmers in Europe came with money they could put toward their farms, while landless people obtained it through a variety of means. Some adult children expecting inheritances sold their rights and used the proceeds to start a farm in America. Immigrants who arrived with little more than their bare hands might rent a parcel of land or work as wage laborers until they accumulated enough savings to start their own farms. But even immigrants who came with some financial resources learned that setting up a family-run farm was a more expensive undertaking than they had expected. Although it was true that land was fairly cheap, buying the necessary implements, work animals, food-producing livestock, and seed to establish their farms could require $500 to $800. In order to get started, many immigrant farmers went into debt and used their land or animals as collateral.

To pay debts or to acquire hard cash, it was not uncommon for men to take temporary jobs. For part of the year when they could not work in their own fields, these farmers became wage laborers. A few poorer farmers worked as hired hands for better-off countrymen; most men, however, found more lucrative employment. During the winter months, immigrants in areas stretching from the upper Midwest to the northern Pacific Coast got jobs in the lumber industry. Men also split rails and laid railroad tracks. In the 1880s, a person could earn at least $1.25 to $1.50 a day laying track and maybe the same amount working for a logging company. In the early 1890s, miners in Michigan could gross $50 a month. Although companies normally subtracted room and board from workers' weekly wages, the net earnings still provided cash-poor farmers with some otherwise unattainable income. Performing seasonal labor unfortunately entailed living in logging camps or traveling with construction gangs as they laid branch lines and extended railroad tracks westward. Consequently, men left their families for months at a time. While men were away in the winter, women and children had to take care of the farm, do all the chores, and handle any emergencies that might arise. When spring came, these farmers-turned-temporary-wage-laborers once again returned to their families and their farm duties.

FAMILY FARMS

The first years were just the beginning of what would be an ongoing challenge for many immigrants dreaming of becoming self-sufficient farmers. In addition to coping with everyday tasks, farm families had to adjust to the perennial **Division of Labor** short supply of labor for hire in the United States. Finding hired help had not been a problem in rural Europe. Population explosions and a tradition of seasonal labor had created a labor pool that owners could tap to help with the heavy fieldwork and other tasks. The situation was decidedly different in America's Midwest and Great Plains. The abundance of cheap land and the availability of good-paying jobs meant comparatively few people sought work as agricultural laborers. Relatives helped one another, but at the same time individual families had their own farms to get into production. There was no choice: the labor shortage meant the nuclear family—parents and their children—made up the workforce on immigrant-run farms. Everyone pitched in whenever necessary, but there were also divisions of labor in which each family member had his or her own tasks. Because cultural traditions could influence which chores men, women, or children performed, not all immigrant groups developed precisely the same system of assigned duties. Still, there were enough similarities among the various nationalities that it is possible to depict the division of labor that shaped the daily lives of men, women, and children.

Men

Men were chiefly responsible for the heavy fieldwork. From spring to early summer, which was their busiest time, men planted crops and cleared land to increase acreage for future cultivation. For men, the second busiest time was the autumn when the crops were ready to be harvested. To take advantage of the daylight, beginning with the spring planting and continuing well into the fall, a farmer's day started with sunrise and ended when the sun set. During a family's early settlement years, women and children normally lent a helping hand in the fields, but men performed the heavy labor. They pushed the plows and then pushed the harrows. If fortunate enough to have a team of horses or oxen to pull plows and harrows, men maneuvered animal-drawn implements through the fields. Men took care of farm equipment, maintained buildings, and built fences to enclose fields. Because people in immigrant communities bartered services or worked in exchange for borrowing a countryman's equipment, a farmer's day was not always devoted to his own farm. He went off to help plow, construct buildings, or perform other chores that were part of a personal bargain. Often farmers simply helped one another with labor-intensive undertakings such as raising a barn. At harvest time, gangs of men moved from farm to farm to thresh wheat or to assist fellow countrymen reap other crops.

When men were not in the fields, there was plenty to keep them busy. They built houses, stables, and barns or enlarged existing structures, especially houses. Until families could afford to purchase items, men typically made the furniture that newly established households needed. It was also not uncommon for immigrant men to do the shopping for goods the family required but could not produce. Depending on where the nearest town was located, a shopping venture could take a short time or entail a good part of the day, with several hours spent just traveling back and forth.

Women

During the early years while families were struggling to start their farms, immigrant women worked in the fields. In addition to removing brush and rocks from uncultivated ground, they helped sow seeds and harvest crops. Although it was unlikely that they would have had to clear land, the practice of women going out into the fields to labor was not unheard of in some European countries. For instance, nineteenth-century observers contended that German women doing fieldwork in America was a continuation of Old World practices. German Mennonite women from Russia, however, had not usually toiled in the fields; thus, engaging in such activity marked a deviation from their traditional patterns. And it was not customary in Scandinavian countries for women to venture into the fields to do heavy work either. The change that took place in women's roles in America was often only temporary. As farming became increasingly more mechanized after the 1870s and farmers found the resources to buy laborsaving machines, there was less need for women to do heavy fieldwork. The continual influx of immigrants in the 1870s and 1880s, however, almost assured that one would always see some immigrant women clearing the land, planting, and harvesting.

Although they occasionally had to join men in the fields, the daily lives of immigrant farm women were shaped by what was viewed as their traditional domestic role. Women's responsibilities usually centered on house-related chores, providing sustenance for the household, and child rearing. Similar to what women did in Europe and what so-called Yankee farm women did, immigrant women prepared meals, baked, preserved foods, cleaned the house, and did the laundry. In addition to spinning and weaving cloth, they sewed new clothes, mended torn ones, knitted, and darned. Women usually made soap and candles. They plucked and dressed chickens and skinned freshly killed rabbits. From summer into fall, they picked berries and gathered wild eatable vegetation. Women's duties also included tending the vegetable garden, taking charge of small animals, milking cows, and helping with the slaughtering. Similar to men, who often could bring only a few farm implements, women arrived with precious few household items. They lacked cooking equipment, utensils, dishes, and housecleaning tools, so farm women had to make do and improvise, for example, by using bottles as rolling pins or borrowing pans and kettles until they could acquire their own. Women also had to teach themselves to do familiar chores, including cooking, in different ways. As an immigrant woman in Iowa put it, "One must readjust oneself and learn everything all over again, even to the preparation of food."

Immigrant women performed many of the same domestic chores they would have done in their homelands, but housekeeping under frontier conditions was a tough challenge. Dust sifting into living quarters was a continual irritation on the dry prairies; rainy weather created worse problems. Sod roofs that leaked when it rained left muck dripping on clothes and furniture. Keeping the house clean was only part of a woman's daily routine, which usually began at daybreak with making breakfast before her husband—or she and the rest of the family—headed into the fields. Describing daily life to her sister back home, Ida Lindgren explained, "There is not time for me to sit and do any handwork." She had "ten [people] to bake and cook and wash up for every day," but, she declared, "worst of all," she had to do laundry for ten people. And without any hired help, she had "to do everything" by herself. Detailing a recent day's activities, she recounted, "After we finished slaughtering, I got started with laundry. . . . *Washing* is the worst work I have to do, for my hands can't take it and they have been so miserable, swollen and raw, that all the knuckles bled."

Ida reflected a common loathing for doing laundry, a task that required immigrant women to learn new methods for doing a customary domestic chore. They used traditional washboards, but because the water was so hard, as one woman explained, "Clothes are washed in a very unusual way" and require "a lot of extra work." So people back home would understand what she meant, she detailed the process: "First one must prepare the lye. This is poured into boiling water, and immediately the lye forms a white scum something like thick sour milk." Because the lye was caustic, "The frothy scum must be skimmed off before one puts the clothes into the water." If there was a stream nearby, women might carry boiled items there to scrub or beat them clean before rinsing them. To get rid of the water, each piece was wrung separately by hand. After all this work, women on the prairie might be forced to watch helplessly as swirling dust coated recently washed clothes hung outside to dry. Doing laundry was tougher yet in the winter. If a family had no well and nearby creeks froze, the large water supply required for washing clothes temporarily vanished and the laundry piled up. One woman who hated doing the laundry nevertheless complained that sometimes in the winter it was simply "so cold" that one was not "able to do any washing for some weeks." When this happened, so much laundry accumulated that, when conditions improved, washing clothes was a more horrendous task than usual. After they finished the laundry, women saved the lye water and used it to scrub floors.

Apparently the only way one woman believed she could convey just how much work a farm woman had to do was to compare it to what was necessary to run wealthy homes in her native land. "Here [in America] the mistress must do all the work that the cook, the maid, and the house-keeper would do in an upper-class family at home. Moreover, she must do her work as well as those three together do it in Norway." As this immigrant woman put it, "We are told that the women of America have much leisure time, but I haven't met any woman yet who thought so!" A shortage of affordable hired help—specifically of domestic servants—made household chores more demanding. And although females pitched in to make up for the short supply of field hands, their husbands typically did not assist with routine domestic chores.

Children

Trying to tell a grandfather something about the grandchildren he would never see, Gro Svendsen depicted, in part, the daily life of immigrant children on a midwestern farm. Describing her family, she related that eleven-year-old Svend, who was "tall and big for his age," was "a great help to his father" around the farm, and eight-year-old Carl "works" fast. Ten-year-old Niels was especially good at caring for his three younger brothers, ranging in age from four to seven, and his two-year-old sister. During the next four years, the number of sisters he cared for increased by two, but only one survived infancy. All told, the young mother had 10 children before she died in childbirth. Large households like the Svendsens' were not uncommon; however, calculations based on a few census samples indicate that the average immigrant farm family probably included four to six children. Apart from how many sons and daughters a couple had, as with the Svendsens, each child played an important role in farm life.

In America, a large number of children was an asset to immigrant farmers because they provided a ready supply of otherwise unavailable or unaffordable laborers. There was no set age when children joined the family labor pool, but it was not unusual for children to begin performing odd jobs at the age of six or even younger. Although there were exceptions, immigrant parents usually were not unreasonable taskmasters; moreover, the chores they assigned children generally corresponded with the young-sters' abilities. Duties changed as sons and daughters became stronger and matured. Similar to Svend, Carl, and Niels Svendsen, most youngsters spent their days doing odd jobs, helping raise younger siblings, or assisting mothers with their domestic and food-related tasks. The specific responsibilities given to males and females depended on where families lived, the children's ages, and cultural traditions carried over from Europe. Both boys and girls were charged with gathering kindling, stacking firewood outside, and carrying in the day's supply of fuel for cooking and heating. They hauled water from the well or nearby stream. Males and females alike assisted with planting and harvesting; they picked and shucked corn, sheaved grain, and gleaned wheat. Young people helped with the gardening, gathered eggs, and scavenged for wild fruits and eatable vegetation. As they grew older, boys worked longer hours in the fields, and, in addition to doing backbreaking labor, they took on farm duties that required more skill, such as operating machines or driving teams of horses or oxen. By helping mothers with household and domestic duties, young girls learned skills they would need when they set up their own homes.

Some children contributed to the family income by taking wage-paying jobs. Lauding the benefits of migrating to Texas, for instance, one immigrant woman assured people that "children are no burden, but a great help to their parents." Elaborating, she related that a child could make "good money picking cotton." An industrious worker could pick two hundred pounds a day, and at 75 cents per hundred pounds that amounted to $1.50 for a day's labor. The work, she assured potential immigrants, was "light" and could "easily be done by children." As early as their midteens, young

Polish father and son cultivating near Wilmo, Minnesota in undated photograph. Courtesy Immigration History Research Center, University of Minnesota.

women took jobs as domestic servants and turned earnings over to their parents.

Traditional views regarding parental authority meant that young people typically had little choice but to do their share of the daily chores. Indeed, most immigrant parents not only expected it of them but also took pride in their children's contributions and approvingly compared them to "Yankee" children, whom they depicted as lazy or ingrates. Immigrants felt justified in requiring sons and daughters to work because, from their perspective, children would ultimately benefit from their own labor. They reasoned that by helping enlarge farms and making them successful, youths were adding to their inheritances and, moreover, ensuring that their parents would not be burdens in their old age. History has not recorded how most children and young adults felt about their parents exerting so much control over their daily lives. When they reached young adulthood, however, many children balked at continuing to serve as a source of cheap labor on the family farm. Believing better prospects awaited elsewhere, young adults might move on to establish their own farms or abandoned farming altogether. Even after they wed, however, some adult children opted to remain with their parents. Despite whatever future decisions they made, the early lives of sons and daughters of immigrant farmers were significantly influenced by the belief that children had an obligation to help the family succeed.

FARMING IN AMERICA

Relying on family members to offset the shortage of wage labor was only one adjustment that immigrant farmers had to make. As a young immigrant explained to his sisters, "Farming is very different here from in Sweden." In the Old Country, farmers had usually tilled small fields, knew which crops grew well, and, moreover, knew how to raise them successfully. Besides cultivating acres and acres of land, in America immigrant farmers had to adapt to new crops, unusual climates, and often quite different agricultural conditions. Also, because the primary reason for emigrating had been to establish a secure future for themselves and their children, immigrants realized from the outset that they had to do more than get by as subsistence farmers producing foods for family consumption. To realize their dream of a landed livelihood, they had to raise animals and produce cash crops that could be sold on the general market and especially to booming cities demanding unprecedented amounts of foodstuffs.

Whatever their nationality, most immigrant farmers did adapt to changed conditions. They learned that grain crops popular in Europe were not equally favored in America, and so, on immigrant farms, barley and rye gave way to wheat. When wheat proved a fickle crop susceptible to diseases and insect infestations, immigrants in the Midwest ultimately followed the example of Americans and planted corn. Since corn was not grown in Europe, immigrants were not familiar with it; however, they learned how to cultivate huge acres of this popular grain. Immigrant farmers also adjusted to the fact that even familiar crops were grown differently. For example, in the upper Midwest, they planted potatoes and sowed seeds more thinly than had been common practice on European farms.

Immigrants did not simply give up their traditional ways of farming. Experienced farmers continued to use Old World methods that had worked for centuries. Some immigrant farmers actually adjusted to America by introducing new techniques and crops that subsequently altered or improved American agriculture. German Mennonites from Russia, who had successfully farmed in the center of what is modern-day Ukraine, brought a hard winter wheat that was well suited to dry prairie conditions. Because the seed was sown in the cool autumn, lay dormant over the winter, and was harvested in the spring, the introduction of winter wheat required American farmers to readjust their farming patterns. Ultimately, this more resilient wheat helped permanently establish the Great Plains as America's wheat belt. When wheat proved an unreliable crop for them, Swiss immigrants in Wisconsin switched to raising dairy animals and developed a thriving cheese industry. Their success prompted other farmers to follow suit, and, as result, by the early 1900s Wisconsin had become a leading dairy-farming state.

Modifying traditional methods and learning to grow new crops were not necessarily difficult for seasoned farmers. Adjusting to weather conditions in America, however, presented a challenge—sometimes a formidable one—for immigrant families. Before they left for the United States, many people knew that the climate would be different. Guidebooks alerted potential immigrants to inclement winters in the Midwest, and, of course, letters described the extreme types of weather. But being forewarned did not lessen the misery people suffered as a result of seasons that alternated between bitterly cold winters and blistering summers. In addition, the extreme weather conditions did more than cause physical discomfort: they could ruin farm families' livelihoods.

Weather and Climate

Winter

For farm households, the onset of winter meant relief from backbreaking field labor, but with winter also came a constant struggle to survive the cold. Immigrants suffered through blizzards the likes of which they had never seen; they endured frigid temperatures they had never experienced. Even hardy natives of Scandinavian countries found themselves in a harsher environment than they had previously known. When they departed for America, one immigrant couple thought to bring a thermometer from Sweden with them; however, such forethought only reinforced the extent to which their new world differed from their old. In their first year, they learned how bitter the winters in the United States could be. The thermometer, the woman wrote, "cannot show anything lower than minus twenty-five degrees, but it was below that." In 1870, they and other families spent the week before Christmas shielding themselves against the frigid weather that swept over northeastern Kansas. "We kept the fire going the whole day through and sat around the fireplace, and still we could see our breath when we talked. We piled everything we could think of on top of us at night and then Gustaf [her husband] got up at three and built the fire up again, and still we were so cold," she related. On the coldest days and in the harshest weather, there were still daily chores to do. Livestock needed care, cows had to be milked, eggs had to be gathered, water had to be hauled from the well, and firewood had to be brought in from outside.

Many immigrant families shivered day in and day out during the winter months; however, intensely cold weather inflicted misery that went beyond personal discomfort. People suffered severe frostbite. Others met the awful fate of the Medgaarden family's second oldest boy who "froze to death out on the [Iowa] prairie" during a terrible snowstorm. Farmers sustained financial losses as livestock died of winter diseases or froze to death during blizzards that lasted several days. One immigrant estimated that the loss of horses, cattle, sheep, and hogs to the cold and to a winter illness set him back "over $200.00," a substantial amount of money in 1873.

Spring and Summer

Spring ushered in farm families' busiest season but at the same time brought an end to the brutally cold months and allowed people to venture outdoors. The pleasant spring weather, however, could be a mere interlude between the extremes of hot and cold that immigrants had to contend with in the West. Descriptions of the horrific heat appear as a recurrent theme of immigrant correspondence from different parts of the frontier. "It is terribly hot here [in Texas], so that one even suffers from the heat," one young man related as he proceeded to explain that during the summer he and his brother slept on the porch because their bedroom was unbearable. Likening summer "breezes" in Kansas to the exhaust from "a heated up steam engine," a woman lamented "that we cannot leave the windows open and pull down the blinds to keep out the dreadful heat." Farmers had no choice but to work outdoors. However, in torrid midsummer months when it was "so hot that you can't go outside in the middle of the day," most men tried to stay away from the fields until "later [when] it gets a little cooler," or they split the fieldwork between the early morning and early evening hours.

Summer rains, which served as temporary respites from the searing heat, created their own problems. Because the houses were poorly constructed, when it rained "the water runs in on us," one man reported. During one rain and hail storm, the wind almost blew his house apart.

His brother, who was inside when the storm began, had to jump out the window because the house was leaning so badly that the doors would not open. Worse yet, this fierce storm damaged "a large part of the crops [and] indeed almost everything was ruined." Nevertheless, too little rain—not too much—was the reality that farmers more commonly faced, especially on the Great Plains. Time and again, immigrants reported losing entire crops to drought or turning out harvests barely sufficient to feed the livestock and family through the winter. Easily sparked during dry summers, massive fires lurked as a constant threat on the brush-covered prairies of the United States. Balls of blazing flames could spread rapidly over entire regions and destroy everything in their paths. People tried to stop their advance, but often they could do little more than flee to nearby water and wait for the infernos to burn themselves out. The ashes fouled local water supplies. Waiting anxiously along a riverbank for a fire to die down, one mother found she could not even get a drink for her children because the water "was black with ash."

For settlers, life was seemingly an ongoing struggle of withstanding one calamity after another. In her own words, Ida Lindgren dramatically recounted the perennial crises immigrants struggled with and the anxieties that characterized their daily existence during the summer. Without rain for nearly three months, "everything has dried up," she moaned to her mother in Sweden. "We have gotten a fair amount of wheat, rye, and oats, for they are ready so early, but no one here will get corn or potatoes. We have a few summer potatoes but many [farm families] don't even have that." The anticipated yield of other potatoes did not materialize, and field crops were not faring well either. Thus, "Instead of selling the oats and part of the rye as we had expected, we must now use them for the livestock, since there was no corn. We are glad we have oats (for many [families] don't have any and must feed wheat to the stock) and had hoped to have the corn leaves to add to the fodder."

Ida then graphically described yet another bane of farm families' lives. "One fine day [in 1874] here came millions, trillions of grasshoppers in great clouds, hiding the sun, and coming down onto the fields, eating up everything that was still there, the leaves on the trees, peaches, grapes, cucumbers, onions, cabbage, everything, everything. Only the peach stones still hung on the trees, showing what had once been there." Clearly unable to resist an opportunity to draw comparisons with her homeland, she hastened to make sure people understood that "They are not the kind of grasshoppers we see in Sweden but are large, grayish ones." It is no wonder that Ida flatly stated, "There has . . . been general lamentation and fear for the coming year." Locusts could be equally destructive, swooping in and, at times, taking only a few days to devour a region's entire vegetation. Ida surely expressed the sentiments of many immigrant families when she lamented at the end of one particularly bad summer, "It is sad and distressing and depressing for body and soul to find that no matter how hard one drudges and works, one still has nothing, less than nothing."

In wheat- and corn-growing areas, there was always hope that crops planted in the fall would produce sizable harvests to offset yields lost to drought, plagues, and other natural disasters. Seeds sown during the cool months had a good chance of germinating and surviving, but, as one immigrant revealed, fall plantings had their own risks. "No sooner had the wheat come out of the ground . . . than we had a severe frost . . . so that I fear the wheat has been ruined." The cycle could seem never ending. Farm families would, once again, struggle through the winter with the hope that next summer the weather would be favorable and the insects would stay away.

Economic Misfortunes

Just as natural forces beyond anyone's control could significantly influence farm families' lives, economic forces also affected their well-being. One immigrant summarized the blend of realities people faced when she reported that farmers "had a fairly good harvest this year, but in spite of this, the times are very hard, since the prices for agricultural products are lower than they have ever been." Recessions in the 1880s and a major economic depression in the early 1890s sent agricultural prices plummeting. Thus, even when crops were bountiful, farmers might not be able to pay their debts, let alone realize a profit. To make matters worse, farmers had to go through middlemen to get their crops delivered to a mass market. Local businesses and railroads that had monopolies on storage and shipping facilities gouged farmers by charging high users' fees. Farmers could also be victims of unscrupulous storage and grain elevator operators who cheated them by grading quality crops as inferior and misweighing sacks of grain. Wanting their grain to reach buyers, some farmers had no alternative but to pay the exorbitant rates and put up with the operators' dishonesty. Off and on, state legislators attempted to protect farmers by passing legislation aimed at putting an end to the worst abuses. More often than not, however, lawmakers fell sway to powerful business interests and ignored the farmers' plight, or their legislative measures were either weak or poorly enforced.

FAMILY AND COMMUNITY LIFE

Health

On the American frontier, immigrants also coped with different and added threats to their health. For instance, they encountered dangerous snakes and insects they had never seen in their homelands. Recounting their recent land purchase in Texas, two brothers reported that they "also got an untold number of rattlesnakes in the bargain." Ida Lindgren, who often complained about conditions in America, actually saw one ironic benefit to winters in Kansas: "It is nice not to have to see snakes during the winter, which I can never think of without a shudder." Snakes, spiders, and insects were more than nuisances, they could be deadly to anyone they bit or stung. Besides dangerous creepy-crawly pests lurking in fields, barns, or crevices of their homes, immigrants had to contend with the usual illnesses. Young people suffered through the normal range of childhood sicknesses, including measles and mumps as well as the more dangerous whooping cough and diphtheria. Poor diets weakened people's stamina and made them susceptible to colds, flu, and contagious diseases. And, during winter, when wholesome food was in shorter supply, common illnesses could be unusually deadly.

Getting sick or being injured was a reality of life regardless of where one lived, but, for immigrants accustomed to different circumstances, dealing with illnesses and injuries could be particularly distressing. By clustering together, immigrants created ethnic communities in the American West; however, because people in settlement areas often lived at a distance, it was difficult to come to one another's assistance in times of illness. To make matters worse, immigration disrupted traditional family networks that had nurtured people through poor health. Comparing her new home unfavorably with her native land, one woman grumbled, "It is no fun to be sick in America!" She wistfully recalled that in her homeland "Everyone looked after [a sick person] . . . and tried to make it as nice and comfortable as possible." In particular, she missed her mother's assistance and attention. Providing a particularly vivid portrayal of farm life, she moaned that if one feels ill, "you must [still] drag yourself around as long as possible and tend to all your many chores."

Remembering being coddled by her own mother and probably wishing for a few days of bed rest, this woman failed to mention that it was the lack of adequate medical care that represented the more serious problem for residents in rural, western America. A few doctors did migrate to the United States and set up practice in areas where their fellow immigrants had settled. In addition, there were American doctors in some towns. When they mentioned doctors at all, however, almost universally immigrants complained about their exorbitant fees. A Norwegian woman listed doctors as being among "what ruins a person here" and added that they "very seldom" got money from her. John Bauer described the situation in America when he explained to people back home that "one doesn't go to the doctor because of minor ailments because it costs so terribly much." This German farmer reported that doctors charged $3 per visit, and he estimated a week's illness might cost $20 to $25. High doctors' fees, together with "the problems one often encounters here," compelled individuals to learn "to be half doctor," he said. To make matters worse, unlike in the Old Country, farm people lived a far distance from towns and thus could not easily get to the druggist. Given these conditions, Bauer's family did what so many other immigrants did when a family member was sick or injured: they relied on home remedies, especially in emergencies.

Even when physicians were available, many immigrants probably trusted their own ancient cures and actually preferred them to anything a doctor might have prescribed. Although each nationality brought its own, often distinct, folk medicines and peculiar healing practices, by and large immigrants used herbs, specific foods, or special concoctions to cure the sick or heal injuries. In addition, the pioneer generation learned about cures from Native Americans and passed them along to fellow immigrants who arrived later. When it came to nursing the sick, all immigrant groups adhered to traditional views about proper gender roles. Mothers assumed responsibility for taking care of ill or injured family members. The most capable person—and often the closest available—treated severe cuts, broken limbs, and other physical injuries resulting from work-related accidents or careless child's play.

Pregnancy was always dangerous. But for women on isolated farms in the American West, bearing children was particularly risky. Like other women in rural America, immigrants gave birth at home and relied on midwives instead of doctors to help deliver babies. Many women chose midwives, in part, because doctors were either unavailable or too costly, but using midwives was also a tradition that immigrants carried over from Europe. Some immigrant communities were fortunate enough to have one or more experienced women who served as midwives. When there was no midwife in an immigrant settlement or she could not be reached in time, expectant parents turned to a woman who had several children and thus had gained experience by having given birth multiple times. If a woman went into labor in the midst of a blizzard, she and her husband had to deliver the baby by themselves. Unfortunately, even when overseen by an experienced midwife, the mother or newborn—or both—might not survive an exceptionally difficult or complicated birth. Although the number of immigrant women who died in childbirth and the number of infants stillborn can never be known, the totals were not insignificant.

Diet   Farmers always worried about producing enough food to fulfill their family's needs and, most important, to survive the nonproductive winter months. When crops failed or were lost to pests, plagues, or natural disasters, immigrant families lived on the brink of starvation; nevertheless, dying from hunger was not common. Despite periodic catastrophes that destroyed or severely reduced annual harvests, immigrants often wrote enthusiastically about the "great abundance" of food in America. C. F. Carlsson proclaimed that "even the greatest gourmet" in his native Sweden "would be amazed" at the bountiful supply and variety of foods in America. Carlsson refrained from enumerating the various foods because, he explained, the list would be "too long." He tellingly admitted, however, that the food "is unfamiliar to us Swedes." Because they often had little choice except to rely on animals, fruits, vegetables, and grains indigenous to the regions where they settled, immigrants did not have the luxury of being overly finicky about what they ate. So, for adults who came with already developed tastes, food concerns centered on the kinds of things available, not just on how much there was.

As C. F. Carlsson implied in his letter, immigrants had to alter their diets. Despite his glowing description of America's agricultural bounty, conditions sometimes necessitated surviving on monotonous, and not particularly nourishing, fare. For example, immigrants ate various types of gruel, made by combining flour, salt, and milk; or, in areas where corn was plentiful, cornmeal substituted for flour in this porridge-style food. Cinnamon, butter, or corn syrup added flavor to these otherwise bland concoctions. Using wheat flour or ground cornmeal, they made pancakes, also called "flapjacks." From the immigrants' perspectives, some changes represented marked improvements over the past. Deviating from habits in their homelands, immigrants reported eating meat two to three times a day. Depending on the households' cooking facilities, the meat was usually fried or boiled pork, beef, or chicken. Fried salt port was standard fare in the corn belt and pig-farming regions of the Midwest. Families also consumed wild game such as deer and rabbit in the Midwest and prairie chickens and jackrabbits on the Great Plains. With any luck, during the growing season, fresh vegetables and fruits were regularly incorporated into the menu. Throughout the rest of the year, most produce on the table had been preserved by a drying or some other process; potatoes, carrots, rutabagas, and cabbage, which still had to be cooked, were the chief vegetables. Apples were the most common fresh fruit eaten year round. To keep produce and other foods in cool storage, people dug cellars under their houses. Until they acquired chickens and a milk cow, families bought eggs and dairy products from neighbors; nevertheless, household larders usually contained eggs and butter. After a farmer purchased a cow, homemade cheeses became part of the daily diet and there was milk for drinking. Beverages also included coffee if it could be obtained, and if not, families made substitute drinks from grains.

Depending on their homeland cuisine, some nationalities had to adjust more than others. Immigrants typically had not eaten corn products in their homelands, but those who settled in Nebraska as well as in other corn-producing areas added ground corn to their diets. Scandinavians generally ate more pork in America than they had in their home countries. For Czechs and Germans, however, consuming pork was part of their traditional eating habits. Norwegians, Swedes, and Danes, especially on the dry Great Plains, missed fish dishes; many pined for salt herring and other specialties that had been regular fare at home. Because breads, especially those made with ground wheat, differed from the heavy grain and rye varieties in Europe, most nationalities had to develop a taste for American kinds. Some immigrants liked the white and lighter wheat breads, but Ida Lindgren was not the only Scandinavian who longed for "Really good sour-sweet rye bread." After a while, though, the family had "gotten more or less used to wheat bread with all kinds of food," she told her sister. It was, however, more a matter of resigning oneself to reality than a happy adjustment, for Ida still often thought about the "good rye bread" in her native land.

Still, immigrants found a variety of satisfying foods that provided essential ingredients for traditional as well as "American" dishes. This was particularly true for those who made their way to the lush regions of the upper Midwest and the Pacific Northwest. Hazel and other nut trees yielded great quantities of nuts; blackberries, blueberries, strawberries, raspberries, cherries, and apples flourished. While reproducing homeland favorites, immigrants learned to make pies, an "American" treat, which one man described as a "wonderful dish . . . that glides easily down your throat." In the Midwest and, where possible, in the Great Plains, Scandinavians fished in local rivers and streams. The types of fish differed from those in their homeland waters; nevertheless, what they caught satisfied immigrants' cravings for a traditional food. During winter, families kept supplies of fresh frozen fish on hand by putting their catches in stone pots and burying them in the snow.

Immigrants rated some new foods as exceptionally good because they resembled a dish cooked in their homeland. Referring to a familiar food, a woman wrote that the yellow peas sold in northeastern Kansas were expensive but worth an occasional indulgence because, when cooked, they dissolved "almost like strained peas." Immigrants who longed for fruits and vegetables not available where they lived tried to import shoots to grow their own. Learning that friends would soon be emigrating, one woman asked them to "bring a few trees." Her wish list included specific pear, apple, plum, and cherry trees. She also wanted gooseberry and current bushes. Just as Mennonites used their expertise to improve wheat production on the Great Plains and the Swiss applied their skills to promote dairy farming, immigrants' desires for familiar foods prompted them to introduce fruits and vegetables that added to the variety of American agriculture.

Food and Holidays In all cultures, having traditional foods was an important part of holiday celebrations. And immigrants on the frontier tried to uphold these customs even as they made adjustments to new circumstances. Although practices differed, in European countries Christmas was a season characteristically steeped in food-related customs. Lavish meals were usually served on either Christmas Eve or Christmas Day. Regardless of which day was more ceremoniously observed, both occasions had their special dishes. At Christmastime, for instance, Scandinavians customarily served *lutfisk*, a dried fish that had been cured with lye. After soaking it in water to draw out the lye, the *lutfisk* was cooked and shared at the Christmas Eve family get-together. Most Scandinavians also included some type of creamy porridge prepared by cooking rice in milk. In addition to customary entrées, all the nationalities had special cookies, cakes, and other distinct delicacies intrinsic to Christmastime celebrations.

Immigrants who expressed dismay that Christmas observances in America differed from those in their homelands often pointed to the inability to have all their traditional dishes. Comparing celebrations in Sweden with those she saw in Utah, one immigrant woman sarcastically observed that eating turkey and drinking liquor on Christmas Day were the only changes Americans made to their otherwise normal routines. Clearly judging the Swedish traditions superior, she reminisced about "the old Swedish custom of living high, wide, and handsome for a few days, with fine bread, fish, and rice pudding." A German farmer in Missouri confirmed the important role food continued to play when he reported that celebrating Christmas differed from what people did in Germany, but, nevertheless, his wife had "baked different kinds of cake."

The continual influx of immigrants into the United States made it easier to produce some homeland specialties. Norwegians in one settlement were finally able to brew ale for Christmas because "the last emigrants brought yeast with them." Residents had not had "such a simple thing as ale up till now because of a lack of yeast," one woman explained. Having been so long deprived of a favored drink, she happily reflected that the traditional Christmas brew "has never tasted so good to me as now." As more people came and stayed, towns sprang up and local shops carried specialty ingredients that catered to immigrant tastes. Describing holiday festivities in his rural community in 1895, one man took pains to note that "Here it is beginning to get like Sweden, at least at Christmastime, for there is both lutfisk and Christmas porridge." He went on to explain, however, that in addition to these luxury items, the day's feast included "a lot of other good things, but the latter are more everyday things." In time, immigrants of all nationalities in the upper Midwest, Great Plains, and farther west incorporated locally grown produce and meats into their Yuletide menus while at the same time reproducing time-honored dishes of the season.

Although the seemingly endless chores of farm life left little time for recreation, youngsters and grownups did find occasion to relax and play. With neighboring homes often spaced far apart in rural regions of the West, family **Recreation and Socializing** members necessarily engaged in recreational activities with one another. During winter, children played in the snow and went sledding or tobogganing. Fishing and hunting let adults and youths combine fun with family needs. Children turned barnyard animals into playtime companions. In addition to his older siblings and two dogs, "little Niels" Nielsen counted "a little pig and two chickens" among his "playmates." Parents taught children games they knew from their childhood days in the Old Country. Families sang songs, and if fortunate enough to have a musical instrument, they could sing and dance to music. Children also played with simple, often handcrafted, toys.

Adults read during their leisure time. Eager to "read everything that pertain[ed]" to their homelands, they devoured newspapers people sent them. When resources permitted, farm families also subscribed to immigrant newspapers, which contained a mixture of homeland and American news. These foreign-language papers published in the United States also printed articles, feature stories, literature, and correspondence. Some people enjoyed reading novels, plays, and other fiction; however, in the late nineteenth century, many nationality groups had to deal with the fact that foreign-language publications were either scarce or expensive. "It interests me so much to see something from our recent authors, but I cannot afford to buy them," one woman admitted as she prevailed upon friends to send her books from the Old Country.

After immigrant communities established their own nationality churches, for those families who could get there, attending Sunday services provided a chance to socialize. People chatted about wide-ranging matters, got caught up on the local gossip, and shared news from their homelands. During nice weather, family and friends occasionally went on picnics or summer outings. And, of course, on special occasions people joined together for a little merrymaking that included traditional music, songs, and dancing.

Weddings offered the best opportunities for immigrant families to mingle and have a good time. After the ceremony, people went to the bride's home or to a larger house owned by a relative or friend to celebrate. Guests enjoyed a complimentary feast of cakes, meats, and other side dishes. Depending on the family's circumstances, postceremony celebrations could be lavish or quite modest. More prosperous farmers had the wherewithal to turn a wedding into an extravagant affair that treated guests in styles reminiscent of Old Country celebrations. For instance, the marriage of a couple in one rural Norwegian community was followed by two days of revelry. The bride's parents held a party on the day of the wedding, and, on the following day, the groom's widowed mother had 130 guests to her house for dinner and dancing. Two hogs, 3 turkeys, and 12 chickens were butchered for the occasion. The leftovers from dinner were served cold as people celebrated and danced late into the night. Comparing the festivities to wedding celebrations in the Old Country, she admitted that she did not serve as many different foods here in America. "We only had roast, stew, several kinds of cake, and pie." Still, she thought, "Everybody seemed to be having a good time." Regardless of whether wedding celebrations were simple or multiday affairs, they brought people together to participate in a happy occasion and served as temporary diversions from humdrum farm life. Instead of going on a honeymoon, though, newlyweds usually went home and the next day did regular farm and household chores.

Homesickness and Loneliness

Despite an occasional social outing or meeting for chitchat after church services, many immigrants suffered from homesickness and loneliness. People who departed their homelands in the 1870s and 1880s to take up farming in the United States realized that they might never again see their beloved parents, favorite relatives, and dear friends who opted to stay behind. Adjusting to strange environments such as the arid Great Plains or the Southwest, which differed so markedly from the hilly and forested areas where many immigrants had grown up, nurtured nostalgia. To make matters worse, the hardships of farm life heightened the already painful effects of missing loved ones. Of course, some farmers had known adverse conditions—crop failure and blights—in the Old Country, and immigrants endured the same conditions as American families who made their way to the West. For immigrants, however, their experiences in America were colored in part by idealized memories and comparisons with their homelands. Coping with disasters, many farmers looked back and realized that life had been hard and prospects perhaps limited but, "at home," they had never encountered the same extreme alternating frigid and sweltering temperatures, prairie fires, or awesome plagues of insects that made farm life so precarious and miserable in America. In the Old Country, they had lived in decent homes that could protect them from inclement weather and ordinary rain showers.

While immigrants suffered from homesickness, nostalgia for their homeland did not blind them to the benefits they had derived from emigrating or prevent them from adjusting well to life in their adopted country. In his own words, one foreign-born German revealed the mix of emotions that immigrants felt. He confessed that it made him happy to "linger in thought" about relatives and friends, and when he did, "a quiet ache creeps into my heart." It was "true," he also admitted, that "be it ever so lovely, a foreign land . . . will never be home." But this immigrant hastened to emphasize that "all at once all the troubles and hardships that a poor though honest laborer must endure [in Germany] pass[ed]" before his eyes. He was then grateful that he had left his homeland. Despite fond memories, he, like so many immigrants, was a pragmatic person who accepted the reality that he now lived in the United States and that his daily life centered on securing a comfortable existence for his family. A Swedish woman in North Dakota, however, revealed that some immigrants were "not burdened with love for the fatherland." She went on to state that, as a poor person, life had been extremely difficult for her in Sweden. This woman expressed no homesickness as she shrugged off how hard she had to work in America.

Apart from bouts of homesickness, life on the farm could be lonely. Indeed, dealing with solitude was one of the hardest adjustments immigrant farm families had to make. Bad weather or chores on their farms led to long intervals when people could not regularly visit with one another. Immigrant women could lead particularly secluded lives. Some women, for instance, might stay on their farms for months on end, rarely venturing farther than the immediate farmyard or fields. They remained at home when husbands traveled to towns to purchase supplies. Wives whose husbands went away on temporary jobs felt isolated when left alone to take care of the farm and children during dreary winter months. Some immigrant women longed for female companionship; some simply missed conversations with people back home. One woman surely expressed the sentiments of other immigrants when, in a letter, she explained to her mother that the reason she wrote about her tribulations was because she felt "a real need to speak with you" so as "to some extent lighten my own cares by so to speak burdening you with them instead." Coping with daily life on the farm, while at the same time missing loved ones, male and female immigrants alike understandably became downcast at times.

CHANGING CONDITIONS AND TECHNOLOGY IN HOME AND FIELD

Houses, Furnishings, and Machines   In spite of adversity, personal struggles, and setbacks, many immigrant farmers saw their lives improve over time. Except during the financial panic of 1907 to 1910, in the early 1900s economic conditions in the United States were good and farmers did reasonably well. During World War I, farmers benefited from the increasing demand for grains by Europe's warring nations. Even if they did not become well-to-do, numerous families could claim, as one immigrant woman earlier had, "We are now well housed, both man and beast. No body must doubt that

Finnish "Man on bridge," near Buffalo, South Dakota in undated photograph. Courtesy Immigration History Research Center, University of Minnesota.

we are living comfortably. . . . We are satisfied and happy with this life." In the upper Midwest and other areas with timberland, white frame houses stood in place of the shanties or other makeshift dwellings where immigrants had passed their first years. Farmers replaced flimsy structures, sod houses, and dugouts with stone dwellings or built homes with wood shipped via railroad to lumber-scarce regions. Homes were also bigger; two-story houses were not uncommon. Curtains dressed windows, wallpaper covered walls, rugs lay on the floors, and nicely crafted furniture filled rooms. In place of crude tables, chairs, beds, and cabinets, there were sofas, upholstered chairs, and chests of drawers. Farm families purchased some American pieces, but they also engaged countrymen with carpentry skills to construct specialty items. Furnishings in most immigrant households thus were probably a mixture of "American" and Old Country styles characteristic of the individual nationality groups. Mirrors, clocks, pictures, knickknacks, and religious articles decorated the rooms. Because almost no rural homes had electricity, families used kerosene lamps and candles for their interior lighting.

As early as the 1880s, washing machines were making life somewhat easier for those farm women whose finances permitted specialty purchases costing $15 or more. This machine, which was a tub equipped with hand-operated paddles for agitating clothes, meant women could put away—indeed, probably discard—the loathed washboards. Rollers to squeeze out water could be purchased separately. Cranking handles on simple devices was preferable to rubbing each item up and down on a corrugated board and then wringing it by hand. However, hauling and boiling water remained part of laundry-day drudgery because, as late as 1920, most farm households lacked indoor plumbing. For families who could afford one, the sewing machine eased yet another of women's domestic responsibilities. The family seamstress merely had to learn to operate the machine's treadle with her feet while simultaneously guiding cloth across a flat surface under the needle. Women still tended the small animals and spent their days cleaning, cooking, and caring for their families, but there was more time for crocheting, knitting, and other handiwork.

Machines had a far more dramatic impact on field labor than they did on domestic work. As steam-powered **Mechanized** machines became more widespread in the 1870s and 1880s, **Farming** they made fieldwork less onerous and more productive for farmers able to afford them. Planting machines, reapers, threshers, and binders allowed grain farmers to cultivate more acres and produce much larger harvests. In his own words, Franz Joseph Loewen provided a farmer's assessment of how mechanized farming affected daily lives. Displaying the tendency common among immigrants, this Michigan German drew distinctions between his native country and America when he reported, "Nothing here is dug by hand." Elaborating on the differences, he noted, "for every kind of work . . . there are machines" that make keeping up land and harvesting crops easier. Farmers nevertheless still toiled long hours in the fields.

Loewen also offered an excellent example of how immigrant farmers at the turn of the twentieth century paced their lives, planned their futures, and gauged their own success. Every farmer wanted to acquire laborsaving devices, he explained, "but it often takes a long time before . . . [he] can buy them because they are very expensive." The reality was that "a new farm that is only partly cultivated often doesn't yield more than what one needs for one's own use." Patience and hard work, however, paid off because, "little by little, as his income increases, a farmer buys the machines he needs." In his portrayal of farm life, Loewen uttered what thousands of other immigrant farmers who had labored for years to make their farms a success were thinking when he admitted that "the strength of my younger years has passed somewhat," and therefore he bought machines that could do the work for him. It would take patience and profitable crop yields before the farmer had every machine he wanted, but "for now" he was "happy not to have to do the hardest work by hand any more."

Prices varied slightly from place to place and over time, but machines Loewen and other farmers wanted were indeed expensive. A farmer had to pay $65 for potato planting machines and between $80 and $120 for diggers. A mower could be obtained for about $80, but a reaper required an outlay of between $100 and $135. Thus, into the early years of the twentieth century, immigrant farmers who could not afford steam-powered equipment still used horse-drawn implements to plant seeds, harvest crops, and mow fields, or they did the work by hand. Moreover, mechanization did not equally affect all types of farming. For instance, corn was picked and shucked by hand until after World War I. Mechanical equipment allowed dairy farmers and those who raised cows, hogs, and sheep for market to grow their own feed; however, livestock still needed year-round tending. Nevertheless, the invention of laborsaving equipment and the spread of mechanized farming significantly improved the daily lives and enhanced the prospects of many immigrants who made their way to the United States with the hope of becoming successful farmers. Satisfied with their lives and progress so far, in the early twentieth century many immigrant farmers were cautiously optimistic that life would continue to get better.

Ongoing Moves and Migration   Although land-seeking immigrants came with the intention of establishing farms and staying in one place, many farm families relocated. Sometimes it took two, three, or more moves before immigrants found a suitable location or determined the kind of farming they would finally pursue. Indeed, the first foreign-born farmers to make their way into the upper Midwest and to states along the rim of the Great Plains during the mid-nineteenth century were immigrants who had initially lived in Illinois, Indiana, Ohio, and rural sections of other eastern states. The abundance of rich land that could be obtained on easy terms lured immigrants to these new areas. After these internal migrants resettled, family and friends who subsequently emigrated from Europe followed them directly to newly established settlement areas.

In the last decades of the nineteenth century, immigrants kept moving farther west into the Dakotas, Montana, and Idaho, and, especially after 1900, they continued onward to states in the Pacific Northwest. Swedes from Iowa and Minnesota migrated into Nebraska and Colorado. These Scandinavians later went on to establish farms as far west as Washington. Norwegians migrated from Iowa, northern Illinois, and southern Wisconsin to Minnesota and the Dakotas. Czech immigrants traveled from Wisconsin into Iowa, Nebraska, and Oklahoma while Czechs in Texas spread throughout the Lone Star State. Germans moved around the corn- and hog-producing region that extended from Ohio westward to Missouri and Iowa. They also scattered throughout Wisconsin and Michigan. As Swedes, Norwegians, Danes, Germans, Czechs, and other land-seeking immigrants kept making successive moves, they created webs of ethnically homogeneous communities that stretched through rural, western America. Of course, starting over meant enduring some of the same miserable conditions that immigrants had suffered during the early years on their first homestead. Farm families that resettled, however, generally did not have to start with nothing. They likely had farm tools and some animals and were experienced settlers better prepared to cope with frontier life.

There were benefits to families moving away from older immigrant communities. Their departure made room for newcomers from Europe and thus fueled ongoing chain migrations that preserved the ethnic homogeneity of immigrant settlement areas. In addition, departing farmers left houses, buildings, and partially cleared land that made life easier for new arrivals. People leaving also freed up land that farmers staying behind could purchase to enlarge their acreage and make their farms more productive.

Immigrant farmers pulled up stakes and moved on for different reasons. Crop failures due to drought, blights, or insect plagues caused people to give up and look for better conditions elsewhere. Some families decided to leave a region because they wanted to try their hand at a different kind of farming; instead of growing crops, they turned to raising animals or to dairy farming. Tired of depending principally on a single crop, some farmers resolved to diversify and raise both crops and animals. Shifting from one type of farming to another sometimes required changing locations. Recruiters also campaigned to convince veteran farmers to head to a new place. For example, in the mid-1880s Dutch immigrants in Nebraska and Kansas responded favorably to recruiting efforts explicitly designed to lure experienced Dutch farmers to Minnesota. Weary of losing out to recurring droughts, they packed their belongings and headed to southwestern Minnesota, where they established farming communities.

An increasing shortage of land in settlement areas also prompted people, especially young adults, to go farther west, where large parcels could still be obtained cheaply.

Many immigrants did what the Johann Witten family did: they moved on simply because they wanted to do better. Fed up with renting in Nebraska and because, in his words, "I want to have my own land," in the summer of 1889 Witten visited a relative in Dakota "to see what the land was like there." Concluding that it was "not very good," he decided that instead of relocating to Dakota, his family would go "far away, where land is still cheap." The next spring, the Wittens sold almost everything and set out for Washington. They went via railroad and then by covered wagon for the last part of the exhausting 1,600-mile trip. Writing with satisfaction a year and a half later, he told family in Germany that not only was the land fertile in Washington but there was also "a nice German settlement" in the county. By 1900, the Wittens owned more than 1,000 acres of good farmland and were doing well. This family's experience shows how immigrants maintained kinship ties and, more important, how chains of ethnic settlements worked both to influence people's lives and shape migratory patterns in rural, western America.

NEW IMMIGRANTS AND ASIANS ON THE LAND

Market and Truck Farms   While land-seeking immigrants largely of the old wave struggled to succeed as independent farmers, other migrants used America's rich resources in different ways to try to better their futures. The country's varied climate and terrain made it possible for immigrants from wide-ranging cultural backgrounds to engage in various kinds of agriculture. Some new immigrants who emigrated before the massive second wave got under way did go west, where they acquired uncultivated acres and labored to turn them into large working farms. Except for Czechs from Austria-Hungary, Poles from the German-controlled section of partitioned Poland were the most likely to take that route. But the number of Poles who became large farm owners was relatively few. In general, new immigrants acquired smaller parcels of land and went into truck farming. Instead of large-scale dairying, crop production, or livestock breeding, this method of farming involved the cultivation of vegetables and fruits for sale in local markets. Truck farms usually ranged in size from 10 to 40 acres. Although this type of undertaking was popular among Italians, other immigrants tried it as well. Small Polish truck farms, for instance, sprang up outside major urban centers in New York and New Jersey.

Immigrants grew an amazing variety of vegetables and fruits on their farms. The kinds of produce depended on the local growing conditions and on the cultural background of the family running the operation. As with the large cash-crop farmers, immigrants cultivated fruits and vegetables indigenous to the United States, but, at the same time, they added variety to existing American agriculture. It would be virtually impossible to itemize the varieties of fruits and vegetables that could be traced to immigrants' native lands. Italians, for example, are credited with adding assorted peppers, artichokes, and eggplants. In addition, immigrants introduced methods that improved harvests. The Italian custom of staking vines resulted in larger yields from individual tomato plants. Using their knowledge and willingness to engage in labor-intensive farming, Poles produced onions and tobacco in the nearly exhausted soil of the Connecticut Valley.

In a manner similar to large-scale farmers in the West, truck farms operated on the philosophy that the family constituted a labor force. While every member helped out as needed, each person usually had his or her own assigned tasks. Families living on untilled acreage pooled their labor to clear the trees, stumps, rocks, and weeds. Men, women, and children hoed, planted, and later weeded around plants. They harvested vegetables and picked fruit. In families that owned animals, women and children were expected to help tend the chickens, pigs, or milk cows. Just as on farms in the West, gender defined duties. Universally, females were in charge of housekeeping and home life. Cooking daily meals, cleaning the living quarters, and washing the clothes added to the drudgery of these women's daily lives. Women also assumed responsibility for child rearing and nursing the ill. So, keeping a watchful eye on youngsters and sitting up with the sick turned already busy days into taxing ones.

Some new immigrants began small-scale farming right away, but more often than not smaller farms were outgrowths of ongoing internal migration. In the 1890s, Poles, in particular, went from the cities and factories to the land. Italians left jobs on sugar plantations in rural Louisiana to settle near New Orleans, where they started growing fruits and vegetables. As a result, by the early decades of the twentieth century, southern Italians dominated truck farming in the region. Although old immigrants and American farmers typically mocked truck farmers as not being real farmers, many families not only produced a year's supply of food for their own tables but also derived a livelihood from these endeavors. Still, new immigrant truck farms were typically not self-sufficient enterprises. It was, therefore, normal for men to get part-time or regular jobs to supplement the families' annual earnings from gardening. Some worked in nearby industries, but it was common for men to leave for long periods to work as seasonal laborers. In the early 1900s, Italian men in northern Wisconsin were away upward of nine months. They as well as other part-time farmers took jobs on construction gangs, with railroad maintenance crews, and in the lumber trades.

Rather than diversified gardening, some immigrants successfully adapted Old World expertise to develop or improve upon existing agriculture. Northern Italians, for example, used their knowledge of viticulture to grow grapes in California, where the soil and climate were especially suitable. In addition, by applying wine-making methods carried over from their homeland, Italians contributed to the emergence of the state's wine industry. Although northern Italians were the pioneers, southern Italians made successive moves that took them from the East or South to the Midwest and onward to California, where they provided knowledgeable labor for vineyards and wineries.

Despite notable exceptions and the marked success of a few, overall, the percentage of new immigrants who took up farming was small. There are no exact statistics, but even among nationalities that boasted farming colonies and truck gardeners, the number of people engaged in agricultural pursuits represented only a fraction of their populations. For example, according to some estimates less than 2 percent of Italian males in the United States in the early twentieth century could be classified as "farm operators," and only about 10 percent of Poles fell into that category.

Japanese

Agricultural Laborers
American agriculture also created opportunities for migrants desiring temporary employment. As early as the 1880s, owners of sugar plantations in southern Louisiana recruited Italians to work in their fields. The demand for hand labor in orchards, vineyards, berry patches, sugar-beet fields, and on vegetable farms attracted immigrants to states stretching along the Pacific Coast or just east of it. Similarly, immigrants did the tedious picking required in the fruit districts of the East and Middle Atlantic states. In the berry regions and cranberry bogs, growers relied heavily on Italians, Poles, and Portuguese workers.

While Europeans took temporary jobs as seasonal laborers, many Japanese emigrated with the intention of finding some type of work in agriculture. The Japanese, who began arriving at the close of the nineteenth century, did obtain employment in construction, railroad maintenance, lumber mills, and canneries, but large numbers preferred agricultural labor. According to a congressional study published in 1911, by 1909 Japanese immigrants did "practically all of the hand work in the berry patches" and "one-half of the picking" in California orange groves. On average, they received $1.40 a day for their labor. As with migrants who crossed the Atlantic Ocean or passed over a land border, many Japanese planned to save their earnings and return to their homelands. At the same time, many hoped to accumulate enough money to buy land in the United States.

Japanese immigrants achieved some measure of independence by entering into various contracts or "share" agreements with landowners. They negotiated terms that either let them raise crops in return for stipulated amounts of money or for a percentage of the profits from sales. For immigrants unable to purchase land, however, leasing was the next-best option. These farmers paid rent, but, because they kept the profits, they reaped the benefits of their labor. While some Japanese hired fellow coun-trymen as field hands, families typically made up the labor pool on farms leased or owned by immigrants. From dawn to dusk, spouses toiled along-side each other. A Japanese cultural tradition rooted in the belief that men did not help with housework or child care meant women spent long days doing essentially two jobs. More than one woman recalled getting up as early as 4:30 A.M. fixing breakfast, passing the day in the fields, and then returning home to cook, put the children to bed, and sort or pack produce until late night. The hours performing tedious hand labor clearly paid off for some Japanese. By 1910, more than 2,500 Japanese either owned or rented nearly 500,000 acres of farmland. Due in part to refrigerator cars and the expansion of America's railroad system, Japanese farms supplied produce to urban markets in California and elsewhere. According to one estimate, by 1910 Japanese farmers grew 70 percent of the strawberries in California.

Chinese

In part because their migration got under way after U.S. law had halted emigration from China, Japanese newcomers replaced aging Chi-nese fieldworkers. By the last quarter of the nineteenth century, however, bigotry—not necessarily free choice—had caused the Chinese to forsake agricultural labor for other livings. Prejudice affected occupational deci-sions and regularly touched the lives of these immigrants more than any other nationality in the post–Civil War era. The escalating pattern of dis-crimination was evident by the early 1870s when the railroads' demand for Chinese unskilled construction workers declined. Barred from many occupations or permitted to engage in only menial, low-paying jobs that "whites" would not take, Chinese initially moved into agriculture and a variety of service industries. Those who turned to agriculture became seasonal laborers in vineyards, orchards, vegetable farms, hop yards, and sugar-beet fields. By 1880, Chinese made up 86 percent of the agricultural workforce in Sacramento County alone; in other areas, they accounted for upward of two-thirds of the farm laborers. Chinese immigrants also became sharecroppers and truck farmers. By one estimate, Chinese accounted for more than one-third of the truck gardeners in California in 1880. Many Chinese, who came with well-honed skills in planting and harvesting, used their knowledge to improve vegetable and fruit produc-tion in the far western states.

Hostility from native-born Americans as well as their willingness to encourage discrimination against minorities significantly affected the lives of immigrants from Asia. Indeed, a blend of economic rivalry and blatant prejudice essentially pushed Chinese agricultural laborers out of California's growing fields in the late nineteenth century. Resentment stemming, in part, from claims that the Chinese were depressing wages and taking jobs from "whites" stirred demands that growers stop hiring

Chinese immigrants. Growers favored Chinese because of their reputation as hardworking, reliable employees. In 1893 and 1894, "whites," determined to drive Chinese laborers out of California agriculture, carried out raids in areas where Chinese worked. Marauding groups stormed into towns and camps. Besides breaking into homes and vandalizing property, they beat, shot, or forced Chinese onto trains headed out of town. Vigilantes terrorized growers and ordered them to fire Chinese workers. There were cases of rioters going into orchards, driving out Asian workers, and cutting down the trees. The anti-Chinese disturbances, which went on sporadically for more than a year, were credited with essentially putting an end to Chinese farm labor in California.

Regardless of where they resided or what sort of work they did, Chinese immigrants lived day to day with the reality that they could be become targets of ethnically based hate attacks. Gangs of young thugs threw rocks, rotten eggs, and spoiled vegetables at them. There were numerous incidents of Chinese being beaten, physically mutilated, and even killed. Recounting life in the 1870s, one immigrant described the Chinese in San Francisco as "simply terrified." Afraid they might be "shot in the back," they did not venture outside after nightfall, he recalled. "Children spit upon us as we passed by and called us rats."[1]

A combination of racism and economic rivalry prompted legislators in some western states to enact discriminatory legislation targeting Chinese and Japanese immigrants. Ironically, the success of the Japanese farmers roused animosity among "American" growers. Disdainful of these foreigners and resenting the competition, growers lobbied lawmakers to adopt measures that would reduce the immigrants' ability to compete. For example, in 1913 California enacted a law preventing "aliens ineligible for citizenship" from acquiring land. Japanese skirted the law by putting deeds in the names of their American-born children. The small number of families and aging nature of their population effectively prevented Chinese from doing the same. By that time, however, many Chinese had opened businesses and become self-employed or worked for countrymen who ran their own establishments.

Immigrant Farmers in the West: 1920 Portraying the experience of early settlers, an immigrant who later took up farming was right when he said that "Making a wilderness into a fruitful place and a wonderful garden takes a tremendous amount of hard work, patience and stamina and often privation too." He was not completely wrong when he added, "the [immigrant] pioneers who go on ahead first to settle uninhabited woods and prairies of America seldom reap the rewards of their work."

Statistics on the number of immigrants who were successful or lived out their years as farmers are elusive. Between 1870 and 1920, the Census Bureau restructured several categories, changed how it tabulated data on farmers, redefined terms, and published different information for each census. Nevertheless, figures culled from census tables show that, despite setbacks and the constant struggles that characterized farm life, scores of immigrant farmers remained on the land. In 1910, immigrants accounted for nearly 19 percent of farm operators in the area embracing Michigan, Wisconsin, and all the states stretching westward from the Mississippi River to the Pacific Ocean. By 1920, the percentage of "foreign-born whites" who owned or operated farms in this region had dipped to 13 percent. This reduction in part reflected new census categories, but the decline in foreign-born farmers was also due to deaths and to immigrants transferring ownership to their American-born children. Taken together, first- and second-generation "white" immigrants made up 21 percent of the farm population in the upper Midwest and western states.

In 1920, foreign-born farmers owned about 100 million acres of what the U.S. census labeled "land in farms" in the upper Midwest and western United States. More than 55 million of the acres in that region were designated as "improved." Immigrant-owned acreage thus amounted to more than 15 percent of the land in farms and about 18 percent of the improved farmland. In some of these states, foreign-born people composed a significant portion of the farmers. In North Dakota, 47 percent of farm operators were foreign born; in Minnesota, immigrants constituted nearly 38 percent of that group; and in Washington, they accounted for nearly 30 percent of people owning or managing farms. Nationality groups also dominated the ethnic makeup of farm populations in individual states. Scandinavians claimed 51 percent of Minnesota's foreign-born farm operators, and they made up 34 percent of the immigrant farmers in both North Dakota and Washington. Some nationalities were more prone to continue farming. First- and second-generation Norwegians, for example, remained more heavily concentrated in agriculture than other ethnic groups.

Many immigrant farm families never achieved success. On one hand, there were those who hung on and spent their lives eking out a living on the land. They remained poor or existed only at a subsistence level. On the other hand, there were those who, unable to keep their heads above water and discouraged by constant setbacks, gave up. How many immigrants abandoned farming can never be known. Some of these disheartened people, like the Lindgren family from Sweden, returned to their homelands; others who had originally hoped to become farmers remained in the United States but found new ways to make a good living. The children of immigrants in particular became part of the massive rural-to-urban migration that took place in the United States at the turn of the twentieth century. They chose to do what recent arrivals from northern and western Europe and new immigrants from southern and eastern Europe were doing. They migrated to cities and towns to work as hired laborers in America's booming industries.

NOTES

Immigrant life stories and quotations included in this chapter were derived from Theodore C. Blegen, ed., *Land of Their Choice: The Immigrants Write Home* (Minneapolis: University of Minnesota Press, 1955); H. Arnold Barton, ed., *Letters from the Promised Land: Swedes in America, 1840–1914* (Minneapolis: University of Minnesota Press, 1975); Walter D. Kamphoefner, Wolfgang Helbich, and Ulrike Sommer, eds., *News from the Land of Freedom: German Immigrants Write Home*, trans. Susan Carter Vogel (Ithaca, NY: Cornell University Press, 1991). Immigrant quotations derived from secondary sources are cited separately.

1. As quoted in Ronald Takaki, *A Different Mirror: A History of Multicultural America* (Boston: Little, Brown, 1993), 208.

3

Life on the Job: Immigrants in the Industrial Workplace

Although America's abundant land had been an important force nurturing the early migration from much of Europe, it was the prospect of a good-paying job that beckoned so many immigrants in the late nineteenth and early twentieth centuries. Immigrants who set out intending to become, at least temporarily, part of America's industrial labor force expected to work hard. Few worried that they lacked the capability to secure employment in America. At the turn of the twentieth century, most jobs in industry required little, or often no, previous training or experience. The capacity to withstand long hours and arduous working conditions was the only significant qualification for the type of employment that most workers sought and, in fact, that U.S. industry was offering.

America's diverse industries presented immigrant workers with a vast array of job possibilities. Immigrants spent their workdays refining raw materials in mills; producing a wide variety of goods in factories; and slaughtering animals, dressing meat, or processing food in plants. Immigrants drudged in underground and open-pit mines where they extracted minerals from the earth. For many wage earners, their work-weeks involved building, hauling, digging, and doing other types of unskilled labor on all kinds of construction projects. Although males and females performed a stunning variety of jobs in industrial America, they nonetheless shared many common experiences. Immigrants typically did terribly hard work, and life on the job often meant enduring dismal, frequently exploitative conditions.

Immigrant workers had to make adjustments, to be sure. Besides confronting cultural differences, non-English-speaking individuals had to cope with language barriers. Still, although they came from less industrialized countries, immigrants were not hindered by backwardness or shocked by the industrial society they encountered. Indeed, for many immigrants, their first day on a particular job was not necessarily their first time on an industrial site. They were, instead, seasoned migrant workers, part of the unskilled international labor force that flowed in and out of the United States, moved from place to place, and worked in different establishments.

INDUSTRIALIZATION AND IMMIGRANT LABORERS

The United States emerged from the nineteenth century as the world's leading industrial power. In the remarkably short span of three decades, America rose from the category of a second-class industrial nation to first place. Several factors combined to bring about such spectacular growth. The country possessed an abundance of raw materials and natural energy resources such as timber, coal, minerals, oil, and water. New technology revolutionized industries and spawned the development of new ones. For instance, the development of more efficient methods to produce steel provided America with large quantities of a durable, more versatile metal than the previously widely used iron. The transformation of steelmaking stimulated the creation of sundry allied industries and affected manufacturing as diverse as the construction of railroad cars and the forging of nuts, bolts, and screws.

The rapid growth of heavy industry had a ripple effect on various sectors of the American economy. Mining expanded as mills and factories used tons of coal to power massive machinery; the excavation of iron ore, tin, lead, and copper increased; and the necessity to lubricate machines promoted America's infant petroleum business. The radiating effect continued as the need for foundries and plants to refine raw materials and manufacture products nurtured a building boom. Technological advances also turned food production and distribution into major industries. The development of the refrigerated freight car stimulated meatpacking enterprises; at the same time improved methods of preserving foods sparked the emergence of a variety of food-processing plants. By providing the means to transport all the raw materials and goods efficiently, the country's railroads contributed mightily to America's rise to industrial supremacy.

No single factor was responsible for the extraordinary industrial growth that took place. It owed much to a complex combination of innovative technology, capital investment, government support, and exploitation of bountiful natural resources. America's industrial expansion also depended heavily on a plentiful supply of cheap labor. The ready availability of unskilled workers encouraged entrepreneurs to invest as well as to continue building and expanding factories. Sheer numbers underscore the significant role that human labor played in America's astonishing industrial growth. Between 1870 and 1920, the number of people employed in what official records labeled "manufacturing" quadrupled. In 1920, more than one-third of the U.S. labor force toiled in manufacturing, mechanical, and mining industries.

Industrial expansion owed much to the country's existing labor force, especially as people abandoned farm life to find work in factories. The internal rural-to-urban migration, which helped boost the population of America's "urban territory" by slightly more than 55 percent between 1870 and 1890, however, could not satisfy the rising demand for common laborers. Instead, as the 1890s gave way to the 1900s and America's industries kept clamoring for cheap labor, more and more it was immigrants who filled the need. The foreign-born contribution to industrialization continued over time as immigrants—and later their children—joined America's industrial labor force. The U.S. Immigration Commission, a joint Senate-House body appointed in 1907 to investigate every facet of immigration, found that in 1908–1909 immigrants composed nearly 59 percent of the workforce in 21 major industries. The Dillingham Commission, as it was subsequently called, calculated that two-thirds of these foreign-born employees were southern and eastern Europeans. In 1910, nearly half of the workers engaged in industries categorized as mining, mechanical, and manufacturing were born outside the United States. By 1920, at least 54 percent of all foreign-born males who were older than 10 worked in these industries. And in that same year, immigrants and their children represented more than half of the laborers toiling in America factories, mills, and mines.

Foreign-Born Workers

It was stories about high wages and a desire to make money that inspired so many foreign-born people to yearn for jobs in American industry. Information on wage scales in European countries is fragmentary; nevertheless, the figures show why—to inhabitants of the southern and eastern regions of the European continent—the wages paid to common laborers in the United States seemed astronomical. People needing work might find employment in Europe, but they typically got little pay in return for their labor. In Hungary, where many Slavs lived, workers in the various trades and industries averaged a weekly pay of $1.55 to $3.00; iron, steel, and foundry workers received a mere $2.75 per week. Farm laborers fared even worse than industrial employees. In 1905, the average daily wage for agricultural workers in northern Hungary was 23 cents for men and 13 cents for women. In Italy, where farm laborers earned 26 cents to 45 cents and common laborers brought in between 30 cents and 96 cents, the situation was similar. Skilled workers such as carpenters, stonemasons, and machinists could expect higher wages. As late as 1908, agricultural workers in Greece received only between 58 cents and 72 cents, while their industrial counterparts took

Lure of Jobs and Wages

home 68 cents to 77 cents a day. By comparison, daily wages for industrial laborers in the United States ranged from $1.05 to $1.80. A steelworker got as much in one day as agricultural laborers in Hungary and Italy could get for an entire week's toil. And in just two days—possibly less—a man working in an American mill could rake in earnings it took industrial workers in southern and eastern Europe more than a week to garner. As news of employment opportunities and higher wages reached Europeans, individuals calculated earnings on the basis of their own countries' currencies. Even taking travel and living costs into account, when measured against incomes that ordinary laborers could expect in their native lands, America held out spectacular possibilities. So, from that perspective, going to the United States became a practical option for pragmatic people.

Migrating in search of temporary employment or engaging in seasonal labor was not unusual for Europeans, especially for the inhabitants of the continent's southern and eastern regions. Indeed, the fact that small landowners and peasants often needed additional income to subsist had created migratory traditions in many countries. Thus, at the turn of the twentieth century, southern and eastern Europeans who had traditionally done seasonal labor or wandered to other parts of the continent to work packed their bags for a much longer journey. For people making the transatlantic voyage, the new trip differed in length but not in objectives. As many immigrants described it, they migrated to the United States "after bread," meaning they wanted to make money to improve their lives.

Kith-and-Kin Networks   Information is sketchy on how people who migrated during early stages of the massive new immigration wave actually found jobs. In the 1870s and early 1880s, some companies dispatched agents to recruit workers in Europe. The number of laborers these agents actually brought to America was small; nevertheless, critics alleged that "contract labor" was hurting American workers. In 1885, Congress passed the Alien Contract Labor Act, which prohibited companies from importing foreign laborers "under contract." As immigration increasingly gained momentum, however, this law, which was popularly known as the Foran Act, was essentially irrelevant. The legislation could not stop steamship companies from advertising opportunities. It could not prevent agents from recruiting immigrants after they disembarked in the United States. Into the early 1900s, agencies at American ports tried to direct recently landed immigrants to their clients' factories, mills, mines, and construction sites. Most important, however, federal legislation could not disrupt the personal relationships fueling immigration and funneling foreign-born laborers into America's industrial cities, mill towns, and mining hamlets. As with earlier immigrants who came to settle on the land, most migrants seeking wage labor already had a destination in mind when they departed their native lands.

The lure of high-paying jobs was even more compelling when potential immigrants left with the knowledge that they would not have to fend for themselves but, instead, could rely on assistance from people they knew. During the initial stages of most migratory movements, recruiters emerged from among the ranks of the various nationality groups. Acting as go-betweens, these individuals channeled their fellow countrymen into particular industries. A Pittsburgh Croatian, for instance, was able to help fellow Croatians because the managers of one local mill agreed to supply jobs for all the men he sent them. Greeks and Italians relied heavily on padrones, who generally were people who had arrived earlier in the United States. The padrones found jobs and housing for countrymen who came later; they also performed other services for fellow immigrants who could not speak English. Recruitment systems with individuals serving as middlemen between workers and employers could be exploitative and even abusive. In return for providing assistance, an intermediary might charge workers an exorbitant commission or sign them to unfavorable, binding contracts with employers. Under some arrangements, employers gave the workers' weekly pay to the recruiters, who then kept a portion for themselves.

As the volume of individual migratory streams increased, the need for agents or padrones dwindled. Immigrants relied instead on family and friends to help them secure employment. The hiring practices followed by many American industries actually reinforced networks built on immigrants' personal ties. Companies usually had some type of employment office at plant sites, but factories and mines also permitted foremen to hire workers. These bosses, in turn, let their workers serve as recruiters or go-betweens. They promised employees that if they sent for their friends or relatives, there would be jobs waiting for them. It was also common for workers to prevail upon their bosses to hire a recently arrived family member or acquaintance. Regardless of how the hiring system operated, once immigrants got jobs in a particular establishment, they knew the hiring procedures and could help or at least advise people who arrived later. A Lithuanian who made his way to Chicago recounted just how beneficial this experienced advice could be. His first day job hunting turned into a miserable failure when he was not selected from a throng of perhaps 200 men vying for what turned out to be only 23 positions in a packinghouse. The next day, after he followed a friend's advice and slipped $5 to the yard policeman in charge of selecting workers, the formerly dismayed Lithuanian got a job.

Personal contacts and networks, in effect, funneled nationalities into specific industries. As a result, many factories and industries became what have been described as "occupational beachheads" for particular immigrant groups. At these beachheads, some nationalities had an advantage when it came to securing jobs for their families and friends. As one foreign-born laborer bluntly put it, in some places "The only way you got a job was through somebody at work who got you in."[1] In the

Ethnic Concentration in Industries

Pittsburgh area, where a large number of new immigrants migrated, Lithuanians were heavily represented in the National Tube Works and the American Steel and Wire Company while Ruthenians and Poles worked in the Oliver Steel Works. At the same time, Poles made up a significant part of the workforce in Jones and Laughlin Steel, a factory where Slovaks, Croatians, and Serbians also made a living. Ethnic concentrations were evident in America's other industrial cities as well. In Chicago, Lithuanians and Poles worked in slaughterhouses and meatpacking plants; in Cleveland, Hungarians found employment in ironworks located in the city's eastern section; in Bayonne, New Jersey, Poles dominated the barrel factories; and eastern European Jews made their way to the same workshops and factories in New York's garment trades.

Forces identical to those that guided the flow of people into America's urban factories propelled currents into the country's industrial towns. Recruiting efforts by agents representing mines set patterns in motion that by the early twentieth century were bringing Poles, Slovaks, Croatians, and Hungarians to western Pennsylvania's coal mines. Similarly, the steelworks in Homestead, a single-industry mill town in western Pennsylvania, relied on a steady stream of foreign laborers from eastern Europe. Over 53 percent of the 6,772 men employed at the Homestead mill in 1907 were eastern European immigrants. More than half of these foreign workers were Slovaks while Hungarians, Romanians, Ruthenians, Poles, and Lithuanians made up the remainder. Similar patterns of ethnic clustering were repeated in mines, factories, and plants sprinkled throughout the East and Midwest.

To some extent, cultural preferences or, perhaps, premigration skills influenced the type of occupations that nationalities characteristically sought. For instance, their skills enabled some Italian stonecutters and stonemasons to acquire jobs with building contractors or to get positions in marble-cutting plants, brickyards, or masonry-related occupations. By and large, Italian immigrants preferred any kind of construction or outdoor labor to working in mills, mines, slaughterhouses, or meatpacking plants. Even Italians hired by factories often worked on construction crews or did what one investigative report described as the "roughest unskilled yard work around plants." Eastern European Jews who had some tailoring skills found work in the needle trades, and, over time Jewish immigrants gravitated into the garment industries. Jews and Italians were not normally found working in deep mines or manning blast-furnace crews in steel mills.

The hiring practices—combined with personal networks and cultural preferences—that brought immigrants to the same factories and mills also created ethnic divisions within them. Indeed, ethnic occupational networks went beyond simply determining at which facility a job seeker might successfully find employment; they often resulted in family and friends working together. It was not uncommon for fathers, brothers, uncles, cousins, or godparents to be in the same departments or even on the same crews. A tragedy involving 12 Slovaks at a steel mill in Pittsburgh in 1906 demonstrated the powerful connection between personal relationships and where people worked. Eleven of the men hurt in the explosion came from the same European village; the twelfth victim was from a neighboring village. The accident involved two brothers from one family and two brothers from another. Such clustering had the effect of causing workers to identify certain jobs with particular nationalities. Take, for instance, the Lithuanian who, in answer to a sympathetic inquiry about whether any of his countrymen had been hurt in a recent furnace explosion, haughtily replied that one would not "catch our people doing such work as that! There you find the Slovak."[2] The tendency to link jobs to immigrant groups both nurtured stereotypes and reflected ethnic animosities that existed in the industrial workplace.

Immigrant networks and cultural preferences were not the only factors responsible for the ethnic bunching in America's factories. Bosses desired ethnically homogeneous crews because they believed it was more efficient to have individuals who spoke the same language working together. But some employers and managers also viewed ethnic diversity as a safeguard against unionization. By having each crew composed of a different nationality, employers thought that ethnic antipathies, such as those expressed by the Lithuanian steelworker, would prevent workers from joining together to support union activities or strikes. Stereotypes also influenced hiring decisions. Companies as well as foremen preferred certain ethnic groups because of alleged cultural or physical attributes. They imagined that some nationalities possessed natural or abilities that suited them for certain types of work.

Although the majority of migrants who left for the United States knew precisely where they were headed and possibly **Ongoing** even where they might be working, they did not necessarily **Internal** stay in one place. Indeed, the migration mentality that char- **Migration** acterized population movements at the dawn of the twentieth century nurtured successive internal migration in the United States. Having departed for America with the intention of getting a job—and perhaps having already made two or more trips to the United States—immigrants willingly moved on when conditions warranted it. Sometimes circumstances beyond their control caused them to abandon a city or town. For example, in 1901 a steel strike in Pittsburgh prompted some foreign-born laborers to leave the city, but the reverse happened in 1902 when a strike in eastern Pennsylvania's anthracite coal region caused workers to migrate to the "Steel City." If a local economy took a downturn that thrust people out of work, immigrants might go in search of jobs elsewhere. The decision to set out for a different locale also stemmed from a practical assessment of available opportunities. Some migrants simply left one place for another because they heard about better jobs somewhere else. Single workers or married men whose families remained in Europe had more options and were probably more geographically mobile than breadwinners whose families lived in the United States.

Immigrants had several ways to stay informed about employment opportunities and working conditions. Nationality groups had their own newspapers that served as important sources of information. Publications carried "work reports," which contained news about wages and jobs in cities and towns throughout the United States. For example, in 1900 one immigrant newspaper reported that work in Pittsburgh was "universally good," but in 1905 this same foreign-language paper warned in large, bold type: "Do not go to Pittsburgh for work." Newspapers might announce when new factories would be opening and, consequently, would be hiring people. In addition, strikes also generally merited coverage in the immigrant press. Besides work-related items, some newspapers printed letters from readers that included commentary on the employment situation where they lived. All this information was helpful to workers who might have been considering leaving their job to find a better one or who suddenly became unemployed.

Although immigrant workers were mobile people willing to move on, they did not wander haphazardly in search of jobs. The same family and friendship ties that first directed migratory chains from homeland districts to specific American destinations affected ongoing internal migration. When they made second moves, workers often went to locations where people from their regions already lived and had, perhaps, established footholds in local industries. Telling his own story, John Ciganik typified the personal relationships that shaped ongoing migration within the United States. Deciding to emigrate, this young man went directly to Michigan, where his father was already working and where so many people from his village and neighboring villages had already migrated that "it was just like home." He later stayed behind while his father responded to news from people in Pittsburgh that there were good jobs in the Steel City. Ciganik subsequently left Michigan to join his father, godfather, and other friends in Pittsburgh's North Side, where he got a job in a factory. A young Lithuanian offered a more poignant example of how personal motives affected geographic mobility. His father, who already worked in a Pennsylvania mine, sent for him and helped him find work in the mine. Unhappy working in a coal mine, the son set out for Michigan, where, with the assistance of a cousin and friends, he was hired by a furniture manufacturing company. After his father was badly maimed in an accident, however, the young Lithuanian returned to Pennsylvania and worked in the dreaded mines. When his father died, he moved again and found work in a Connecticut factory.

Immigrant mobility contributed to a high rate of labor turnover in American industries. The employment office for a machine works highlighted the extent of worker mobility when it reported that, in the particularly prosperous year of 1906, the firm had hired 12,000 people in order to maintain a stable workforce of 10,000. At the same time, the superintendent of a mine in western Pennsylvania alleged that he had hired 5,000 workers to sustain the necessary 1,000 laborers he needed. Although the manager of the region's largest mining operation questioned such a high figure, he, nevertheless, underscored the large number of laborers industries had to hire. He estimated that to keep 1,000 labor slots filled, an industry had to take on 2,000 workers during the course of a year.

It must be emphasized that, despite the extensive mobility that occurred within the United States, many immigrants remained in the same place. And if they finally decided to stay in America, most foreign-born workers settled down. These permanent residents provided a solid base of support for ethnic institutions and stable immigrant communities. Still, transient workers, together with individuals planning to return to their homelands, formed an especially large contingent of the early stages of the new immigration. Moreover, these mobile people remained part of the second-wave migration throughout the pre–World War I era.

LIFE IN THE WORKPLACE: IMMIGRANT WORKINGMEN

The fact that most industrial jobs called for no experience and required minimal training made it easier for immigrants to abandon one geographic area and go elsewhere. In addition, the wide variety of industries and the diverse jobs available meant that laborers dissatisfied with one type of work could try to find something different. Regardless of where they were employed, however, most unskilled immigrant laborers worked in mines or massive plants under corporate ownership. And after workers passed through company gates, the business philosophy and management principles of employers had a significant impact on their workaday lives.

Business Philosophies and Popular Stereotypes

Philosophies promoted by Andrew Carnegie, the tycoon who helped spearhead the American steel industry's phenomenal rise, were among the most important principles shaping conditions for immigrant mill workers. Indeed, the views of this titan influenced the overall outlook of steel producers and their allied industries. As one partner put it, Carnegie was not interested in profit reports; he wanted to see the cost sheets. His objective was to maximize productivity in steel mills by increasing efficiency and trimming labor costs. In a nutshell, Carnegie believed that keeping costs down—not focusing on profits—was the key to success. One way to achieve this goal was to install laborsaving machinery that not only reduced the number of workers needed to do a task but also improved individual worker output. To Carnegie's way of thinking, mechanization justified lowering wages or at least keeping them in check while, at the same time, extending the workday. Thus, as the nineteenth century gave way to the twentieth, the country's steelworkers experienced a gradual lengthening of both their workday and their workweek. And although Carnegie sold his holdings to financier J. P. Morgan, who formed the U.S. Steel Corporation in 1901, his labor policies continued to shape the steel industry.

While Andrew Carnegie's philosophy was a driving force behind the fixation with costs in steel manufacturing, competition created corresponding pressures for other industries. Corporate employers across the broad spectrum of American industry operated on a mentality of keeping production costs low and reducing them whenever possible. Driven by this mindset, businessmen wanted to get the maximum productivity per worker, and this meant paying the lowest possible wages. Hence, technological advances, and especially the growing use of assembly-line and mass-production methods, changed the workplace but did not necessarily improve working conditions for industrial wage earners.

Stereotypes and popular attitudes also had an impact on immigrants' workplace experiences. Americans of the day commonly felt antagonism and superiority toward southern and eastern European immigrants. Many people expressed disdain by alleging that these new immigrants were "stupid" or "lacked intelligence." Such contempt made its way into the workplace. Unless they held a supervisory position, native-born Americans balked at working with individuals they considered inferior "foreigners." This aversion was one reason that employers reserved low-level, disagreeable jobs for new immigrants. Stereotypical views also led some to prefer certain nationalities. Eastern Europeans, in particular, were characterized as people of brawn and, therefore, naturally suited for heavy or intense labor. One contemporary claimed that employers also liked "Slavs" because of their alleged "docility, their habit of silent submission, their amenability to discipline, and their willingness to work long hours and overtime without a murmur." Although popularly held images of ethnic groups were generally ill founded and distorted, the credence given to them affected immigrants' lives in the workplace.

Steel and Allied Industries   At the beginning of the twentieth century, more than one-third of the people employed in mills where steel was manufactured and in foundries where it was turned into durable products were foreign born. In western Pennsylvania's Pittsburgh District, the center of America's steel industry, immigrants reportedly made up two-thirds of the steelworkers. Moreover, the majority of foreign-born day laborers employed in the steel industry were eastern Europeans. Although a small percentage of new immigrants held skilled positions, native-born Americans and old immigrants typically claimed most of the skilled and supervisory slots in steel mills and foundries. The Carnegie steel plant in Homestead, Pennsylvania, offered a striking, yet representative, example. "Slavs" and Hungarians constituted more than half of the mill's labor force, and 85 percent of them were unskilled day laborers. Regardless of where they were employed, immigrant steelworkers shared much in common. There were variations, but in general, they worked similar hours, received equivalent wages, and endured comparable working conditions.

Wages and Hours

By 1907, the typical steelworker spent 12 hours a day on the job. Departments normally operated on two shifts, a day turn and a night turn. Laborers in most departments could expect to be off during the day on Sunday, but, depending on their shift, by six o'clock in the evening they might have to be back on the job. Because blast furnaces ran continuously, men on the furnace crews worked a seven-day schedule with only one day off during a two-week period. In order to switch from one shift to the other, every two weeks blast-furnace gangs were required to work a straight 24 hours, go home for 12 hours, and then return to begin their next shift. From management's view, the long turn, as it was called, was the most labor- and cost-efficient way to handle the shift change, but from the workers' perspective it was grueling.

Even when they worked in different departments, unskilled steelworkers could expect to earn approximately the same money. Most companies established a standard pay rate for ordinary labor. Some newly hired workers reportedly accepted wages as low as 13 ½ cents an hour, but by 1907 men employed by U.S. Steel received 16 ½ cents per hour; laborers in a few independent mills got an hourly rate of 15 cents. This 1907–1908 scale was a two-cent increase over the 14 cents per hour the industry had paid unskilled workers in 1892. Depending on how many hours they actually worked, unskilled steelworkers living in cities and mill towns earned between $1.65 and $1.98 a day. A few men assigned to hauling gangs were paid by the ton. Under this tonnage system, metal wheelers and cinder pitmen could anticipate $2.28 to $2.41, which amounted to approximately 19 cents to 20 cents an hour for moving heavy loads all day long. Immigrants promoted to skilled jobs in foundries fared better than common day laborers. A machine operator could get up to $2 per day. Riveters, punchers, shearsmen, and pressmen, who were paid by "the piece," could amass $35 to $50 in a two-week period.

Workplace Conditions

From the time they entered factories and foundries, immigrants passed their days in surroundings fraught with danger and under conditions potentially damaging to their health. Typically alternating between the day and night shifts, workers began their workday at either six o'clock in the morning or six o'clock in the evening. Every two weeks, men on a seven-day schedule faced the dreaded long turn. They started work early on Sunday, remained on the job until Monday morning, went home, and returned 12 hours later to begin the night turn. A week later, they finally got a twenty-four-hour rest while men on the day shift worked the long turn. This schedule was exhausting for the blast-furnace crews, who labored day and night in intense heat. In 1907, when industry officials and stockholders moved toward eliminating Sunday work, blast-furnace departments were explicitly excluded from the proposed reform. Even people calling for change argued that, because the blast furnaces had to run constantly, "it was not practicable" to abolish the seven-day schedule for the furnace divisions. So, except possibly for some "cooling spells" during the day, the blast-furnace crews—which "seldom [comprised] any but Slavs and Hungarians"—got little relief from the blazing heat and drudgery of their jobs.

Regardless of which department they were assigned to, steelworkers toiled either in "intense heat or the din of machinery" and often in both. In foundries where steel was turned into massive rolls or durable products, the screeching created as "the cold saw bites into the steel" was "fairly maddening," an outside observer declared. Cranes moving loads overhead added to the crash and roar that pervaded steel plants. Offering a vivid firsthand account of factories, this eyewitness proclaimed it a "world filled of men in greasy overalls." In places where crews moved around furnaces or molten metal, one saw "faces reddened by the glare of fire and hot steel, muscles standing out in knots and bands on bare arms."

Some jobs were hot, dirty, and arduous; others were dangerous. Each department carried its own risks. Men working near the infamous "skull cracker" in steel mills needed to be especially alert and agile. Hoisted about sixty feet in the air, this pear-shaped iron weight came down with sufficient force to crush balls of hardened metal that had accumulated in ladles. With no protective barrier around the operation, the shattered chunks of metal were thrust distances of 200 feet or more. Men who repaired overhead cranes might work on runways with no railings. While standing on ladders, crews replaced cooling plates in blast furnaces, a process that carried the danger of powerful spurts of gas suddenly gushing out. Because there was no means of quick escape, when this happened laborers were asphyxiated. Each day, as they went about their jobs, workers moved under dangling loads of heavy or hot materials being transported by overhead cranes. In addition to the danger of possibly suffering bodily harm, there were health risks connected to working in America's steelworks. Laborers in finishing mills and fabricating plants handled dangerous chemicals. Dust permeated the foundries where steel was cast, ground, or polished. Besides irritating one's eyes, nose, and throat, breathing the grit made workers more susceptible to lung ailments, especially tuberculosis, which afflicted a large number of immigrants in the early twentieth century.

Workplace Facilities

A contemporary survey of factories in the Pittsburgh area documented conditions characteristic of the steel industry at the onset of the twentieth century. Investigators discovered that most plants lacked basic convenien-

"Filling moulds with steel, Pittsburg[h], Pa.," ca. 1905. Courtesy of Library of Congress.

ces. There were no lockers for coats, packed lunches, or other personal items that employees might have carried with them. Workers brought their own food for the day, but there were often no facilities where they could eat. Because time off to eat was not necessarily built into daily schedules, even if there were cafeterias, laborers might not use them. Instead, they ate on the job.

In the steel mills and older foundries, washrooms and lavatories were few, inconveniently located, insufficiently equipped, and poorly maintained. Managers often supplied neither soap nor toilet paper and, in addition, refused to put bulbs in light fixtures. They alleged that workers stole supplies and that too much light encouraged them to fritter away time reading instead of getting back to their jobs. As an alternative to employing an attendant to oversee these rooms, plant managers chose not to provide sanitary products. In a few plants where someone was hired to supervise lavatories and washrooms, the overseer reportedly took the check number of each worker who used these facilities and recorded both his entry and exit times. Workers who accumulated too much time in these areas had their pay docked. Often with no showers or other washing facilities available, at the end of their shifts, laborers covered with grime poured into the streets. One contemporary critic charged that these filthy men rubbing against people on public thoroughfares were "nuisances" to the community. By 1910, some new plants had improved eating and sanitary conveniences, but, for immigrants in mills owned by large steel companies as well as in older foundries, coping with inconvenient and unsanitary conditions was part of life on the job.

Mining Industries   At the turn of the twentieth century, thousands of immigrants spent their days in mines both above and below ground. Nearly half of the country's miners were foreign born, and in some mines managers estimated that less than one-fourth of their workforce could speak English. This pattern held true for mines in the eastern United States as well for those in the upper Midwest and western regions of the country.

Mining industries had long relied on immigrant labor. As German, Scandinavian, and Czech immigrants were striving to establish farms in America's Midwest and western regions during the 1870s, Cornish, Irish, Swedish, and northern Italian males took unskilled jobs in the areas' iron-ore, copper, or coal mines. In the mid-1880s, Finns began migrating into the mining districts of Michigan and Minnesota, where they worked as common laborers. The earlier immigrant groups moved up to skilled and supervisory positions in the mines. Into the twentieth century, Finns continued to dominate the unskilled labor force, but mining in the upper Midwest and western United States gradually attracted more diverse peoples. Slovenes, Italians, Croatians, Montenegrins, Bulgarians, Czechs, Greeks, Serbians, and even some Syrians worked in the regions' open-pit and underground mines. Besides enhancing the diversity of the unskilled force in Minnesota and Michigan's iron-ore regions, these groups added to the ethnic mix in the copper mines of Michigan's Upper Peninsula and in the silver and copper operations in Montana, Colorado, and Arizona. They did the same to the makeup of the population in the coalfields of Illinois, Kansas, and Oklahoma. Although Slavic immigrants made their way to western mines, in general Slavic groups, Hungarians, and Lithuanians tended to gravitate to the anthracite (hard) coalfields of northeastern Pennsylvania and to the bituminous (soft) coal region stretching from western Pennsylvania into West Virginia.

Slovak miners at the entrance to coal mine near Pittsburgh, Pennsylvania, 1904.
Courtesy Immigration History Research Center, University of Minnesota.

Workplace Conditions

They unearthed different minerals, but for immigrants who went down into the coal, iron-ore, and copper mines, the experience was notably similar. Once miners entered the mine shaft, they did not exit until their shift ended. They ate, drank, and performed necessary bodily functions in the depths of the earth. Describing his days as a miner, one immigrant recalled, "I never saw the sunlight, because we went down in the mine before the sun came out and we finished work after the sun had set." The miners' day began the moment they started their descent to perhaps 1,000 feet below the surface. Depending on the setup, in some mines "a cage," which was "a flimsy, shaky elevator, devoid of walls or anything else . . . [to] cling to," transported the men "down into the darkness."[3] At the end of this wobbly ride, they made their way on foot to their workstations. In sites without cage transport, miners wound their way on foot down into the deep, "black pit" below. While there were often "man entries" and separate "hauling entries" for rail cars bringing coal or iron ore aboveground, in some places men squeezed between cars and walls as they marched into and out of the mines. Regardless of whether men walked the entire way or descended into the mines in a cage and continued on, the trek by foot was usually the same. "Stooping to avoid overhangs [and] . . . scrambling on hands and knees" on paths covered with chunks of coal and slate, miners made their way through dark passages probably no more than five-and-a-half feet high.

Before they could begin work, the men had to check overhead for loose slate, rock, or coal and construct temporary ceilings to protect themselves from falling debris. Realizing they got paid by the amount of coal they extracted or loaded onto cars, workers kept busy. With electric drills or handpicks, miners bored holes into the walls, prepared the deposits for blasting, and then detonated explosives. Common laborers cleaned away the rock and loaded coal into cars that transported it aboveground. The harsh clack of explosives detonating, the rumble of loaded cars, the banging of implements against hard surfaces, and the clang of rock, slate, and coal being thrown around all combined to create an oppressive atmosphere. The dust and grit that pervaded underground mines added to the already grim conditions workers faced every day. Mining was not only noisy, dirty, and strenuous work, it also was dangerous. There was the constant threat of a cave-in. Besides these catastrophic collapses, volatile dusts and gases increased the likelihood of deadly explosions in coal mines. In addition to being on guard against falling slate and rock, miners had to be on the lookout for frayed electric cables—or "live wires" as the workers dubbed them—that powered the electric drills used in the mines.

Wages and Hours

The type of job a person did determined how his wages were calculated. Common laborers were usually paid by the hour while the men who actually extracted the iron ore, coal, and copper or loaded it into cars and

Mine cage located in South Pittston, Pennsylvania coal mine, 1911. Courtesy of Library of Congress.

containers for transport were paid by the ton. In the early 1900s, the pay in copper and iron-ore mines amounted to about $1.65 to $2.08 per day. Unskilled workers in nonunion coal mines received daily wages ranging from $1.50 to $2.25, whereas laborers and skilled miners in unionized coal mines negotiated slightly higher pay scales. By 1906, common laborers in some union mines earned $2.35 to $2.56 a day, and " pick miners," who got 90 cents per ton, could anticipate wages averaging around $2.70.

At the outset of the twentieth century, miners generally worked a nine- to ten-hour day and a six-day week. Like the steel mills, mines usually operated on two-shift schedules, so the men could expect their workweeks to alternate between day and night turns. Unionization, though, led to a reduction in hours for some miners. By about 1908, laborers in unionized mines normally worked an eight-hour day and a six-day week; those at nonunion mines most likely had a ten-hour schedule. At the same time, men mining copper stayed on the job for nine hours and were off for one-and-a-half days on the weekend. Workers unearthing iron ore on ranges in the upper Midwest usually remained in the mines 10 hours each day and had Sundays free.

Thousands of immigrants passed their workdays doing unpleasant, even grisly, jobs in America's slaughterhouses and meatpacking plants. In Chicago, which by the turn of the twentieth century was the center of the meatpacking industry, immigrants formed the mainstay of the city's slaughterhouses and processing plants.

Slaughterhouses and the Meatpacking Industry

One congressional investigation of Chicago found that over 78 percent of the employees surveyed were foreign-born males and more than half of them were new immigrants. These mainly unskilled workers suited the needs of an expanding industry, which, by the late nineteenth century, had developed efficient assembly-line methods for slaughtering animals and dressing the carcasses. In addition to processing meat for the mass market, meatpacking nurtured a host of by-product industries dependent on the remnants of butchered animals. Blood, bones, hooves, horns, and hides were turned into usable goods such as fertilizers, glue, soap, and tanned leather items. Nothing was wasted. The dressing process thus involved assembly-line workers taking out the internal organs and removing other parts from the carcasses and throwing them into chutes that sped the retrieved elements to the by-product departments.

Workplace Conditions

Whether in Chicago's huge establishments or in smaller ones elsewhere, daily life in meatpacking plants was a similarly horrid experience. From the moment they entered the plants and until they left, workers were assaulted by dreadful noises, awful odors, and appalling sights. The squeal of animals in the "killing rooms" mixed with the jarring sound of machinery splitting flesh and sawing bones. These dissonant noises reverberated and

"Dressing the beeves, Armour's great packing house, Chicago, U.S.A.," ca. 1892.
Courtesy of Library of Congress.

the smells persisted as workers sat or stood at their stations and rapidly
performed their assigned tasks on the line of carcasses that passed in front
of them. There is no better description of these immigrants' everyday lives
on the job than the one Upton Sinclair provided in his powerful 1906 novel
The Jungle. Offering an eyewitness account, Sinclair takes his readers to the
dressing tables, where with remarkable efficiency immigrant workers cut
and cleaned the slaughtered animals. As the dangling carcasses moved
along "between two lines of men," each man did "a certain single thing" to
each passing carcass. "One [man] scraped the outside leg; another scraped
the inside of the same leg. One with a swift stroke cut the throat; another
with two swift strokes severed the head, which fell to the floor and vanished through a hole. Another made a slit down the body; a second opened
the body wider; a third with a saw cut the breastbone; a fourth loosened the
entrails; a fifth pulled them out—and they also slid through a hole in the
floor." Each man was "working as if a demon were after him."

Remaining at a single post all day, workers did the same tedious scraping, slitting, and gutting maneuver over and over and over again. And
they did it under the watchful eye of foremen eager to reduce costs and
speed up the process. Looking to gain recognition for their own department's productivity and perhaps receive a bonus, the bosses drove workers to perform tasks ever more rapidly. Individuals knew they had to
work quickly; otherwise, they might be fired. An immigrant, whose job
in the killing room was to push blood along a gutter, believed he was let

go because he was "too slow." Maybe, he surmised, someone had bribed the yard policeman in charge of selecting workers that day, but there was no doubt in his mind that "The foreman in that room wanted quick men to make the work rush, because he was paid more if the work was done cheaper and quicker." Another immigrant sized up the mentality of pack-inghouse managers when he cynically told a coworker, "They get all the blood out of those cattle and all the work out of us men."

Upton Sinclair's *The Jungle* sparked a national outcry and demands for reform. The public uproar prompted Congress to enact both the Pure Food and Drug Act and the Meat Inspection Act in 1906. The law established an inspection system to protect the country's food supply, but Sinclair's shock-ing exposé did not lead to major improvements in working conditions.

Wages and Hours

Packinghouse workers received approximately the same hourly wages that day laborers got in the steel industry. By 1904, the pay for unskilled positions in meatpacking, which most immigrants held, had risen from 15 cents to 18 ½ cents an hour but then dropped that year to 16 ½ cents, where it remained for at least the next decade. The seasonal nature of food-related industries meant the number of hours or days that individu-als worked varied. During particularly busy times, workers could stay on the job until late at night. On slack days, people might be sent home midday or arrive at the plant only to be told to leave because there was no work that day. Thus, when they set out in the morning, packinghouse employees did not know for certain what time they would start or how late they would remain on the job. Recalling his own experience, one immigrant offered a typical example when he explained that on his first day at a meatpacking plant he and fellow countrymen worked "from six in the morning till seven at night." The next day, they started at the same time but remained an hour later. The extended days turned into an unfore-seen benefit because on the third day the men "had no work." Describing the men's schedules, he observed, "we had no good, regular hours."

Some immigrants demonstrated a decided preference for outdoor work, and if possible, they avoided heavy indus- **Construction** try and underground mines. As an alternative, they sought **and Railroads** employment in construction, public works, and railroad yards that needed unskilled workers and had a vast array of jobs to offer.

Foreign-born workers made up crews that constructed roads, bridges, mass-transit systems, skyscrapers, and all types of private or public build-ings. They dug ditches and laid gas lines and sewer pipes. Immigrants built scaffolding and did much of the excavation work on construction projects. All day long, they mixed mortar or carried bricks and other building materials. They cleaned up the debris on building sites. Since it was not uncommon for utility companies and factories to establish separate units to do construction, carpentry, and repair work, immigrants filled the payrolls of maintenance departments. Cities contracted private companies to handle public works projects, but municipalities also had public works divisions responsible for community construction projects and services. They attracted sizable numbers of the foreign born. Indeed, in some cities, immigrants made up a significant portion of the common laborers on the payroll in these departments.

Local ordinances often stipulated how long city employees could be required to work. They generally limited the workday to eight hours. Governments also required construction companies awarded city contracts to abide by local regulations. On private projects, however, laborers put in longer days, especially during warm weather. In areas where craft unions successfully negotiated maximum hours for skilled workers, these agreements had the ripple effect of regulating schedules for unskilled laborers as well. On the whole, at the turn of the twentieth century, immigrants employed in the various types of construction probably averaged an eight-hour day and did limited work on the weekends.

Railroads also provided opportunities for unskilled immigrants who preferred outdoor labor. They laid tracks or worked on section gangs responsible for maintaining them. The foreign born were employed in the railroad yards, where massive carloads of freight were received and distributed each day. As trackwalkers, section men, and ordinary laborers, they loaded and unloaded shipments, cleaned cars, and took charge of the yards' general upkeep. Shipments arrived and were dispatched around the clock and railroad yards typically operated twelve-hour shifts; however, it was not uncommon for yardmen to put in longer days.

Railroad companies and the construction trades generally paid low wages. A study of Pittsburgh's industries, for example, concluded that railroads and contractors had "the distinction of being the industrial employers who paid the lowest wages for a day." In 1907–1908, section hands in railroad yards—large numbers of whom were foreign born—earned 13 ½ cents an hour or $1.35 a day; by 1913, the daily wage had risen to roughly $1.65. Pay for construction workers varied. Again, as with ordinances regulating the length of workdays, companies with city contracts had to comply with established pay scales. Private employers could set their own rates on other construction projects. Despite variations, unskilled construction workers could expect approximately the same wages as the railroads' section gangs. By 1913, common laborers averaged between 16 ½ cents and 18 cents an hour. At the same time, in unionized building trades, the unskilled workers on a project could command up to 25 cents an hour.

LIFE IN THE WORKPLACE: FEMALE WAGE EARNERS

Attitudes and Female Labor Immigrant women and the daughters of immigrants also made up an important segment of America's unskilled workforce. These female workers were typically unmarried and young. Many women sought employment as domestics in hotels or private residences, but specific nationalities tended to take these jobs. For instance, 10 percent of the female domestic workers in Chicago in 1880 were Swedish. As late as 1920, more than 80 percent of the females from Ireland who were employed outside the home were in domestic service. By and large, other nationalities gravitated toward the factories. In 1910, slightly more than 1 million first- and second-generation immigrant women worked in the manufacturing and mechanical industries, and they represented well over half of the female labor force for those sectors. Throughout the next decade, the number of these first- and second-generation female factory workers remained constant. In 1920, they represented slightly over 54 percent of the women engaged in America's manufacturing and mechanical industries. Women belonging to old immigrant groups usually held supervisory or better paying skilled positions while new immigrants and their children occupied the unskilled ranks.

Complex factors determined if and where immigrant women or their daughters worked. With the notable exceptions of some Irish and Swedish women, most females did not migrate with the intention of becoming hired workers and establishing their own independent existence. Women more likely traveled to America to join their husbands or fiancés; single women also came on their own with the long-range plan of working temporarily, getting married, and leaving the workforce. Cultural mores significantly influenced whether females—especially married women—took paying jobs outside the home. In most cultures, married women working for hire was frowned upon. In some societies, the disapproval of women working outside the home bordered on taboo. Italians and Jews, for example, strongly disapproved of married women accepting paid employment. Traditional attitudes regarding women's "proper roles" also deterred the daughters of some immigrants from seeking jobs in either domestic service or in light industry. Still, in many families, financial needs superseded conventional views; consequently, once they reached young adulthood, daughters added to the family income by joining the workforce.

When they sought employment, women relied on the same kith-and-kin networks that men did. Relatives and **Kith-and-Kin** friends provided information or had connections that **Networks** helped them find jobs. As a result, women often followed sisters, cousins, and aunts into the same workrooms. Some women labored in the female divisions of establishments that employed their fathers, brothers, cousins, or uncles. Ethnic occupational networks, which channeled women into specific industries, meant that, even if she did not toil alongside a relative, a young woman possibly still worked with someone of the same nationality. In Pittsburgh, for example, Jewish, Irish, German, and "Americans" were employed in garment factories while "Slavic" girls were on the payrolls of canneries and laundries. Slovak, Hungarian, Polish, and Croatian females represented two-thirds of the workingwomen in the city's metal trades. When options were available, traditional cultural attitudes and premigration experiences also affected women's employment decisions. For instance, Italian and eastern European Jewish women gravitated to the garment industries.

Immigrant female workers were usually less geographically mobile than men. Differing from the male migrant force, women were more likely to be part of a family unit and not prone to set out in search of better opportunities. So, instead of leaving a city or town, women typically abandoned one local company to work for another. Regardless of whether immigrant women merely changed jobs or made the more drastic decision to abandon an area, personal networks guided them to a new destination and to a new job. Sadie Frowne reflected the common pattern when she moved from Manhattan to Brooklyn. On her own in New York after her mother died, this young Jewish female from Poland went to the garment district of Brownsville where, in her words, there were "so many of my people" and where she had "friends." She soon began a job in a factory that made cheap underskirts.

Women's Jobs and Workplace Conditions   Cultural traditions and family needs influenced whether females sought jobs outside the home, but the specific type of work they did could depend on the town, city, or region where they lived. Small factory towns and especially those with single industries offered fewer opportunities for female employment; the same was true for cities that lacked a variety of industries. For example, work was scarcer for women in Pittsburgh and Buffalo than in New York or Chicago. Although options varied considerably, America's diversified economy nevertheless meant that women could be found doing a wide range of jobs in various industries. By and large, immigrant women and their daughters held unskilled jobs that required doing a single task repeatedly.

As they went off to work each day, then, most female wage earners could expect to spend hours standing or sitting while performing the same motions over and over again. They also knew that a boss most likely would be pushing them to keep busy and do their repetitive tasks rapidly. In addition, they could anticipate doing them in unpleasant and, often, terrible conditions. Because most establishments that hired foreign-born women or the daughters of immigrants consigned these females to the least desirable jobs, they typically endured the industries' worst workplaces. Although each industry had unique characteristics, female wage earners usually endured overcrowded, poorly lit, and badly ventilated environments. Moreover, their workplaces were typically dusty and either damp and cold or hot and dry.

Food Processing and Laundries

First- and second-generation women did a wide array of jobs in the food-processing industries. They washed bottles, sorted raw produce, and filled containers. Young female workers grew weary standing all day in front of conveyors and doing the same back-and-forth or up-and-down motions as food and containers passed in front of them. They hulled berries and prepared fruit, filled cans, labeled containers, or slipped a piece of pork into each can of beans moving by on high-speed belts. In coastal areas, women and children cleaned and processed raw fish and seafood. Providing an eyewitness peek into everyday life on the job, one observer recounted that "Slavic girls" in canneries worked "without turning their heads or changing their positions . . . [and] they can keep pace with the chains." In cracker factories, where workers' "muscles" had "to be taught to keep pace with the machine," female packers worked in more unpleasant conditions. The packing rooms had huge cooling fans that blasted cold air as workers lifted crackers from the fast-moving conveyors and put them in boxes. Conditions for female employees in meatpacking plants were often worse than in other food-related industries. In the sausage divisions, they twisted the ends of stuffed casings and linked the sausages; women also worked in the lard, chipped meat, and several other by-product departments. They stood entire days on platforms and performed their often single task in dismal, damp surroundings. Even when they wore leather aprons, there could be so much water that the workers still got wet; in winter, the meat was so cold that ice formed on it.

First- and second-generation females provided unskilled labor in commercial laundries that serviced hotels, factories, railroads, and private residences. The young girls who operated the mangles passed their days feeding wet sheets into hot metal rollers while someone stood on the other

Processing shrimp in Biloxi, Mississippi, 1911. Courtesy of Library of Congress.

side and folded them as they came out. Steam spewed from these sizzling cylinders and from huge washing vats while exhaust from gas-heated machines filtered through the facilities. The tendency for some laundry managers to ignore regulations meant that, on some days, women could endure perhaps 15 hours of extreme heat, steamy atmosphere, and fumes.

Garment Industries

Thousands of first and second-generation women also spent their time doing some type of work in the garment industry. In 1900, a U.S. Senate investigation found that three-fourths of the women involved in manufacturing men's clothing were either foreign born or the children of immigrants. Instead of making entire garments, though, female workers usually did something to an unfinished shirt, blouse, jacket, trouser, skirt, or other item. They made cuffs, neckbands, and pockets; they sewed seams and hems, added buttons, or stitched together various parts of a garment.

Whether they climbed up the stairs or went down into a workroom in New York, the center of the U.S. garment industry, or anywhere else, female workers entered a noisy, shabby environment. Sewing machines lined the length of stark workrooms. Some rooms accommodated a huge number of machines, but in smaller places managers made use of all the available space by cramming people together. One immigrant woman described the typically crowded conditions when she recalled that in the factory where she worked, 14 machines were squeezed into a room 20 feet long and 14 feet wide. Once the work began, for the rest of the day people were subjected to the roar of sewing machines and the "sound of many needles being driven through cloth." They felt the floors quiver as the machines' wheels spun furiously.

The operators' day usually started at seven o'clock when the foreman brought each person a pile of items from the cutting room. For at least the next 9 to 10 hours, workers bent forward over their machines and repeatedly performed the same tedious task as they pushed cloth under the needles and pumped the treadles with their feet. Before they could go home, they had to finish the stack the boss had set beside them in the morning. If the "work is not all finished by six o'clock . . . then the one who is behind must work overtime," one seamstress explained. A "slow" employee who wanted to keep her job had no choice but to stay until she was done. Other employers paid workers by "the piece"; so, the more cuffs they sewed or pockets they attached, the more money they got. Paying according to individual output meant, "The machines go like mad all day, because the faster you work the more money you get," one immigrant declared. Since "the machines are all run by foot-power . . . at the end of the day one feels so weak that there is a great temptation to lie right down and sleep," she added.

Contemporary investigators consistently underscored the miserable conditions in garment factories where people, especially females, toiled. Some employers positioned a lightbulb over each machine, but poor lighting was

The sewing room of a Troy, New York shirt factory, ca. 1907. Courtesy of Library of Congress.

nevertheless a characteristic common to the workrooms. Besides sitting in a bent position for hours on end, workers breathed air heavy with lint and dust. Strips of cloth and threads falling constantly from the machines made work areas littered and unsightly. Relating conditions she witnessed, one visitor described the workroom floor as scattered with "rubbish." When windows were either located high in the rooms or closed—sometimes both—ventilation in the work areas was extremely poor.

Light Manufacturing and Heavy Industry

Women were also employed in diversified light manufacturing industries that fabricated lamps, brushes, lightbulbs, paper boxes, pencils, hats, toys, and sundry other items. In Pittsburgh's glassworks, Slavic girls worked in the decorating department where they prepared glass for etching or stamping. In stogie factories, women stripped leaves or rolled the dried tobacco into cigars. Dust and fumes permeated factories, especially those that produced cigars, soap, and garments. In stogie factories, a fine gray-brown powder from dried tobacco leaves filled the air and covered everything in the rooms where workers sat in stalls and stripped the stems from tobacco leaves. The air was heavy with nicotine fumes emitted by drying tobacco. Soap packers coped with a stifling environment as well. In the packing rooms, as women continually scooped powder from tubs and dumped it into boxes, dust floated through the air and settled on tightly closed windows as well as on the workers. Unswept floors strewn with debris contributed to the disagreeable atmosphere in cigar and soap factories.

Compared to the number of females engaged in food processing, light manufacturing, and the needle trades, relatively few women worked in America's heavy industries. In cities such as Pittsburgh, which had a large number of foundries, however, first- and second-generation eastern European women acquired jobs as unskilled laborers in the metal trades. Although men dominated the steel industry's workforce, some foundries employed young women to perform lighter, monotonous tasks. They formed cores, which were baked sand molds used to produce brass machine parts. They made small coils, split mica, trimmed bolts, soldered tin, or dipped pieces of tin in enamel. They ground threads into bolts by pushing the smooth metal into grinding machines; they screwed nuts on to bolts. Young women also packed the finished nuts, bolts, and screws into boxes for distribution.

Working in heavy industry was exceedingly unpleasant for female wage earners. With screeching sounds pounding in their ears, young women stood for ten-and-a-half hours and fed the machines that ground threads into screws and bolts. The women who trimmed up to 16,000 bolts a day by pushing one after another into machines heard the same high-pitched grating sounds 16,000 times. Meanwhile, crews of possibly 200 women screwed nuts onto the bolts under dripping spouts of fish oil. They stood because they could work faster and perhaps finish 4,000 each day. Operators of the threading machines also used fish oil to facilitate the grinding process. To protect their hands against the oily compound, the women bound their fingers with rags. After working with the stinking oil all day, at the end of their shifts these female employees left wearing smelly oil-spattered clothes.

Women's Wages and Women's Hours   Investigators who studied wages in the early 1900s estimated that female industrial workers probably earned, on average, between $3 and $6 a week. These are, however, rough calculations not precise figures. For several reasons, it is difficult to determine the hourly or weekly wages working women received. First, because a large number of women were put on a "piecework" scale, both their daily and weekly pay varied considerably. Under this system, women's earnings depended on the number of items they produced, packed, or hand finished. Second, even within the same industry, pay rates and policies varied by plant and locale and changed over time. Finally, determining female wages is complicated by the fact that women were employed to do so many different jobs in diverse industries.

Even when women performed comparable tasks, their pay rates varied. Female packers at a cracker factory received 50 cents a day. The "bottling girls" in canneries could make from $1.30 to $1.50 for stuffing food into containers. Those who labeled the jars were paid about 3 cents a dozen and averaged around 98 cents a day. Women who packed cigars in some stogie factories worked at rates ranging from 7 cents to 50 cents per 1,000. In the early 1900s, stogie packers probably earned $4 to $6 a week, or what amounted to between 75 cents and $1.00 a day. Workers who filled boxes with soap powder averaged $3.50 to $4.50 a week while individuals who wrapped and packed soap bars could anticipate getting between $6.00 and $9.00 for a week's labor. Most soap packers likely got the lesser amount because to get the maximum a worker had to package nearly 11,000 bars each day for six days.

Women employed in the metal and garment trades also normally received a piece rate. Core makers, who worked on a scale of 10 cents for every 1,000 brass molds, could anticipate daily earnings of $1.25 to $1.40. Forming some larger molds paid a higher rate of 12 cents per 100, but, because making them took longer, workers still reaped only $1.00 to $1.20 a day. On a scale of 6 cents for every 1,000 bolts they squared, women who operated trimming machines usually managed to eke out about 96 cents for the 16,000 bolts they handled each day. Piece rates also applied to female workers in departments where machines ground threads into bolts and where nuts were then twisted by hand onto the bolts. At 15 cents per 1,000, individuals usually managed to realize between 90 cents to $1.00 for feeding 6,000 to 7,000 smooth bolts into the threading machines all day long. Paid at a higher rate of 40 cents per 1,000, women who screwed nuts onto the finished bolts could expect daily earnings of up to $1.16 on an especially productive day. Weekly incomes in the garment industry varied, but piece rates meant that women in workshops might get paid anywhere from $4.50 to $6.00 a week.

Workers employed in factories that had pay scales based on weight did not fare any better than females paid strictly by the piece. Employees in stogie factories usually got 1 ½ cents a pound for stripping the stems from dried tobacco leaves. The tobacco, though, was weighed after the stripper had removed the thick center stem. The amount that an individual worker could strip daily usually ranged between 19 and 33 pounds; so, at the end of the week, women could expect between $3.60 and $4.80 in their pay envelopes.

At the dawn of the twentieth century, more and more employers tried to establish pay scales based on worker output. By 1907, for instance, Pittsburgh's laundry owners were moving toward instituting piece rates in ironing divisions. Instead of weekly wages of $5 to $9, women who ironed shirtfronts, collars, and cuffs went on piece rates ranging from 6 cents to 35 cents for each 100 items they ironed. "Our girls know," one laundry foreman explained, "that they are paid for what they do, and if they don't do much they don't get paid much."[4]

Paying by the piece drove people to work quickly and continuously all day long. Women who received hourly wages usually took their full lunch breaks while those paid by the piece or given a daily quota were less likely to use the allotted time. Realizing that by shortening their lunch hour they could make more money, women allocated perhaps only 15 minutes to eat, ate as they worked, or skipped eating altogether. The rationale underlying piecework was to increase worker output; yet, ironically, efficient workers could be penalized. For example, managers in one factory reportedly reduced the per-piece rate for core makers when they learned that particularly speedy employees could garner $2 a day. At the same time that they cut rates so individuals would almost certainly receive no more than $1.50 a day, they capped the amount of money a worker could actually earn. The maximum was put at $1.85 a day. Other establishments also developed scales that effectively limited how much money a pieceworker could be paid in a single day.

Low wage scales—not the number of hours they put in on the job—caused workingwomen to receive a thin pay envelope at the end of the week. By the first decade of the twentieth century, several states had enacted legislation regulating the number of hours females could work. Laws usually restricted their workday to 10 hours and the workweek to between 58 and 60 hours. Despite state maximums, women still put in long hours on the job. Immigrant women or their daughters employed in factories, workshops, or laundries could expect to leave their homes six days a week and head off to work. They could anticipate staying on job at least 10 hours on Monday through Friday, possibly working only a half day on Saturday, and then having the entire day off on Sunday.

Some industries ignored state restrictions or evaded them during seasonally busy times. When supplies of ripe, perishable produce arrived, canning industries forced employees to work overtime and stay on the job well into the evenings. Investigators found that, in the early 1900s, during some seasons, laborers in canneries toiled from seven o'clock in the morning until nine o'clock at night. This meant workers clocked 72 hours or more in a single week. Other industries also used loopholes in their states' laws to require female employees to put in longer days or to work, at least occasionally, beyond the legal weekly limit. Operating on schedules that suited hotels and customers, laundries compelled some workers to put in 15 hours on certain weekdays when the demand for clean, ironed goods was particularly high. Thus, even in states where the legislature imposed maximum lengths, neither the ten-hour workday nor the fifty-eight- to sixty-hour workweek was universal.

Regardless of how long their workdays were, first- and second-generation immigrant women employed in factories, food-processing plants, and laundries could not expect to earn a living wage. Even when they "k[ept] at it just like horses," as one cannery supervisor described the "Hungarian girls" who pared fruit in his division, women's accumulated earnings were next to trifling. On average, unskilled female laborers made about half the money that unskilled male laborers did. There were several reasons for the huge wage disparity between male and female laborers. It was due in part to the fact that employment opportunities available to first- and second-generation females were limited to low-level, unskilled jobs often done at piece rates. In industries with a mixed male and female labor force, men standardly got positions ranked superior to those open to women. But contemporary investigations also revealed a pattern of wage discrimination in factories where men and women worked together and did the same jobs. A survey of "women and the trades" highlighted a common policy in American industry when it reported that male employees summoned to help with a rush order in one foundry's coil-winding room received double the wages for doing the same work as their female coworkers.

The measly wages that foreign-born women and the daughters of immigrants were paid, in part, reflected popularly held beliefs about females and why they sought employment. Although many married women and, of course, widows worked out of necessity, the common view was that women sought only to supplement a family's income or perhaps to acquire money for personal use. The notion that neither married nor single women were breadwinners but, instead, had men to support them helped perpetuate the idea that women's work should be compensated at the lowest possible rate. A box manufacturer revealed a general attitude when he told an investigator that "We try to employ girls who are members of families . . . [because] we don't pay . . . a living wage in this trade."

Instead of going into factories or workshops, many foreign-born women opted to earn money by doing piecework at **Homework** home. For nationalities whose cultural traditions discouraged or even prevented women from accepting outside employment, "homework" offered a way for them to contribute to the family income. Italian and Jewish women were heavily involved in the homework industries. The practice let mothers take care of their children while they earned money. By enlisting family members to help with the piecework, women essentially turned their living quarters into tiny factories. From the employers' perspective, using "homeworkers" was highly profitable because it lowered both overhead and labor costs. Besides paying lower piece rates for homework, factory owners saved on rent, heating, and lighting. The homework system reduced the number of machines that employers in the garment industry, in particular, had to buy and maintain.

Homeworkers performed an enormous variety of jobs at piece rates. For instance, they made artificial flowers and feathers used to decorate bonnets; they shelled nuts, sorted coffee beans, rolled cigars, and assembled toys. The garment industry in particular relied heavily on outside piecework and engaged females to perform a huge array of tasks. They made vests or seamed cut cloth to make jeans, skirts, and other clothing items. Homeworkers did much of the hand finishing on garments, such as adding buttonholes, buttons, pockets, collars, and cuffs to coats, shirts, and sweaters. They sewed the unfinished edges of hems, armholes, and necks; they did the fancy embroidery and detail work on children's clothes.

Women beaded buckles, covered curtain rings, or strung thread or twine through holes in tags. Fingers got sore from attaching thousands of safety pins, snaps, buttons, and hooks to cards. Hands ached after hours of cutting rag remnants into strips, sewing them together, and rolling them into balls that would be sent to factories to be woven into rag rugs.

There is no way to determine the number or percentage of female immigrants who did homework. People worked out of sight in the privacy of their living quarters. In addition, a wide variety of industries relied on outside pieceworkers, and many used them on an irregular, seasonal basis. Still, the practice was common and the number of foreign-born women or children of immigrants who did homework was significant. In New York alone, estimates placed the number of homeworkers in 1910 at perhaps 250,000. In areas where industries routinely used homeworkers, at almost any hour of the day women could be seen carrying bundles and bustling back and forth between factories and places where they lived.

Workdays and Pay Scales

Because they set their own hours, homeworkers decided how much time they wanted to give over to their tasks. Individuals developed routines such as dedicating the early mornings and evenings to their piecework jobs while giving over most of the day to family responsibilities. It was, however, not uncommon for homeworkers to put in long days and continue working into the wee hours of the night. During the day or in the

Woman, with child in her lap, and two neighbors cracking nuts in a tenement flat in New York City, 1911. Courtesy of Library of Congress.

early evening, children kept busy alongside their mothers and, perhaps, fathers who also lent a helping hand. Sons and daughters as young as six years old put in hours carding safety pins, snaps, buttons, and hooks. They strung tags, shelled nuts, and did other odd jobs to assist their mothers or, maybe, their older sisters assemble products or finish garments. Children also served as couriers. They ran bunches of finished products to the workshops and returned home with another batch of items to be worked on.

It is difficult to determine how much homeworkers earned. There were no established rates for outside piecework; instead, each shop determined what it would pay. Piecework scales fluctuated, especially in industries that experienced seasonal demands for their goods. Rates also changed without notice; consequently, workers could not be sure what they would make from one day to the next. Overall, however, the monetary rewards for piecework were paltry. Take, for instance, the Italian woman who reported in 1910 that, with the help of her children, she could assemble five bunches of artificial flowers a day. At 15 cents a bunch, she and her young assistants got 75 cents for their combined labor. Women and children who carded safety pins could possibly fill 100 cards in two hours. If they kept up that pace, their earnings amounted to around 6 cents an hour. In the early 1900s, home seamstresses in Pittsburgh received less than 75 cents a dozen for seaming cheap jeans. As it gained more power, the International Ladies Garment Workers Union negotiated terms that led to a decline of homework in the women's garment industry, especially in New York after 1910. In other industries, however, homework remained common, and, into the 1920s, the daily routine for many immigrant families included working where they lived.

Sweatshops

The demand for inexpensive, ready-made clothes also nurtured the "sweating system," which was another type of nonfactory work akin to homework. The system was most commonly identified with the clothing trades, but it was used in cigar making and the manufacture of small household wares. Sweating went hand in hand with homework and the cultural traditions that nurtured it. Although immigrant women made up a significant portion of the "sweatshop" workers, entire families got involved in this particular income-producing activity. Briefly described, "sweating" involved several people working in an outside shop to produce apparel or other consumer goods. In the garment industry, independent contractors, who were immigrants, bargained with factory owners to make clothes. The "sweaters" then set up shops in tenements or buildings in the foreign districts and recruited fellow immigrants to turn bundles of cloth into finished garments. In the sweatshops, the contractor divided the process into several tasks, and, as in the garment factories, each employee performed a specific operation. Because the sweaters' financial returns

Making artificial flowers in New York City for 8 cents per gross, 1908. Courtesy of Library of Congress.

rested on producing goods at the lowest possible cost, they paid the lowest wages possible. Indeed, the system's descriptive name originated in the idea that contractors sweated their own profits from the miserly compensation they gave employees.

Despite the meager wages for hours of toil in cramped, generally unpleasant conditions, large numbers of immigrants worked in sweatshops. They were seemingly everywhere in New York's garment district, which was home to vast numbers of eastern European Jews. Sweatshops were also prevalent in Chicago's Little Italy. Their exploitation and downsides notwithstanding, the sweating system gave immigrants a measure of freedom while allowing them to engage in wage labor. Working in a sweatshop let immigrants observe the Sabbath and religious holidays not recognized by American society. In addition, it meant women could take children with them to their jobs and entire families could work together. The system, therefore, found willing hands among the foreign born desperate for money and yet wanting to uphold cultural traditions.

LIFE IN THE WORKPLACE: CHILD LABOR

At the same time that many girls and boys were helping with piecework at home or in sweatshops, other young children were going out to get jobs

Sweatshop workers in New York City, 1908. Courtesy of Library of Congress.

in industries. Just as there is no way to determine the number of women who turned homes into piece-rate workshops, it is impossible to know how many first- and second-generation immigrant children worked in factories and mines at the turn of the twentieth century. Responding to public outcries denouncing child labor, industrial states passed laws regulating the age that individuals could enter the workforce. Minimum-age legislation, together with compulsory education laws, typically meant that children could not legally work until they were at least 14 or, usually, older. Nevertheless, contemporary investigations discovered adolescents—and sometimes younger children—working long shifts in industries. Employers and immigrant parents either ignored or found ways to evade the various compulsory education and child labor laws. Parents, for example, obtained certificates that falsified children's ages. Employers who wanted child laborers accepted flimsy documentation or none at all. Clever children learned to dodge inspectors who occasionally came into the factories to enforce the laws.

Job possibilities for youths varied from place to place. Single-industry towns provided few employment options **Jobs and Wages** for young people while larger or more economically diverse cities held out more prospects. Where opportunities existed, it was not unusual to find first- and second-generation youths doing unskilled jobs in heavy industry. Children as young as eight years old worked in New England's textile factories. Although employers denied that they

hired underage children, a 1908 survey of western Pennsylvania uncovered labor practices in that region that typified patterns in American
industry. Investigators discovered that boys as young as 12 held regular
positions or labored a few days a week or after school in mills, glass factories, and mines. They also found that "Many boys . . . of Slavic parentage
worked in Pittsburgh's spike, nut and bolt, and steel wire factories."

Despite laws in several industrial states that limited the number of
hours individuals younger than sixteen years old could be on the job,
full-time child laborers usually worked shifts of 8 to 12 hours. These
young workers did a wide range of "boys jobs." In the mills, "pull-up"
boys opened and closed furnace doors; "shear boys" cut cold iron into

A Portuguese girl tending spinning machinery in Fall River,
Massachusetts, 1916. Courtesy of Library of Congress.

strips; and other young laborers operated light machinery such as cutting or punching machines. In the glassworks, "cleaning-off boys" cleaned the end of blowpipes; "mold boys" opened and closed the molds for the skilled blowers; "sticking-up boys" reheated bottle necks so they could be finished. In 1908, boys jobs in the metal industries paid between 90 cents and $1.50 a day while young workers in the glass industry got between 75 cents and 95 cents. In coal mines, boys as young as eight worked as "trappers," opening and closing doors so coal cars could move through underground passages, and as "runners," putting wood wedges under wheels to secure the cars. "Breaker boys" picked through mined coal and threw out the slag.

Girls, especially those younger than 18, were less likely to work outside the home than boys, but the daughters of some immigrants did take wage-paying jobs. In Pittsburgh's cracker factories, Italian and Polish girls just 14 years of age packed crackers and wrapped paper around the boxes. When highly perishable fruits were in season, canneries added schoolchildren to the workforce to hull berries or peel fruit.

Although employers who hired underage youngsters violated laws, the children of immigrants who worked for hire did so, in large part, because that was what their parents wanted. Like foreign-born farmers who expected sons and daughters to do regular chores on the farm, working-class immigrants also believed their children should contribute to the family's welfare. By turning all their wages over to their parents,

Breaker boys at work in South Pittston, Pennsylvania, 1911. Courtesy of Library of Congress.

children helped hard-pressed families make ends meet. Some immigrant families needed additional earnings to augment a regular income that was too small to live on. Other youths went to work because the father—the family's chief breadwinner—was disabled or killed in a job-related accident. Whether parents sent youths into the workplace or enlisted their help with piecework at home, economic necessity meant that sons and daughters in many immigrant families spent their youthful years drudging at menial jobs.

ACCIDENTS IN THE WORKPLACE

Males

As they entered the workplace each day, male and female immigrants of all ages faced the possibility they would be injured or killed on the job. In 1904, one authority calculated that annually 1,664,000 workers either were hurt or died as result of accidents. Statistics for Pennsylvania typified what was happening in industrial America at the beginning of the twentieth century. From 1903 to 1913, official figures placed the number of fatal accidents in the state at 2,037 and the number of nonfatal accidents at 19,909. The accident rate in western Pennsylvania's highly industrialized Allegheny County offered an even more revealing illustration. From the summer of 1906 to the summer of 1907, at least 526 industrial workers were killed in the county's factories, mines, and railroad yards. During the same period, 167—nearly 57 percent—of the 294 men injured were in some way disabled. The types of injuries that workers sustained fell into three general classes. The least severe category was "no permanent injury," which meant the individuals might possibly have been disfigured but were not left physically incapacitated. It also included minor cuts, bruises, burns, and broken bones reported to the company physician or infirmary. "Slight permanent injury" identified workers who had perhaps lost a finger or had been left with a slightly crippled foot, arm, or leg but had not been totally disabled. Individuals who were blinded, severely crippled, or had lost a leg, foot, arm, hand, one eye, or two or more fingers were placed in the "serious permanent injury" category. It included workers left disabled and thus likely incapable of securing gainful employment.

The majority of people injured in the heavy industries were immigrants. Critics blamed the foreign-born workers themselves for high accident rates. They maintained that the frequent mishaps were due to the immigrants' poor English, backwardness, or allegedly inferior intellects. Perceptive analysts, however, pointed out that, since there were so many immigrants in America's industries, they naturally made up a large proportion of the accident victims. Moreover, investigators who studied the workplace determined that accidents were more often due to unsafe working conditions than to worker carelessness. Take, for instance, Andrew Antonik, who worked on the "skull cracker" in a steel mill. Describing the circumstances surrounding the accident that ultimately required his leg to be amputated, he explained, "The scrap always flies . . . but in the daytime we can dodge the pieces. At night you can't see well enough to dodge them." It was too dark, he recounted, to see the huge chunk of scrap that crushed his leg.[5] Then there was the young "Slavic" immigrant who, after protesting to his boss that he did not want to work under a moving crane, nevertheless complied with the foreman's order because he did not want to lose his job. The man was killed when the three-and-a-half-ton bucket crashed down on him. In 1906, slate and rock falling from overhead caused 50 percent of the fatalities in coal mines.

Life on the job was also risky for immigrants who labored mainly out of doors. Besides being injured in falls, construction workers were either crushed to death or severely maimed by heavy building materials accidentally dropped. Diggers on construction sites were hurt when explosives misfired or gas pipelines burst. Investigators ranked railroad yards, where laborers worked alongside fast-moving trains, among the most dangerous places for immigrants. A 1906 report revealed that nearly one-third of the workers killed in a series of railroad accidents were run over by a train and that the majority of these deadly mishaps occurred at night. In some instances, the victims were at fault. The death of an Italian railroad worker was but one of many examples in which inexperience or poor language skills probably caused a tragic death. A warning whistle apparently befuddled the young man, who had been in the United States for just over two weeks and on the job less than three days. Instead of dodging an oncoming handcar, he jumped in front of it and was killed. Reports also documented incidents of men losing their lives because in "a hasty confused attempt to get out of the way of a train" they darted in front of one coming from the opposite direction. In other cases, however, there was no signal warning of oncoming trains, and, consequently, men were run down while they knelt working on the tracks.

As they made their way daily to mills, manufacturing plants, mines, and construction sites, immigrants were aware that they might see or fall victim to a dreadful accident. An immigrant priest gave voice to this awareness when he referred to a local industrial plant as "the slaughter house; they kill them [workers] every day."[6] Although probably an overstatement, such exaggerations nevertheless revealed how immigrants perceived the places where they and their loved ones passed their working hours. Even when immigrants tried to relax by reading a newspaper in their own language, they could not escape the stark reality of immigrant workers' lives. Mutilations and disabling accidents were so common that companies specializing in prosthetics regularly placed foreign-language ads for artificial arms and legs in immigrant newspapers.

Women were less likely to be permanently maimed or killed in workplace accidents, but, even so, they still toiled in unsafe, **Females** sometimes hazardous environments. Females employed in laundries and food-processing plants suffered minor as well as major burns. Women and girls who used sharp implements were vulnerable to cuts, including the loss of fingers or a hand. Relating her own experience, Sadie Frowne vividly depicted how female garment workers coped with the reality of injuries on the job. This young sewing-machine operator related that, sometimes in her haste, her finger got caught and the needle went "right through it." When this happened, the needle pierced so quickly that it did "not hurt much," and so the young woman simply bound her finger "with a piece of cotton" and continued working. Sadie nonchalantly shrugged off such injuries by observing, "We all have accidents like that." Her account revealed, however, that not all injuries could be so casually dismissed. "Where the needle goes through the nail it makes a sore finger, or where it splinters a bone it does much harm. Sometimes a finger has to come off. Generally, though, one can be cured by a salve," she explained.

The massive fire at the Triangle Shirtwaist factory in New York City in 1911 tragically revealed that the buildings where females worked posed a greater danger than the machines they operated. The fire, which started on the eighth floor of the factory and rapidly spread through the premises, left 146 people dead. Employees could not escape because managers had locked the exit doors from the outside to prevent employees from leaving work early. The fire escapes could not handle the rush of 700 fleeing persons. As women with clothes and hair on fire leaped to their deaths, horrified onlookers watched and heard "the thuds faster than we could see the bodies fall." Inside the factory, firemen discovered bodies "burned to bare bones." Most of the victims were Jewish and Italian women. In the aftermath of this horrific event, public outrage led to some reforms and laws regulating workplace safety.

IMMIGRANTS AND WORKPLACE CONDITIONS

Acceptance   While investigators and social reformers documented industries' exploitative practices and exposed the "evils" of the workplace, immigrants continued their daily trek back and forth between factory and home. The questions that contemporary observers and historians alike have asked are: Why did immigrants tolerate wretched, perhaps even inhumane, conditions in their workday lives? Why did they endure long hours and accept wages that, based on American standards, were outrageously low? There are no simple answers to these questions. Indeed, whether new immigrants, in particular, were indifferent to workplace conditions and ambivalent toward unions are subjects of historical debate. It is evident, however, that new immigrants' responses to the realities of the American workplace were as diverse as the people who made up the country's industrial workforce.

The fact that so many foreign-born workers planned to return to their homelands was one reason for their willingness to accept long hours and put up with awful conditions. For temporary workers hoping to make as much money as possible during their stay in America, the long shifts meant greater earnings. And, although based on American standards, they did not receive a living wage, migrant workers thought in terms of the future and what the fruits of their labor in America would mean in remittances to families and to their own lives back home. These immigrants resented the dangers, exploitation, and hostile attitudes they encountered in their day-to-day lives on the job, but they also viewed the situation as short term. Even immigrants who planned to return home, however, did not necessarily or universally put up with undesirable or exploitative conditions. Many immigrants protested "with their feet" by quitting and acquiring another job or going to a new place.

It is also a mistake to stress immigrants' submissiveness in the workplace. Both permanent and temporary immigrants became embroiled in battles with employers over wages and working conditions. Indeed, confronting upheaval in **Strikes and Unions** the workplace was part of immigrant working-class life. For instance, in 1892 mostly Slavic immigrants participated in a strike at the Carnegie mill in Homestead, Pennsylvania, that turned into a pitched battle between workers and Pinkerton detectives brought in by the company to quash the strike. Nine workers and three detectives were killed. In the fall of 1897, immigrants protesting wages and conditions in Pennsylvania's northeastern coal regions led to a bloody confrontation in Lattimer. Violence erupted when an armed posse fired into an unarmed crowd of Poles, Slovaks, and Lithuanians who were urging workers to strike. The Lattimer Massacre, as the incident was later dubbed, left at least 19 workers dead and another 39 wounded. Throughout the decades spanning the late 1870s to the eve of World War I, strikes, protests, and lockouts occurred in mills, mines, foundries, meatpacking facilities, textile plants, garment factories, railroad yards, and on construction sites where immigrants worked.

Turmoil in the workplace and especially strikes, which at times seemed to reach epidemic levels, were often connected to the expanding labor movement. Immigrants' attitudes toward labor unions, though, ranged from indifference to fervent support. The reasons for this varied reaction and why foreign-born workers did not throw their support en masse behind labor unions are additional subjects of scholarly dispute. Temporary migrants possibly demonstrated little or no interest because they planned to return home; unions were irrelevant to their futures. All the same, it appears that some sojourners backed unions and participated in attempts to organize them. The evidence is impressionistic, but it also appears that, once temporary workers decided to stay in the United States, they were more likely to support union organizing efforts. In addition, there are clear indications that some nationalities were more likely than others to engage in union activities. Italians, Finns, Germans, and Jews (especially Jewish women) tended to become involved in worker protests. Historians who have studied these groups link their willingness to support unions to cultural backgrounds and to social values as well as to political attitudes cultivated in their homelands.

There were practical reasons why workers shied away from unions. Efforts to organize workers encountered fierce opposition from employers who did not hesitate to use bare-knuckle tactics to prevent unions from gaining a foothold in their industries. Owners, managers, and foremen planted spies who reported on union activities among employees. Individuals guilty of trying to organize workers or suspected of union sympathies could be fired and blacklisted, which meant other firms would not hire them. Thus, both native- and foreign-born workers knew that union-related activities could jeopardize their jobs.

The power employers had over workers' jobs gave them an advantage in battles with labor unions, but they also relied on ethnic differences to undermine organizing efforts. For instance, to thwart unionization and counter what they saw as a Finnish penchant for organizing, employers on Minnesota's Mesabi iron-ore range created multiethnic work crews. Some nationalities unwittingly became strikebreakers when employers brought in gangs of immigrants to take the place of employees on strike. It was also true that ethnic tensions, which immigrants carried into the workplace, could hurt efforts to unite against employer exploitation. At times, immigrants voluntarily crossed picket lines consisting primarily of other nationalities. Stories abound of clashes occurring as workers went into mills, mines, and factories and took over jobs previously held by now desperate strikers. In some communities, ethnic animosities sparked by strikebreaking endured for years.

Despite employer hostility and strong obstacles, by World War I unions had enjoyed success in some industries. It was the onset of the war in Europe in 1914 and the subsequent entry of the United States in 1917, however, that triggered some changes in the workplace. The combined effect of a high demand for goods, a labor shortage created by young men enlisting in the military as well as the slowing of transatlantic immigration, and the threat of strikes caused pay scales to escalate. Although wages did increase during the war, in 1920 laborers in nonunionized industries still put in long hours on the job. And each day, male and female immigrant workers kept doing what they and the children of immigrant parents had been doing for the past half century. They tried to secure their futures by working hard in the present.

SEASONAL LABOR

While millions of immigrants toiled in factories and mines primarily in the industrialized areas of the North and East, thousands worked in various types of construction and in the lumber trades in the country's Midwest and Pacific regions. They were employed to build canals, aqueducts, reservoirs, and bridges. New immigrants and Mexicans replaced Irish, Scandinavians, Germans, and Chinese as the chief source of unskilled labor for railroads. Most of the major railroad lines had been completed by the time the second-wave migration got fully under way, but later arrivals helped build branch roads. They also did most of the repair work on existing tracks. Maintenance crews dug ditches, sloped the ground alongside tracks, shoveled sand and gravel under the rails, carried wooden cross ties, and used heavy bars to shift or reposition existing tracks. As in the lumber industry, most jobs for the railroad and on the assorted construction projects were seasonal. They were also located in remote places far from the ports of entry or urban areas. Thus, to secure enough unskilled laborers to fill these out-of-the-way jobs, companies typically relied on middlemen. The practice of using go-betweens, together with the fact that immigrants—who usually could not speak English—were sent to far-off locations, had exploitative ramifications.

Occasionally, countrymen who came during the early stages of migratory movements became intermediaries **Employment** seeking laborers for temporary projects. For instance, the **Agencies and** same padrone system that channeled Italians into urban **Abuses** jobs also funneled them into seasonal labor in the country's middle and western regions. The same abuses occurred as well. Many immigrants also got jobs through private employment agencies that recruited gangs of unskilled laborers for railroads, construction companies, mine operators, and lumber industries. Although agents assisted migrants who preferred to work outdoors instead of in mills or underground mines, the foreign born often became victims of an unscrupulous system. In return for their services, agencies exacted fees that ranged from reasonable to outrageous. By charging each member of a gang of 65 immigrants a modest $3.50, one agency still made a tidy sum. To reap higher profits, others out-and-out fleeced their customers. The bureau that assessed 70 Bulgarians $15 each and another that required a crew of 40 Italians to fork over $11 per person were merely illustrative examples of such fleecing. The fees siphoned money from migrants who had precious little cash and, consequently, meager resources to live on until they received their first pay from, as yet, a future employer.

Besides sometimes exacting exorbitant fees, agents overcharged workers for the cost of transportation to a work site and then pocketed the extra. But these were not the worst abuses. It was not uncommon for employment agencies to promise more than they could deliver. There were instances of dispatching men to places where no jobs existed. Investigators uncovered cases of migrants being sent from Chicago to as far away as Arkansas, Nebraska, and Wyoming, where, it turned out, there were no jobs. Unable to speak English and with practically no cash, these deceived individuals had to fend for themselves in an unfriendly environment. Because agencies recruited for certain companies, the possibility of legitimate agencies sending immigrants to places where there were no jobs at all was probably less likely than the probability of encountering other unexpected circumstances. Take the case of the 18 Bulgarians who got to their destination in Arkansas and learned that only 10 were needed. Having very little money, the other eight walked back to Chicago to try to get another job. Men arrived only to discover that the wages were less than what had been promised or the jobs were not the ones they had contracted for. Despite assurances of steady work, construction jobs, in particular, possibly lasted only a few weeks or a couple of months. Although men who engaged in seasonal work realized that work periods were temporary and, moreover, expected to move around, most migrant laborers no doubt hoped that stints in one place would last longer.

Peonage   Seasonal laborers risked essentially being turned into peons. Peonage, the system whereby an individual was bound to another person until he or she had worked off a debt, was illegal in much of the United States. In 1908, however, the Dillingham Commission uncovered evidence that some employers engaged in the practice. They did it by giving immigrants an advance on their wages or paying their transportation to work sites. Arriving already in debt, workers had to stay on the job until employers determined they had worked off all the money received up front. To make sure men did not run off, armed guards patrolled work areas. When immigrants did flee, local authorities typically supported the employers and forced the runaways back to work, imposed fines, or jailed them.

Immigrants simply dissatisfied with working conditions or angry over the fact that the wages were lower or the job was not the one promised also found themselves in a state of involuntary servitude. Living in remote, isolated camps, laborers could not easily escape oppressive situations. Employers determined to prevent workers from quitting used the same kind of measures as the "bosses" who engaged in peonage. Mike Trudics, a Hungarian immigrant in his mid-twenties who contracted to go to Georgia to work in a sawmill, offered an illustrative example. Unhappy that instead of being employed in a sawmill at $1.50 per day he was put to sawing and carrying logs in the woods, Trudics decided to run away. Armed men with dogs tracked him down, twice horsewhipped him, tied him up, put him in a buggy, and returned him to the camp. After that, Trudics recalled, "hardly a day passed . . . without some one being run down by the bosses or bloodhounds and returned and whipped." Reflecting on his own terrible experience, he starkly underscored a reality of life in camps run by ruthless men. "In the woods they [the bosses] can do anything they please and no one can see them but God." Even if they were not forced into peonage, some immigrants labored an entire season for nothing. More than one underhanded employer swindled immigrants by paying them in scrip. When, at the end of the season, workers went to the designated locales, they discovered that the offices supposedly equipped to exchange their scrip for money did not exist.

For seasonal laborers, the work was hard and the living conditions were rough. Given the pressure to complete projects **Camp Life**
while the weather was still good, the workday stretched from
sunrise to sunset. In many camps, a seven-day workweek was routine.
In places where men put in six days, they used Sundays to wash their
clothes or relax. Summing up life in the labor camps, one contemporary
observer put it simply. "The men worked, ate, and slept, day in and day
out," he declared. Living conditions were often deplorable. Some companies provided stark but nevertheless livable quarters for their workers;
however, the temporary nature of most jobs meant that, in the main, workers dwelled in makeshift housing. On some railroad sites, employees were
put up in company-provided boxcars. In these oversized metal containers,
men sweltered in the summer and nearly froze in the winter. Immigrants
also slept in tents or hastily thrown-together shanties. Investigators found
20 to 50 individuals crammed into various types of dwellings. Whether
immigrants lived in a converted railroad car or some other the type of
housing, they often shared their quarters with roaches, bedbugs, and
other creepy crawlies. Washing and toilet facilities were generally crude
at best, if they existed at all. One visitor reported seeing a man washing his
feet in a ten-pound lard can. Trying to portray the "barbarous" situation at
sites where foreign-born workers were employed, one eyewitness perhaps
somewhat overstated the case. Still, his claim that he saw "men crawling
into pens" that few people would permit "their dogs [to] occupy" con-
veyed the often deplorable and degrading circumstances in construction,
railroad, and lumber camps.

In addition to miserable living conditions and grueling work, the everyday existence of seasonal laborers was a lonesome one. Individual nationalities normally worked on the same crew with fellow countrymen and
then clustered together in the boxcars and shanties. But living as they
did, far away from towns and even farther from cities, immigrants had
little contact with the world beyond. It was difficult, and at times impossible, to send or receive mail. There were precious few diversions or entertainment. Men played cards and other games of chance, they probably
drank alcohol purchased from the commissary that served the camp, and
they listened to or sang along as a fellow countryman played music on
an instrument. Many migrant laborers possibly spent their time thinking
about loved ones in homelands they planned to return to while others,
no doubt, dwelled on seeing families waiting for them somewhere in the
United States.

The natural bounty in America's coastal waters provided
means for immigrants to adapt skills they had learned in **Coastal and**
their homelands and, thus, move into occupational niches **Fishing**
that mirrored their backgrounds. It also let them avoid **Industries**
punishing jobs in mills, factories, and mines. Finns, Croatians from Dal-
matia, and Italians moved in sizable numbers into fishing industries in the

United States. Teams of Dalmatians fished the waters from Los Angeles to Alaska; Finns caught salmon in the ocean beyond Oregon's shoreline; Italians went out from San Francisco Bay in search of crab and fish. On the East Coast, immigrants joined fishing crews and ships trolling for shrimp and crab. Greeks from the Adriatic and Bahamians from the Caribbean manned the boats and dove for sponges in waters west of Florida. Cape Verdeans and other Portuguese worked in New England's whaling industry. For immigrants from Portugal's mainland, though, whaling usually represented a new line of work, whereas the islanders were falling back on premigration skills. The entry by some Portuguese paved the way for others to move into the fishing and whaling industries as well.

Even though immigrants who chose to make their living by fishing or diving worked with crews of countrymen, going out onto the water sometimes for two or three days and often a week or more made for a lonely existence. One man probably expressed the inner thoughts of many when he admitted that it was not "the work" that was the "hardest side" of their jobs. Instead, "it's the long, lonesome nights . . . the murk and storm days, when there is nothing for us" to do. "We've got to sit around on deck, or be driven below by the rain or smell." At these times, he explained, even talking with countrymen was "dull." There was nothing to discuss with fellow crewman, for, after all, "we know all they know, all they've got to say to us." If, when he returned to land, this young man went, as so many immigrant workers did, to the "foreign district" where fellow countrymen and countrywomen lived, he surely found people to converse with and activities to occupy his time.

Immigrants spent long hours in the workplace, but their jobs consumed only part of their daily lives. When the workday was over, single migrants and married men on their own made their way to temporary lodgings; people with families in the United States went home to them. The trip from wherever they worked to their living quarters was normally short and, more often than not, on foot. Immigrants who resided in cities and towns usually lived in the multiethnic "foreign districts" located close to mills, factories, workshops, railroad yards, or mines. On payday, workers walked away with one or two weeks' wages. When they opened their pay envelopes, immigrants with families in America knew that the contents would go toward supporting them, but these permanent residents hoped they could put a little aside for the future. When they looked into their envelopes and perhaps mentally apportioned the enclosed cash, migratory workers and married men without their families knew they had to use part of the earnings to settle their room-and-board accounts, but they intended to save most of the rest. Some temporary migrants were building nest eggs so they could enjoy a better life in their homelands; other workers were stashing away money so their wives and children could join them in America. Because bachelors and married men without their families not only dominated the early stages but also remained important elements in the ongoing movement into the country, the crowds exiting America's workplaces into the early twentieth century continued to include a mix of sojourners and permanent immigrants.

NOTES

Immigrant life stories and quotations were derived from Hamilton Holt, ed., *The Life Stories of Undistinguished Americans as Told by Themselves*, 2nd ed., with new introduction by Wernor Sollors (1906; New York: Routledge, 1990); Bruce M. Stave and John F. Sutherland, eds., *From the Old Country: An Oral History of European Migration to America*, with Aldo Salerno (New York: Twayne, 1994). Immigrant life stories, quotations, and translations from original documents were also taken from June Granatir Alexander, *The Immigrant Church and Community: Pittsburgh's Slovak Catholics and Lutherans, 1880–1915* (Pittsburgh: University of Pittsburgh Press, 1987). Life stories and quotations derived from other secondary sources are cited separately.

1. As quoted in John Bodnar, *The Transplanted: A History of Immigrants in Urban America* (Bloomington: Indiana University Press, 1985), 61–62.

2. As quoted in Peter Roberts, "Immigrant Wage-Earners," in *Wage-Earning Pittsburgh*, ed. Paul Underwood Kellogg (1914; repr., New York: Arno, 1974), 45.

3. As quoted in Phylis Cancilla Martinelli, "Pioneer Paesani in Globe, Arizona," in *Italian Immigrants in Rural and Small Town America*, ed. Rudolph J. Vecoli (New York: American Italian Historical Association, 1987), 164.

4. As quoted in Elizabeth Beardsley Butler, *Women and the Trades: Pittsburgh, 1907–1908* (1909; repr., New York: Arno, 1969), 185.

5. As quoted in Crystal Eastman, *Work Accidents and the Law* (1910; repr., New York: Arno, 1969), 75.

6. As quoted in Roberts, "Immigrant Wage-Earners," 43.

4

Life in Urban America: Migrants and Immigrant Families

Whether they intended to remain in the United States or return to their homelands, immigrants grappled each day with the realities of life in a rapidly changing foreign country. They generally had to deal with abominable physical environments and terrible housing in the crowded "foreign districts." In these neighborhoods, the lives of transients and permanent immigrants became intertwined as they fought to survive on low—often near-starvation—wages while working to secure a better future for themselves and their families. The lifestyles immigrants fashioned and the living conditions they endured reflected, in part, a determination to live as cheaply as possible. New immigrants had, one contemporary correctly noted, a "mania for saving." As they strove to achieve the goals that had prompted them to migrate and simultaneously struggled to cope with life in an urban-industrial society, both permanent immigrants and sojourners adopted the same strategies they had used to choose a destination and to decide how they would earn a living. They relied on family and friendship networks and drew on their premigration cultures.

URBANIZATION AND IMMIGRANT NEIGHBORHOODS

Urban Growth During the half century spanning 1870 to 1920, the United States underwent spectacular urban growth. The number of people living in "urban" areas skyrocketed from 9.9 million to 54.1 million. The number of cities boasting 100,000 residents rose from 14 to 68 while the total with populations exceeding a half

million jumped from 2 to 9. Because the U.S. census defined "urban territories" as incorporated areas with populations of 2,500 or more, America's
urbanization involved more than the emergence or rapid expansion of
big cities. The process included villages evolving into towns and small
towns developing into larger ones. The growth of medium-sized towns
was especially robust. In less than 50 years, the number of municipalities with populations ranging from 10,000 to 25,000 tripled from 116 to
465. Cities contributed to the mushrooming of towns. As urban industries grew and transportation improved, burgeoning metropolises became
the cores of industrial districts that encompassed huge geographic areas.
Single-industry towns containing factories, foundries, manufacturing
plants, chemical works, brickyards, and textile mills sprang up throughout
America's urban-industrial regions. Some "satellite" towns provided fuel
and raw resources for urban factories while others developed industries
vital to the cities' physical growth, such as material for the construction
of buildings, roads, mass transit systems, bridges, and public facilities.
Besides being marketplaces, cities served as distribution centers for the
industrial and mining towns in their regions.

　　Although municipal governments welcomed the wide-ranging benefits stemming from their physical, demographic, and industrial growth,
they were not prepared to deal with the complex, often enormous, problems wrought by fast-paced change. Expanding industries, coupled with
booming populations, put tremendous pressure on physical facilities and
public services. In addition to constructing new streets and surfacing the
unpaved ones, cities had to build public transportation systems. Existing
water and sewer systems could not handle the rising needs created by
the population increases. Sewage from overflows or bursted pipes spilled
onto streets; in many areas, public sewer lines fed directly into rivers. To
make matters worse, industries poured their wastes into urban water-
ways. Garbage removal and disposal became daunting tasks. Many cities
dealt with the escalating rubbish problem by establishing public dump
sites that became no more than massive heaps of smelly, rotten matter
along riverbanks or somewhere on a city's periphery.

　　As the nineteenth faded into the twentieth century, municipal governments continually wrestled with a wide range of nagging problems. Even
as they sometimes made impressive progress, city administrations could
not keep up with the demand to improve the physical environment and
provide better services. Thus, despite the economic opportunities that
beckoned people to them, America's cities and towns were generally not
pleasant places to live.

Immigrant Populations　　Although the migration of native-born Americans from
rural regions contributed to urban growth, the country's
ongoing urbanization owed much to the influx of newcomers from outside the United States. In 1890, census takers
found that seven major cities in the country's industrial corridor—Pitts-

burgh, Cleveland, Buffalo, Detroit, New York, Milwaukee, and Chicago—had populations that ranged from nearly 29 to 41 percent foreign born. While labor-seeking migrants were naturally drawn to industrial centers east of the Mississippi River, cities farther west also attracted large numbers of immigrants. With 42 percent of its residents coming from outside the United States, San Francisco had the largest nonnative-born population of any city west of the Mississippi in 1890. That same year, Seattle, Minneapolis, and Portland all claimed populations that were 31.9 to 37.3 percent foreign born. Official tallies showed that immigrants made up about one-fourth of Omaha, Nebraska's residents. Overall, by 1910, more than half of America's immigrants and the children of immigrants resided in urban areas; a decade later, three-fourths of the country's first- and second-generation immigrants were urban dwellers. And in 1920, about one-fifth of the more than 54.3 million people residing in urban territories had been born in another country.

Many "urban" immigrants, however, lived in medium-sized and small towns. Indeed, similar to big cities, industrial towns owed much of their growth to the influx of working-class immigrants. In the early 1900s, immigrants might compose somewhere between one-tenth to nearly half of the residents living in towns located in America's northern industrial zone. In fact, in some industrial and mining towns foreign-born peoples claimed a larger percentage of the population than in several American cities. By way of example, nearly two-fifths of the people residing in McKee's Rocks, Pennsylvania, in 1910 were immigrants while in nearby Pittsburgh they represented slightly more than one-fourth of the inhabitants. Over time, immigrants continued to make up a significant portion of the population in medium-sized and small towns. For instance, in 1920 census takers discovered that more than two-fifths of the people living in Aliquippa, Pennsylvania, were immigrants and that at least one-fifth of the population of Steubenville, Ohio, and of Plainfield, New Jersey, had been born outside the United States. These three industrial towns located in separate states were illustrative of patterns throughout the country.

Complex factors influenced precisely where immigrants chose to live. Still, it was true that the availability of cheap housing, coupled with the convenience of being close to their jobs, drew the foreign born to the more undesirable sectors of urban America. This meant that, by and **Slums, Ghettos, and Ethnic Succession** large, immigrants who chose an urban destination ended up in "slums." Broadly defined, slums were densely populated areas with poor quality housing and generally bad living conditions. They usually contained a mix of residential dwellings, workshops, and industrial establishments. Besides being located in the inner cities, by the end of the nineteenth century slums had also emerged in the cities' scattered industrial districts and on their peripheries. Historically, slums had been home to the working-class poor and impoverished residents of both native and foreign birth. Because the old immigrant groups tended to settle together, either ethnic clusters developed within existing slums or additional enclaves emerged as newcomers gravitated to the same sections of the city and its environs. "Swede Hollow" in Saint Paul, Minnesota, was but one of countless examples. The area and its name had their roots in the pre–Civil War era when Swedes first moved into a valley along Phalen Creek. In subsequent decades, the district remained such a popular destination for Swedish immigrants settling in Saint Paul that it became popularly known as Swede Hollow.

At the onset of the new immigration, southern and eastern Europeans followed a path similar to earlier immigrants. They moved into districts that had previously attracted successive waves of Irish, German, Czech, or Scandinavian immigrants. The massive nature of the new immigration, however, created an unprecedented demand for living space. The volume of second-wave immigrants ultimately caused existing slums to spread outward and, often, in a number of directions. This creeping expansion sparked a mixed, but mostly hostile, reaction by older immigrants and "old-stock" Americans. Resistance to the new immigrants could trigger violent confrontations, especially as residents or gangs of hoodlums harassed and physically assaulted them. Longtime inhabitants also reacted by leaving. As the number of southern and eastern Europeans increased or the foreign districts seemed to be nibbling at the fringes of adjoining neighborhoods, older residents fled to residential areas away from these strange peoples whom they deemed "inferior." The process of ethnic groups displacing nationalities that had been dominant in particular areas is often described as "ethnic succession."

At times, the "old" ethnic groups stood their ground in the face of what they considered an intrusion by undesirable "foreigners." Indeed, in some places, particular streets became implicit boundaries between older inhabitants and unwanted "foreign" intruders. People of different nationalities who lived on each side of these informal borders dared not set foot in neighborhoods across the street. As more new immigrants poured into the "foreign districts" and spilled into the peripheries, many inhabitants finally gave up and departed. All this displacement occurred at different rates; nevertheless, over time, substantial numbers of old-time residents moved and left behind more space for later arrivals. Pockets of old-stock Americans and old immigrants remained, but new immigrants ultimately made up the majority of slum dwellers.

Although slums existed well before new immigrants began trickling into the country, by the start of the twentieth century slums became synonymous with the multiethnic districts inhabited by them. Terms—"foreign quarters," "foreign districts," and "foreign colonies"—that contemporaries used when referring to places where new immigrants concentrated all stood for slums. Beginning in the late 1890s, neighborhoods where large numbers of Russian and eastern European Jews clustered were generally called "ghettos," a term that likewise was equated with slums. Regardless of which term was used, each one conjured up images of heavily populated, congested areas characterized by abysmal housing and abominable surroundings. In the main, the imagery was accurate.

Visitors and residents alike were struck by the hustle and bustle that characterized the immigrant districts. Men and women hurried along, peddlers maneuvered push- **Physical** carts, and children played in streets swarming with people **Environment** going about their daily business. Day after day, however, this flurry of activity took place in unpleasant and, in fact, deplorable settings. While it was true that conditions in cities were generally bad, residents of immigrant neighborhoods experienced the worst of them. Even as municipal governments made strides toward expanding services, upgrading transportation systems, and improving the physical environment, districts inhabited by the foreign born were considered low priority.

The tendency for city officials to neglect immigrant neighborhoods and, especially, their failure to provide adequate services such as regular garbage collection contributed to the vile circumstances that made these districts repulsive to sight and smell. In the immigrant quarters, people regularly navigated around overflowing barrels of garbage or the contents of tipped-over receptacles. Trash littered the streets and the alleys between residential buildings. Fluid wastes from open drainage systems or broken pipes trickled into streets. During heavy rains, a combination of water and sewage gushed out of drains and left unsightly and foul-smelling pools of slime on the ground. Everywhere in rainy seasons pedestrians waded through muck, and in northern and western cities during the winter they had to hike through snow mixed with filth, sewage, and rubbish. Snowplows that did wind through the streets left a string of dirty, filth-laden piles of snow. In unpaved alleys, there was mud in the icy mixture. When snow covered the streets and prevented dump carts from collecting trash on even their normally irregular schedules, ordinary garbage problems became worse. Cans filled with ashes and rubbish accumulated along passageways in front of buildings.

Year round, as immigrants made their way through their neighborhoods, they could not escape the horrible stenches that filled the atmosphere. While foul-smelling odors and hard-to-breathe air plagued most turn-of-the-twentieth-century cities, the nastiest of these hung over the foreign quarters. The combined stink from slaughtered animals, their wastes, and fertilizers that emanated from the stockyards and meatpacking plants constantly assaulted the residents of Chicago's "Packingtown." People living in mill districts could not escape the industrial smoke, soot, and fine dust that irritated their eyes, noses, and throats.

Tenements

Immigrant neighborhoods were filled with unattractive buildings. In addition to an assortment of ugly workshops, **Housing** plants, or mills, one encountered a range of unsightly residential

Garbage in the East Fifth Street tenement area of New York City, ca. 1890. Courtesy of Library of Congress.

structures. The dilapidated and poorly constructed dwellings character-istic of immigrant slums were, in part, products of the serious housing shortages that plagued cities. As the throngs of immigrants flooded into urban areas, there were not enough residential buildings to accommodate them. At the same time, the exodus of people from these older neighbor-hoods freed up single-family houses that speculators turned into two or more apartments; if possible, they remade basements into living quar-ters. Developers converted former commercial or industrial buildings into residential dwellings. Landowners established back-to-back living units by constructing buildings on what was originally a yard behind a house. All too often, they created these "rear houses" by actually push-ing an existing house to the back edge of a lot. To cope with the housing problem, entrepreneurs also put up apartment buildings. Although these multilevel dwellings were commonly called "tenements," most munici-pal governments defined any structure configured to house three or more families as a tenement. Areas thick with multiple-family dwellings were often referred to as simply the "tenement districts," which at the dawn of the twentieth century became another term synonymous with immigrant neighborhoods, slums, or ghettos.

New York "Dumbbells"

The kinds of housing available to immigrants differed from place to place and changed over time. New York City dealt with its escalating population by replacing older dwellings with buildings that essentially let the city expand upward. Double-deckers, as contemporaries called multistory residential structures, provided a way for landlords to maximize profits by cramming a growing number of people into a shrinking amount of space. The trend toward constructing multilevel tenements was already under way but gained real momentum in the 1880s when the "dumbbell" design was introduced. Resembling hand-held exercise weights that had two metal balls joined by a center bar, the dumbbells provided a way to accommodate twenty or more families on a small lot. For immigrants who lived in the dumbbells, life was a trying ordeal.

The standard dumbbell had four apartments on each floor. Two living units were located on each end of the building, and stairs, communal toilets, and a dumbwaiter were situated in the elongated central area connecting the apartments. On the side, there was an airshaft that was normally 5 feet wide and, depending on the building's height, could run 60 feet deep. The dumbbell design allowed light to shine into only one side of each apartment. Despite the original intent, airshafts did not let air into the dumbbells; moreover, because there were only a few feet between the tenements, it was nearly impossible for air or natural light to enter the rooms situated directly opposite and quite close to another building. So the individual living units were dark and poorly ventilated. To make the situation worse, airshafts provided a way to get rid of garbage quickly and thus became sources of offensive stenches that flowed into the apartments. The putrid matter attracted vermin and roaches. Further construction of dumbbells in New York City was banned after 1901; nevertheless, the building boom that had fueled the erection of these atrocious dwellings left its mark on the city's slums. Although the foreign districts contained various types of housing, rows consisting of the hideous dumbbells stretched for block after block through New York's immigrant neighborhoods.

Common Styles

While developers in other cities built double-deckers, the multistory brick tenements usually identified with New York's densely populated slums were not as popular elsewhere. Immigrants in other urban areas more likely lived in badly dilapidated one- and two-floor houses than in tall brick buildings. A few three- and four-story dumbbells could be found in some Chicago neighborhoods, but high-rise tenements did not become commonplace in that city's slums. A concern that high residential structures were fire hazards prompted Chicago's government to adopt measures designed to discourage the construction of dwellings taller than three floors. Even though buildings were lower to the ground and contained

"Airshaft of a dumbbell tenement, New York City," ca. 1900.
National Archives and Record Administration NWDNS-196-GS-14.

fewer families, Chicago's immigrants typically lived in tumbledown old houses that had been carved into several units. Single-family homes adapted to multiple-family use were common in Milwaukee's immigrant neighborhoods, but back-to-back dwellings were also near-universal features of that city's scattered foreign districts. Often, the rear buildings were no more than single-floor cottages consisting of two or, perhaps, three tiny rooms. It was not unusual to find several of these structures on a single small lot. In Cleveland, the practice of stuffing several dwellings into a tiny space was out of the ordinary; instead, in most areas, the one- and two-story frame houses inhabited by the foreign born generally had at least a bit of a yard. Because lots in Omaha, Nebraska, were bigger and usually contained only two houses, there was more open space surrounding the multiple-family dwellings in that city's foreign districts.

Although most of the converted structures in immigrant neighborhoods had previously been single-family houses, the foreign born might also end up living in what had formerly been commercial or industrial buildings. With little effort and minimal expense, entrepreneurs partitioned massive old structures into separate rooms. This was how "Tammany Hall," a run-down former wood-planing mill, became home to 25 or more of Pittsburgh's foreign-born families. Immigrants also lived in urban shantytowns. In Minneapolis, new immigrants lived in "Bohemian Flats," a shantytown located along the Mississippi River and close to mills and factories. By the end of the nineteenth century, new arrivals were also making their way to the shacks of Saint Paul's Swede Hollow, which earlier immigrants had abandoned for better housing.

Interior Conditions

The residential structures in immigrant districts were as unpleasant to live in as they were to look at. Poorly ventilated multiple-story tenements were dreary and received little fresh air. Noxious odors drifting in from courtyards or the airshafts aggravated already terrible living environments. Immigrants in the back-to-back houses spent their days in dank, dark rooms. With nowhere to put privies except in the yards behind the new buildings—and between them and the houses in the back—the stench in the rear houses was horrible. When the weather became unbearably hot during the summer, some residents slept on tenement roofs or, perhaps, tried to snuggle down on fire escapes. Probably already serving as storage areas for families with insufficient space in their tiny apartments, the cluttered escapes posed a safety hazard. More specifically, they hindered people's rapid exit in the event of fires or other emergencies. In Manhattan alone, 80 of the at least 250 people who died in fires between 1902 and 1909 lived in the city's Lower East Side tenements; countless others, no doubt, suffered burns ranging from minor to major. Old mills, commercial sites, or warehouses transformed on the cheap were even more ill suited for human habitation. Pittsburgh's Tammany Hall represented some of the worst housing in the city. Dingy overhead skylights were the only sources of light and air for several interior apartments. Despite the lack of exterior windows, the industrial dirt and nauseating odors that pervaded the neighborhood filtered into Tammany Hall's dismal living units.

Inadequate plumbing facilities made life even worse for immigrant renters. Because it was difficult to put pipes and fixtures into older buildings, residents of many converted houses had to get their water from a pump outside. Even when landlords added faucets in kitchens, the reconfigured structures lacked private bathrooms and toilet facilities. Tenants, therefore, had to go out into the hallway to use water closets—the contemporary term for enclosed toilets—or into an exterior courtyard to use privies. Going outside one's private quarters was more than inconvenient;

it was degrading when residents in two or more households had to share a single water closet. People unable to wait to relieve themselves resorted to the nearest private corner or vacant lot. Daily life, though, was particularly dreadful for inhabitants of cellar apartments. Besides being windowless, poorly lit, and damp, sewage from backed–up lines—especially in the winter when pipes froze—and seepage from privy vaults located in the outside courts oozed into the below-street-level rooms.

Reforms and Codes

Pressure from social reformers, together with public outcries in the aftermath of graphic exposés, prompted local governments to try to remedy some of the worst conditions in America's slums. Concerned about the health threats that unsanitary conditions posed, urban lawmakers passed ordinances requiring builders of new tenements to install indoor plumbing. The newly enacted guidelines, though, did not always compel owners of existing structures to do the same. Some city codes stipulated that individual apartments be equipped with a water faucet but specified only that water closets be located within the building. Moreover, even when municipal governments mandated that private bathrooms be included in each unit, builders and landlords often ignored them or devised ways to skirt the rules. Take the case of New York's tenement law of 1901, which required owners of old buildings to upgrade them, in part, by modernizing toilet facilities. When the Dillingham Commission conducted its survey

"The tenement bath tub," ca. 1905. Courtesy of Library of Congress.

eight years after the legislation went into effect, it found that only 6 percent of New York's immigrant households had private toilets. The majority of dwellings, though, did have running water. Overall, based on its seven-city survey, the commission estimated that more than four-fifths of immigrant households in urban areas had running water but only slightly over one-fourth of these had their own toilet facilities.

City regulations and popular clamor did lead to some changes—if not always improvements—in slum housing. After a barrage of costly citations from city inspectors, the owner of Pittsburgh's infamous Tammany Hall decided to demolish the building rather than make mandated improvements to the abominable tenement. The bad publicity created by a 1908 report published in *Collier's Weekly* forced officials of a Pittsburgh steel company to improve conditions in "Painter's Row," a cluster of dilapidated houses the company owned and rented to its foreign-born employees. Pressured by a powerful, socially conscious stockholder, they ordered the most ramshackle houses be torn down and others renovated. The mixed results of the directive offered a representative example of the callous halfhearted way owners tackled the housing problems that made everyday life so miserable in immigrant districts. Within less than a year, the worst houses in Painter's Row were gone and some dwellings had been significantly upgraded, but others were left untouched. Families in the neglected company-owned homes still had no drinking water on the premises and had to use outdoor privies. People living in one row of houses disposed of wastewater and garbage by throwing everything into wooden chutes that fed into open drains in the yards. There, all the slop formed putrid puddles just outside people's living quarters.

Although situations varied from place to place, to enter the foreign districts of an American city was to enter a physical world distinguished by filth, foul air, congestion, and dilapidated or inferior housing. Such were the living conditions of millions of migrant laborers and immigrant families in the late nineteenth and early twentieth centuries.

Housing and Physical Environment

Immigrants who found their way to industrial towns also entered a world where the physical environment was generally awful. Mills emitted fumes that filled the air with potent smells; huge smokestacks belched thick smoky clouds that dimmed the surroundings and showered towns with soot. There were layers of grit everywhere. Backed-up sewers spewed swill aboveground, and revolting fluids trickled through open drains alongside public streets. So as people moved about, they not only smelled nauseating odors but also walked through slime and mud or along gritty thoroughfares.

Industrial Towns

Foreign-born peoples clustered together in industrial and mining towns in much the same way as they did in cities. And similar to residential patterns in large cities, new immigrants displaced old-stock Americans and peoples of the old immigration who fled to areas farther away from industries and mines. To get to the foreign districts of an industrial town, instead of fighting through bustling streets, people might well have walked down a cinder path and ended up in "an alley, bordered on one side by stables and on the other by a row of shabby two-story frame houses." In general, these dwellings were either poorly constructed or in the same rundown condition as those rented to the foreign born in metropolitan areas. Some developers erected a few four- to six-floor buildings, but multistory tenements were not common in towns. Rather, people squeezed into single-family houses that had been reconfigured to handle multiple families or several individuals. Trying to put every bit of available space to residential use, enterprising contractors built tiny dwellings on small lots where converted houses already stood. Besides housing owned by speculators eager to capitalize on an area's rising working-class population, immigrants might also have the option of living in a "company house." Usually located near work sites and belonging to the company, these houses were either modified old structures or, more likely, thrown-together shacks employees could rent.

One investigator graphically revealed that town dwellers had to cope with the same revolting circumstances that characterized life in the cities. Walking through a typical immigrant neighborhood in an industrial town, she saw water hydrants and communal toilets located in small courtyards behind "smoke-grimed houses." One pump supplied water to 20 families. A circular wooden building, which had 10 enclosed compartments and was located in the center of the courtyard, served as toilet facilities for the estimated hundred people living in three houses. Because the toilets were not flush style, the individual stalls fed waste into a vault, which was essentially a pit in the ground. There was no way to eliminate the disgusting stink emanating from these crude facilities or prevent it from filtering into people's living spaces. With affordable housing in short supply, immigrants who toiled in the local mill had no alternative but to make the best of a terrible situation. The foreign born in this industrial town were not alone; similar conditions plagued the lives of immigrants in towns throughout industrial America.

Patches and Company Housing

Immigrants also bunched together in tiny settlements located on the outskirts of a town or, more typically, near a mine. "Patches," as contemporaries called these unincorporated hamlets located beyond the boundaries of "urban" America, consisted primarily of residential dwellings that housed day laborers. Depending on its size, a patch might include a company store, but often residents traveled to the nearby town to purchase goods, attend church, or take care of other needs.

In the patches as well as in some mining and single-industry towns, the local mining company or mill owned most, if not all, of the residential dwellings. The quality of the company-built housing varied. An eyewitness description by one investigator, however, offered vivid testimony as to why, in his words, company housing generally deserved its "unenviable reputation" as awful. Traveling through the towns and patches of eastern Pennsylvania's coalfields in the early 1900s, he found immigrants renting tiny two-room shanties that measured 16 by 16 feet. The worst buildings were ones that were a half-century old or older. Constructed of pine boards with flimsy weather stripping nailed over crevices, these "huts" or "shells," as he called them, had no plaster or interior wallpaper. Despite taking measures to insulate their houses and constantly burning their stoves, tenants spent the winters suffering from the cold. To escape the summer's heat, they slept outside or on roofs. New company houses erected at the beginning of the twentieth century were normally much better than the dilapidated older ones, but they nevertheless were cheaply constructed, dreary abodes. Even though they built new houses—and charged higher rents for them—companies rarely tore down the ramshackle older structures. Instead, they reaped substantial profits by refusing to make repairs and just letting the old rickety houses deteriorate until they were no longer habitable.

In addition to deriving financial benefits from being an area's chief rental agent, because employers monopolized the housing in patches and company towns they had a decided advantage over their workers. Without other options, immigrants had no choice but to rent what the companies had to offer. It was an irony that not only did company-controlled housing contribute to the discomfort of their daily existence but dependence on this housing also added to the precariousness of immigrants' lives. Individuals who lost their jobs, engaged in union-organizing activities, or took part in labor strikes faced eviction.

TEMPORARY IMMIGRANTS AND MIGRANT WORKERS

The horrendous physical environments in the foreign districts were due in part to the combined industrialization and urbanization that transformed American society. The deplorable living conditions immigrants suffered could also be blamed on landlord greed or—in the case of company towns—employers' crass disregard for their workers' welfare and comfort. Poverty was also a root cause of the miserable circumstances. In some ways, however, immigrants contributed to the unpleasantness and deprivation that characterized their lives. Indeed, immigrants' lifestyles were shaped, in no small degree, by personal factors. These included self-imposed aspirations and cultural values they brought with them. Practically from the moment migrant laborers set foot on American soil, their standard of living was affected by a determination to save money to return home or to support families left behind. So, besides immediate employment, recent arrivals naturally sought inexpensive housing. To accommodate the constant influx of migratory workers, settled immigrants established boardinghouses or took lodgers into their homes. In turn, the money these migrant laborers put toward their own upkeep benefited people who had decided to remain permanently in America but needed help to get on with their lives. Thus, to realize their future goals, both permanent and temporary migrants made tremendous sacrifices in the present.

Types

Boarding
During the earliest stages of most migration movements, foreign-born workers stayed in cheap lodging houses operated by old-stock Americans or people who had come in the previous old immigration wave. Fellow countrymen who acted as middlemen and found jobs for newcomers often either ran rooming houses or had connections to individuals who did. For example, immigrants from southern Italy roomed in establishments run by northern Italians who had arrived earlier. Relatives or friends also joined together to rent rooms or a small house. In these "stag boardinghouses," four, six, or more men shared expenses and did their own cooking and laundry. The migration waves also brought immigrants who quickly seized on opportunities created by the flood of unattached males streaming into the country. Probably planning to stay in America, these enterprising individuals rented or bought dwellings and turned them into all-male rooming houses that catered to their own nationalities. A boardinghouse operator—often referred to as the "boss"—who had no wife hired females to cook, do laundry, and perform various domestic chores. Finally, in immigrant communities with more families, husband-and-wife teams opened boardinghouses to serve migrants streaming into and out of America's cities and town. Operations managed by either an individual or a husband-and-wife team could have between 20 and 60 occupants. Couples also took lodgers into their own rented apartments or small houses. Often, newlyweds seeking extra income began married life with lodgers paying to share their quarters.

In Households

The steady influx of foreign workers ensured that boarding would continue to be a widespread aspect of immigrant life. In the pre–World War I era, stag boardinghouses with a large number of inhabitants could be found in regions that attracted male workers but far fewer families. For instance, health officials in South Omaha, Nebraska, discovered 46 Greek males residing in a small house; 60 Romanians lived in a two-story dwelling in a town in northeastern Illinois. The Dillingham Commission calculated that, in 1908–1909, more than one-fourth of the immigrant households in cities had lodgers. Boarding was also prevalent in small and medium-sized industrial towns. According to one finding, at least one-third of new immigrant families in the coal regions of northeastern Pennsylvania had boarders in the early 1900s. Four of every 10 eastern European households in Homestead, Pennsylvania, took in lodgers while in other industrial towns nearly 60 percent of immigrant families reported having roomers.

For large numbers of job seekers, boarding was simply part of life in America. And whether they resided in cities or towns, most immigrant families, at some point, accepted lodgers or provided temporary housing for new arrivals. As a rule, boarding was not an impersonal situation with strangers sharing the same living space. Because people often took in relatives, frequently households with boarders were actually extended families made up of adult siblings, aunts, uncles, and cousins. Indeed, before they set out for America, many migrant workers arranged to stay with kin. Even when roomers were unrelated, they were perhaps godchildren or individuals from the same village as the family that took them in.

It is impossible to determine how many lodgers individual families regularly accommodated. Trying to assess boarding practices at the start of the twentieth century, investigators estimated that, on average, immigrant households had three or fewer lodgers. There were countless instances, though, of families sharing their quarters with more people. Critics were shocked when they came upon incidents such as the Bulgarian parents with two babies who put up 20 boarders in their two-room apartment or the Pittsburgh family with seven children who shared three rooms with 11 lodgers. These situations were not atypical. In addition, the number of lodgers sharing a family's quarters was higher for particular immigrant

Immigrant extended family, New Bedford, Massachusetts, 1912. Courtesy of Library of Congress.

groups. So, although there were no clear-cut patterns, it was not unusual for families of all nationalities to house between 6 and 12 individuals.

The Boarding Business

Immigrant families and boardinghouses accommodated so many people because they packed rooms with as many beds or cots as space would allow. They then rented them on double shifts, which meant lodgers with different work schedules shared a bed. A boarder on night turn slept in the bed during the day, and another lodger scheduled for the day shift used it at night. Stories about one man rolling out of a bunk as another crawled into it became part and parcel of immigrant oral and written recollections. One investigator found two boarders using a bed that their host family had "squeezed into" a walled-off area under a staircase that was no more than a "hole in the wall." Even though an extreme example, this family's ingenious use of space was nevertheless indicative of the lengths to which immigrants would go to keep lodgers.

Boarders were often less concerned with sleeping arrangements than with bottom-line costs and the kind of services available. For their part, boardinghouse operators and families who accepted lodgers wanted to ensure not only that they received proper payment but also that roomers understood what services they could expect. These mutual interests turned boarding into a business based on clear-cut understandings. Men and women who operated the boardinghouse specified what services they would provide and how costs would be calculated. Boarders promised to pay their share of expenses.

Although agreements between keepers and lodgers varied, common features nevertheless characterized boarding practices. Roomers normally paid fixed rates for a place to sleep. Personal laundry services might be included in the basic price or were provided for an additional charge, but keepers were responsible for washing the bedclothes. Meals and food represented the most flexible and most complex aspects of boarding agreements. In stag boardinghouses, residents might cook their own meals; people living with families sometimes had that option. As a rule, however, when a married couple either operated a boardinghouse or took boarders into their homes, the woman did all the cooking. At regular intervals, grocery costs were totaled and the bill was divided equally among the lodgers. Agreements with female boarders were, perhaps, slightly different. Only a comparatively small number of women sought temporary housing, and most were unmarried. They typically moved in with married relatives. These young females usually contributed something toward their upkeep, but they also paid in part by doing light housekeeping.

Women and Boarding Businesses

In family-run operations, and particularly in individual households with boarders, women assumed chief responsibility for providing agreed-to services. Women usually did all the cooking and cleaning. In addition to mending, they washed boarders' work clothes, underwear, and bed linen. When lodgers returned covered with grime from factories, mills, mines, or construction sites, it was not unusual for women to wash the men's backs and legs. Food preparation occupied much of the women's time. Female boardinghouse keepers cooked breakfast for the men leaving for the day shift and for workers returning from night turn. They prepared the communal meal. The female in charge determined what foods went onto the table, but she also made special dishes for individual boarders who requested and agreed to pay for the ingredients. Lodgers could negotiate for food to take to work. When they consented to prepare food for roomers to eat on the job, the women's days included packing lunch buckets for men departing in the morning as well as dinner pails for workers heading out for the night turn.

For immigrant women, then, providing services for lodgers was an occupation. Wives stayed home and oversaw the boarding business while husbands left to toil in factories, workshops, mines, or on construction gangs. Women kept a record of expenses and calculated each boarder's share of the total bill. Men who had received specialty items or packed lunches were given separate statements and required to reimburse the cost of their extras. Even with family members as boarders, women found they had to be deft business managers and weigh conflicting demands. They knew that their lodgers watched closely to ensure they were neither overly extravagant nor cheated them. So, on one hand, women had to keep food and other costs low, and on the other hand, they realized that, in addition to personal services, they had to provide food that satisfied their roomers. Unhappy individuals might leave, and, when that happened, families lost vital income.

Children also contributed to the family's boarding business. Similar to what happened on immigrant farms, parents expected sons and daughters to help out by performing assigned tasks or pitching in when necessary. Daughters, in particular, assisted their mothers with the marketing and domestic chores. Young females helped in ways similar to six-year-old Rose Popovich. To give her mother a hand on laundry day, the young girl recalled that she would "stand on a box to reach the washboard so . . . [I] could do some socks." When the number of boarders declined from 12 to 6, Rose could still reap up to $1.50 on Saturdays by charging boarders a quarter to shine their shoes. She gave all the money she earned to her mother. Boarding thus provided a way for immigrants to turn their families into a private workforce and avoid sending children outside the home to earn often desperately needed money.

Critics versus Immigrant Perspectives

Contemporary critics deplored the boarding practices in America's foreign districts. They abhorred the congestion, which aggravated unsanitary conditions in slums that were already breeding grounds for diseases. Crowding people into small apartments equipped with but one faucet, no toilets, and no regular bathing facilities forced yet more residents to use the limited number of communal water closets or outdoor privies. Social reformers also decried the general lack of privacy, especially when families used their kitchens as bedrooms, living rooms, and even bathing rooms. Their moral sensibilities were offended by the habit of letting children sleep in the same room with parents or lodgers. In the view of straitlaced reformers, a system based on wives staying home to look after unattached young males while husbands went off to work created an immoral climate.

Many criticisms of immigrant boarding practices were accurate. It was certainly true that roomers and their hosts lived in severely congested, frequently squalid conditions. Municipal governments tried to reduce the crowding by enacting codes limiting the number of nonrelated people who could occupy an apartment or house. Boardinghouse keepers as well as individual families, however, either evaded or were ignorant of the codes. With men away at work and beds rented double shift, it was nearly impossible for inspectors to determine how many individuals actually inhabited the premises. So, despite restrictive ordinances, families continued to accommodate migrant workers or assist recently arrived relatives by providing room and board.

Critics harped on all the alleged downsides, but, from the immigrants' perspective, boarding was a practical necessity that benefited both temporary and permanent migrants. First of all, critics' emphasis on immorality was generally misplaced. Although there were documented incidents of adultery, when the huge number of immigrants who either boarded or took in lodgers is taken into consideration, the cases were relatively few. Because immigrants hosted relatives, often households with boarders were actually extended families sharing expenses and pooling their resources to help out one another. Familial relationships reduced the potential for immoral behavior. Sharing quarters with a family or rooming in a boardinghouse run by someone of their own nationality was a practical solution to where migrant workers would live during their stay in America. Boarding also facilitated ongoing migration within the United States. When workers set out for a new location, they left with the expectation that they would find some type of inexpensive housing at their new destinations.

Accepting lodgers provided a way for the foreign born to accommodate the constant influx of people into their communities and, at the same time, let couples turn their living quarters into a source of income. And in the world of immigrants struggling to make ends meet or to save toward a better future, every little bit helped. Immigrant families used the proceeds to supplement a breadwinner's inadequate wages and stashed away any extra in savings earmarked for buying a house or starting a business.

Boarders' fees provided the added revenue newlyweds needed to get a foothold, while widows who opened their quarters to lodgers did so out of necessity.

From the immigrant vantage point, boarding also met the pressing needs of temporary migrants whose primary goal was to accumulate money. In the early twentieth century, on average, boarders probably spent between $10 and $12 a month on room and board. Calculated on a daily basis, expenses for meals and a place to sleep could be as low as 33 cents. Some men reportedly got by on less than 10 cents a day for food. Thus even with other expenditures, frugal laborers who earned between $9 and $11 a week—or, when working full time, $36 to $40 a month—could put away a hefty portion of their wages. Overall, the personal relationships that nurtured boarding practices among the country's foreign born were yet another example of immigrants putting familial and friendship ties to sensible use.

Besides providing inexpensive housing that let them save money, staying with family, friends, or fellow countrymen had emotional and psychological benefits. When they returned from work each day, men could converse with people who spoke their language. The more literate among them wrote letters or read newspapers for those who were less educated. Men played cards or engaged in familiar games and other leisure-time activities. A person with a musical instrument might play tunes for fellow lodgers, and if the mood struck them, they could sing along. Chain migration patterns meant that people from the same regions—and often from the same villages—lodged together. A letter to one boarder carried news that kept others informed about happenings in their native villages. Recent arrivals brought firsthand reports and gossip from the homeland; they might even carry personal greetings from loved ones back home.

Living with compatriots meant migrant workers would eat accustomed foods or that at least their meals would be prepared in familiar ways. While it was true that, concerned about costs, boarders usually wanted simple, cheap fare, they nevertheless preferred food cooked in traditional styles. "I am inclined to believe," one recently arrived immigrant wistfully reflected, that a certain dish "with the right kind of seasoning, touches more channels of memory than . . . a lullaby or even a picture of the homeland." To migrants on their own, "The sweet smell of well-known dishes recalled home and its comforts." Regardless of what foods were put on the table, mealtime reflected homeland customs. For instance, Slavic migrants could regularly count on soup as the first course of their main meal. On weekdays, the soup was made with a simple broth; however, when roomers sat down to Sunday dinner, they could anticipate something with a tastier, richer base. Typical were the Romanians who recalled eating soup and fried meat during the week. On Sundays, though, these residents of a Cleveland boardinghouse got pork, noodles, dumplings, or other favorites cooked in a customary style. Men of other nationalities could similarly expect that countrywomen who planned their meals would try to adhere to Old Country cuisine and mealtime traditions.

Despite the familiar foods and personal services that foreign-born persons could count on in communal households, boardinghouse life was a generally dismal existence. Rooming with relatives or countrymen fulfilled the immediate needs of single migrants or married males temporarily on their own, but, in return for the convenience, people tolerated nasty conditions. Overcrowding, lack of privacy, and occasional verbal sparring or outright fistfights were unpleasant counterparts to the camaraderie and other psychological or emotional benefits derived from living with compatriots. The fact that boarders knew their situation was temporary made life more bearable. At some point, an immigrant worker's years as a boarder ended. For some immigrants, this happened when they returned to their homelands; for others, it occurred when their wives and children joined them in America; for others, it came about when they changed their minds and decided to remain in the United States. If they stayed, immigrants went from dealing with life as transients to striving to build a permanent life in America. In many instances, this meant that immigrants who had once been lodgers themselves now took boarders into their homes.

IMMIGRANT FAMILIES

Uncertain Work and Wages

The Family Economy   Migrant laborers and working-class families carried on their struggle for existence in an often precarious world. Despite the demand for unskilled labor, sporadic downturns in the economy created temporary layoffs or, worse yet, caused workers to lose their jobs permanently. During a nationwide depression in the early 1890s, at least one-fifth of America's labor force was thrown out of work. A decade and a half later, the panic of 1907 ushered in a three-year economic recession that again forced large numbers of people into the jobless ranks. Although countrywide crises wreaked abrupt havoc on immigrant families, irregular employment was the constant menace in their lives. Individuals who took seasonal jobs in construction or any type of food processing were regularly laid off during slack periods. Sporadic slumps in industries meant that, at any given time, segments of the workforce were unemployed. Joblessness varied, but contemporaries estimated that, in the early twentieth century, between one-fifth and one-third of the U.S. labor force did not work a full 12 months.

While unskilled immigrants made up the largest number of the temporarily jobless, the various foreign groups recorded different employment rates. A 1908–1909 survey of the manufacturing and mining industries discovered that only about 6 percent of Serbs and approximately 7 percent of Bulgarians had worked a full 12 months. Variations among nationalities were due in part to chain migrations that took immigrants to particular geographic areas and in part to the tendency for nationalities to domi-nate certain industries or local plants. People from countries where mass emigration got under way later were also less likely to work full time than groups that came earlier. Regardless of where they lived, where they worked, or when they arrived in America, many unskilled immigrant laborers could expect to be unemployed sometime during the year.

Periodic joblessness reduced workers' annual incomes below what—based on established hourly or piece rates—they could reasonably expect. An industrial worker averaging $1.65 a day and putting in a six-day week should have totaled approximately $515 in yearly wages. In the first years of the twentieth century, however, the annual income for unskilled work-ers ranged from $300 to $450. As the decade progressed, the situation for laborers did not improve. The Dillingham Commission determined that in 1908–1909 nearly 44 percent of all foreign-born workers took home less than $400 a year. Foreign-born residents of cities fared a little better than the immigrant population on the whole, but their annual earnings were still less than what pay rates suggested they should be. The yearly average for urban dwellers was $452. The commission concluded that "lost time" was the major reason total earnings dipped below anticipated amounts.

Income and Standard of Living

In the early twentieth century, there was no official "poverty line." Experts nonetheless established guidelines for what constituted "living in poverty" and what was required to achieve a "decent standard of living." They basi-cally agreed that, for the average five-member family residing in the North, the poverty line was $460 per year; for families in the South, it was $300. Authorities generally concurred that, to maintain a minimal standard of living in the urban-industrial North, a typical family needed $600 annually. With this annual "living wage," a five-member household could suppos-edly afford what experts considered were the basics of a decent standard of living: a dwelling with indoor plumbing and an adequate supply of food and clothes. Whether immigrants worked irregularly or steadily through-out the year, many wage earners did not bring home enough money to meet this minimal standard. The Dillingham Commission calculated that, in 1908–1909, over 70 percent of the foreign-born married workers employed in manufacturing and mining had annual incomes of less than $600. The annual earnings of more than three-fourths of the male heads of immigrant families residing in cities fell below that amount.

The male parent's annual income, however, was not necessarily an accurate gauge of an immigrant household's financial situation. When the chief bread-winners' pay barely provided enough to make ends meet, families devised strategies to bring in more money. The funds they derived from taking in boarders, homework, or child labor significantly increased immigrant fami-lies' incomes. For example, according to the Dillingham Commission's tabu-lations, revenues obtained from several sources boosted the annual income of ironworkers' and steelworkers' families from the $409 that the husband earned to a total of $568; the amount in coal-miners' households jumped from $451 to $577. Earnings from these supplementary sources technically lifted immigrant families above the poverty line—but barely. Households with no outside revenue were mired in the ranks of the impoverished.

Expenses and Budgets

Managing tight budgets was part of everyday life for immigrant families constantly teetering on the brink of poverty. Because landlords had the upper hand, rent was usually the most inflexible expenditure they had. In cities and towns alike, proprietors exploited immigrants' limited housing options and their desire to reside in neighborhoods where relatives, friends, and people from their homelands had clustered. How much families spent for housing, though, depended on where they lived and how many rooms they rented. The Dillingham Commission's survey of several U.S. cities revealed that New York, where immigrants paid between $10 and $20 per month, had the most expensive rents while Cleveland, where monthly rates ranged from $5 to $7, was the cheapest. In other cities, monthly outlays for rent fell between these two extremes. On average, renters in Chicago paid $9; in Buffalo, they expended around $7.45. With the foreign born generally paying between $6.50 and $12 for a single- or two-room house, rent was, on average, a little cheaper in industrial towns. Regardless of where they lived, immigrants knew that failure to pay the rent would result in eviction from even the most tumbledown housing. So, in order to keep a roof over their heads, people set aside money for housing and then adjusted expenses to fit their means.

Each family devised its own strategy for managing money. Still, a 1907 study of weekly expenditures by inhabitants of a western Pennsylvania mill town offered a rare glimpse into the lifestyle of households struggling to subsist on a day laborer's wages. Families of the town's foreign-born mill workers who earned the standard daily wage of $1.65—or $9.90 per week—spent $10.03 for rent and basic necessities. Although ranging in size from three to five members, families nevertheless averaged $4.64 for food, 27 cents for fuel, $1.57 for clothing, and 13 cents for "other housekeeping expenses." They reported buying 62 cents worth of tobacco and liquor. The fact that families paid 77 cents for "insurance" demonstrated that they were acutely aware of the dangers they faced each day, especially in the workplace. By joining an ethnic mutual aid society that provided insurance benefits, married couples, in particular, sought to lessen the potentially devastating effects that illness, disability, or death could have on families. Church donations probably accounted for at least part of the 41 cents listed under the "other" category. It is also likely that a few cents went into savings accounts or were sent to families back home. People recorded spending nothing on medical expenses or furniture. As these budgets revealed, during normal times when employment was steady, even the thriftiest of money managers had to pinch hard to purchase bare necessities on a single income. Temporary joblessness or an unexpected medical expense could destroy even the most carefully watched budget and push a worker's family from the edge into the depths of poverty.

Women and Family Economies

A combination of cultural attitudes, together with local job opportunities, determined how families acquired additional money. In cities and towns where there were few jobs for females or when immigrants' cultural mores hindered married women from working outside the home, women still made substantial economic contributions. They did this by agreeing to take in boarders, assuming primary responsibility for meeting contractual agreements, and doing most of the routine work linked to a couple's lodging business. Some women, however, refused to accept boarders. They either did not want the burden or had several small children to look after. In many instances, strongly held convictions about women's "proper role" caused couples to forgo the extra money they could derive from a wife's activities. Cultural traditions stood in the way of married females looking after other men, or husbands refused to brook their spouses engaging in any type of gainful endeavors. Since, in most cultures, men dominated family relationships, women acquiesced when either traditional values or their husbands' opposition prevented them from earning money.

Immigrant women who devoted their days to domestic duties instead of to income-producing activities still contributed to the family's economic welfare. They did this, in part, by finding ways to reduce household expenses. Women living in mining regions cut fuel costs by searching for dropped lumps of coal near railroad tracks. They also scavenged areas around mines for culm, a refuse of coal that could be cleaned and burned. Although coal companies hired guards to stop such scavenging, they were apparently unable to put an end to it. According to one reporter, women outwitted the company's security people by getting up before dawn and finishing their gleaning before anyone arrived. In cities, women and children also foraged for coal along railroad tracks and looked for wood they could burn or sell. From spring to midsummer, children living in Bohemian Flats could be seen gathering the waste floating downstream from sawmills. The yards behind the shacks of this Minneapolis shantytown were covered with pieces of wood and whole logs salvaged from the Mississippi River. Women rummaged through city dumps for items the family could use or dispose of for a profit. In summer, women who lived near rural areas might take their children berry picking and sell the fruit and other wild produce they gathered.

Plot Farms

Immigrant families also survived on starvation wages by relying on their peasant skills and by adapting traditional gender-based divisions of labor to urban-industrial life. This happened when women became overseers of kitchen gardens and, hence, continued to perform what had been a customary female role in their homelands. Where possible, in cities they planted on bits of land near their living quarters. In towns and mining villages, they turned vacant lots into gardens or cultivated plots on surrounding hills and flatlands. What immigrants grew reflected the cuisine distinctive to their groups. Cabbage, potatoes, turnips, onions, beets, celery, garlic, and poppy seed filled the plots cultivated by eastern Europeans while herbs, garlic, lettuces, beans, tomatoes, and various types of squash flourished in Italian gardens. Even when families had to pay for use of the land, having an additional source of food outweighed the usually nominal rental fees.

In addition to gardens, some immigrants kept a few animals. By the early 1900s, municipal governments had generally banned raising farm animals within city limits; but, similar to other codes, these regulations were not always obeyed. And in industrial towns such as Johnstown, Pennsylvania, it was not unusual for a family to own chickens and, perhaps, a few geese. Some immigrants also kept a cow or a pig (and sometimes both). To accommodate their animals, families rented an acre or two or built a shed on the small parcels where they had gardens. In some immigrant neighborhoods, chickens and geese roamed freely during the day and found shelter at night under porches or beneath staircases. And, often coming from agricultural backgrounds—as the majority of the foreign born did—immigrants sometimes let animals enter the family's living quarters. The added work of tilling the soil and tending animals paid off. A modern-day scholar has estimated that immigrants who planted gardens and owned a few animals in one Pennsylvania town trimmed $5 to $6 from their monthly food bill.

While having homegrown produce and animals made life a little better for immigrants struggling to get by, it also helped families survive bad times. Immigrants in northeastern Pennsylvania offer but one illustrative example. It was generally acknowledged that their gardens and small farms contributed to the families' ability to hold out during the 1902 anthracite coal strike. Tiny plots and animals that provided nutritious food for the family table were also valuable sources of revenue. Families that owned chickens or a milk cow sold eggs and dairy products, including cheeses and butter, to other families, boardinghouse keepers, or grocers. The proceeds, which in ordinary times provided households with much-needed extra cash, became crucial to families facing desperate straits if their chief breadwinner was killed or severely disabled in a workplace accident. Even with the additional money garnered from several sources and creatively paring their budgets, many immigrant families lived at subsistence levels and many remained poor.

Cleaning and Laundry

Housekeeping in an Urban-Industrial Environment

Just as they affected the lives of immigrant farm women, deeply rooted beliefs about women's domestic responsibilities helped shape the everyday existence of females in urban areas. By and large, when they made the journey to America, immigrants of all nationalities took it for granted that married women would center their daily lives on house- and family-related duties. Women who engaged in homework or had boarders were still expected to handle all the routine housekeeping chores, take charge of child rearing, and supervise the families' home life. For both nongainfully employed females and those who engaged in income-producing activities, the home was always a workplace.

Immigrant women found that keeping house in urban America required adjusting to different, often difficult circumstances. Some adaptations were minor. Women from villages where residents normally took their loaves of raw bread dough to local bakers who completed the baking process had to learn to use modern stoves. Because there were no cellars or cold storage areas in America's tenements, women had to market more regularly and become skilled at storing perishable foods such as milk, eggs, and meat. Other adjustments were major. The filthy environments created by overcrowded living conditions and industrial dirt turned ordinary housekeeping into a formidable task. Women with lodgers faced a particularly difficult challenge. One twenty-three-year-old woman surely voiced the frustration of many female immigrants when she lashed out, "How can you keep the house clean with 20 men to take care of, and [three] children?"[1] Housekeepers without boarders still had to contend with the grime and grit that permeated industrial areas and filtered into their homes. The lack of laborsaving devices such as washing machines, together with deficient indoor plumbing, turned routine domestic chores into grueling exercises.

When immigrant women took up housekeeping in urban-industrial America, adapting to poor water supplies and disposing of waste were among the least anticipated lifestyle adjustments they had to make. Many came from villages or towns where getting water and throwing away refuse posed no problem. In America there was typically water to be had in their neighborhoods, but it was often difficult to get the large quantities necessary for the type of cleaning required. Badly installed or faulty equipment meant that water piped through public systems might not efficiently reach kitchen faucets or the communal hydrants. When weak pumps did not produce sufficient pressure to force water into tall tenements, up sharply slanted streets, or into hilly regions, residents could not get enough for regular cleaning. People also discovered that, especially in the summers when water levels dropped, industries in low-lying districts siphoned off water before it flowed into pipes leading to residential districts. Inhabitants of hilly sections of a heavily populated Pittsburgh neighborhood went out before dawn to get their day's supply for cleaning, cooking, and bathing, They had to go early because, once the day shifts started in mills along the riverbank, there would be little water available until evening.

Hauling water was part of daily life for housekeepers. Sometimes women had to go only a few steps to the kitchen sink; at other times, they had to trudge up and down one, two, or several flights of stairs to get the amount needed for their tasks. "The marvel was," one investigator reported, "not that some of the homes were dirty but that any . . . were clean." Her visit to one woman's home revealed the lengths to which some housekeepers went to provide a dirt-free home environment. According to this reporter, the mother kept her family's two-room apartment on the top floor "spotless" by carrying water "many times a day" and "day after day." While offering no comment about her domestic chores, she nevertheless probably expressed the sentiments of many immigrant women when she told her visitor, "God! Miss, but them stairs is bad."[2]

Although ordinary cleaning required a few buckets of water, doing the laundry called for tubs of it. As was the case on farms, washing clothes in urban America was a laborious task that devoured a woman's entire day. Laundry day involved carrying pails of water from a kitchen spigot or outside pump to the stove, where it was heated and then usually poured into tubs. Using a standard corrugated washboard, women scrubbed, wrung, rinsed, and rewrung each item by hand. Clothes covered with grime from factories, mills, and construction jobs required extra scrubbing, probably several rinses, and, of course, additional wringing. Wet items were then hung to dry on lines in the kitchen, in an exterior yard, or stretched between buildings. With no easy place to dispose of huge amounts of liquid waste, women lugged tubs or buckets outside and dumped the dirty, soapy contents onto the street.

Ironically, although housekeeping kept women inside and alone for long periods, the inconvenient exterior water pumps provided opportunities for them to mingle with people. As they stood in line waiting their turn to get water, neighbors conversed with one another, exchanged news, and gossiped. During warm weather, laundry day also offered a chance to socialize as women gathered in the yards outside their living quarters and combined a detested task with neighborly visiting. Children playing and women working in a courtyard "covered with tubs, wringers, clothes baskets, and pools of soapy water" was a common scene, especially in the foreign districts of towns and patches.

Food and Diet

Immigrant groups carried their own culinary traditions and distinct cuisine to America. Adjusting to the rhythm and demands of an industrial society, though, caused them to modify some mealtime and dietary habits. Customary eating patterns were disrupted in part because daily meals revolved around the male breadwinners' work schedules. The fact that men needed substantive food to withstand long hours of grueling labor encouraged changes in traditional diets. Thus, as with farm families, urban immigrants probably ate meat more often than had been normal in their homelands. Working-class families also incorporated some low-cost processed "American" foods into their diets. As a rule, however, insufficient incomes, irregular employment, and the "mania for saving" meant

"Yard of tenement, New York, N.Y."; image created between 1900 and 1910. Courtesy of Library of Congress.

that immigrant homemakers regularly stretched their food budgets by relying on inexpensive but filling dishes.

The drive to economize did not alter immigrants' palates or their preferences for certain foods prepared in familiar ways. Although there were marked variations among the nationalities, eastern Europeans favored similar types of food. Their diets relied heavily on cabbage, noodles, and dumplings. Boiled or fried beef, pork, and sausages were the most popular meats; chicken and goose were reserved for special occasions. Low-priced canned sardines or herring were among the other well-liked fare. Soup was an important part of the day's main meal. Cabbage, potato, and a variety of vegetable soups were customary, but women boiled bones to make meat-based stocks as well. Barley was the grain normally used to add substance to thin broths. Although immigrants from northern and southern Italy brought recipes unique to their respective regions, macaroni was a staple of the Italian diet. Formed into different shapes and sizes, cooked macaronis were normally covered with some kind of light sauce. Beans, smoked meats, dried cod, marinated vegetables, crusty breads, and cheeses were also found in Italian households. Greek women relied on the oils and cheeses that characterized their traditional cuisine; Syrians continued to eat distinctive breads, cheeses, and grains; Russian and eastern European Jews kept kosher. Other nationalities also maintained Old World culinary traditions.

Marketing

When it came to what they ate, urban immigrants had a decided advantage over foreign-born farm families in the rural Midwest and on the Great Plains. Instead of being dependent upon foods indigenous to the regions where they settled, urban cooks normally could acquire necessary ingredients at shops in their neighborhoods. Often local grocers and butchers were immigrants who had scraped together enough capital to open a small business. These shopkeepers catered to their own nationalities and, additionally, served a multiethnic clientele. This was especially true among eastern European groups whose cuisines were similar. A Polish grocer, for instance, might carry items that Slovene, Czech, Croatian, Slovak, Bulgarian, Serbian, and nonkosher Jewish cooks needed. Easy access to railroad or shipping distribution centers let owners of small businesses import exotic items from immigrants' homelands.

For immigrant women in urban areas, marketing became a regular part of their lives. It was normal for a woman seeking unusual ingredients, the best buys, and possibly special service to visit several shops during a single outing. Shopkeepers, who knew many of their customers, added personal touches that pleased female patrons. They extended credit that allowed their regulars to purchase needed items but delay payment until husbands got their wages or boarders had settled their accounts. With the help of obliging shopkeepers, women who took in boarders were able to accommodate requests for special foods and keep their lodgers happy. At the same time, boarders' cravings for familiar fare benefited permanent immigrants striving to build successful grocery stores and butcher shops.

Although women went out into the community and frequented several shops on their market days, they also bought goods from vendors who moved through their neighborhoods. Pushing carts loaded with fruits, vegetables, assorted dried foods, eggs, live poultry, and even fresh fish on ice, these peddlers brought supplies almost directly to the women's kitchens. Although food could be purchased in nearby stores and practically on their doorsteps, most working-class immigrant families nevertheless subsisted on scanty diets lacking adequate nutritional value. And with immigrants and their children sometimes going hungry, it was not uncommon to see malnourished individuals among the throngs of the foreign born moving about in urban America.

HEALTH IN AN URBAN-INDUSTRIAL ENVIRONMENT

Individuals who migrated to the United States were generally robust and in good health. Examiners surely missed some cases, but medical inspections at immigrant receiving stations went a long way toward ensuring that the sick or physically disabled were denied entry. Although the people who crossed unmonitored borders to enter the country could avoid medical screenings, they were most likely healthy and in good physical condition. Migrants from the Western Hemisphere were, after all, primarily young people seeking wage-paying jobs and thus ready and able to work. After immigrants had lived and worked in the United States for a while, however, their health often deteriorated.

In addition to fighting off the normal variety of colds, flu, and childhood sicknesses, immigrants in urban America had to deal with serious illnesses and infectious diseases. Sicknesses that afflicted the foreign born could be traced, in part, to the abominable conditions in the neighbor-

Physical Environment and Work

hoods where they lived. Poorly ventilated living quarters, contaminated water, pervasive filth, and congestion created settings ideal for breeding and spreading germs. Diphtheria, typhoid, tuberculosis, smallpox, and other communicable diseases menaced immigrant communities. Unfiltered water and inadequate sewage lines made cholera a persistent threat. Respiratory and gastrointestinal disorders were universal afflictions. Pneumonia, which could either be contracted or develop as a side effect of injuries or other illnesses, was regularly listed as the cause of death.

For many immigrants, there was a link between their health and their work. Beyond falling victim to work-related illness, the very nature of their jobs made them not only less resistant to normal infections but also less likely to fight off those they contracted. Backbreaking labor drained immigrants' vitality. Twelve-hour schedules and six- to seven-day workweeks left people dead tired. Construction gangs spent long hours toiling in hot weather. Alternating between day and night shifts caused industrial laborers regularly to lose sleep as they adjusted to new schedules and tried to rest during noisy daytime hours. Mill and foundry workers often experienced extreme temperatures in quick succession, especially in the winters. After finishing their shifts, men dripping with sweat and wearing damp clothes ventured out into the cold and made their way home. Toxic substances contributed to anemia and a variety of other energy-sapping disorders. To make matters worse, workers might carry communicable diseases such as tuberculosis or viral infections home. Often with no place to wash before heading out, laborers working in factories, workshops, and mines brought chemicals and any germs they might have picked up on the job into their living quarters.

Women who made the home their workplace also suffered the adverse physical effects of a demanding job that kept them constantly busy throughout the day and often well into the evening. Married females who engaged in homework or spent their time primarily keeping house and rearing children were worn out after putting in fourteen- to sixteen-hour workdays. Daily life for women charged with taking care of boarders was particularly grueling. They worked long, hard hours seven days a week. Preparing meals at all hours, packing lunch pails, washing filthy work clothes, mending, marketing, and, perhaps, preparing hot baths for lodgers left women fatigued at the end of the day. As they performed their sundry boardinghouse responsibilities, mothers also looked after young children and babies. When one observer declared that "the burden of motherhood and the ceaseless toil of home" left miners' wives "worn out, their frames shattered" and made them "look prematurely old," he was, in reality, stating what was true for many working-class immigrant women at the time.

Pregnancies, Infant Mortality, Childhood Diseases

Besides fatigue and the usual illnesses that struck urban communities, females faced dangers during pregnancy. Foreign-born Canadian and eastern European Jewish women had, on average, fewer pregnancies than Italians and Slavic immigrants from the Austro-Hungarian Empire. Still, even though birth rates differed among the various immigrant groups, most foreign-born women of child-bearing age could expect to confront the risks of pregnancy at least four times during their life in America. Personal recollections and contemporary accounts testify to the fact that, by and large, expectant mothers continued doing routine household chores—including fulfilling their obligations to lodgers—almost to the time they went into labor. Moreover, just a few days after giving birth, most mothers returned to their regular domestic chores but with the added burden of caring for a newborn. There are no reliable figures on how many immigrant women died during their pregnancies or at the time of delivery, but the numbers were considerable.

Because births often went unrecorded, data on stillbirths or the number of infants who died soon after being born are also elusive. Church burial records, however, contain evidence that the death rate for children younger than two years of age was high. Diarrhea, nutritionally deficient diets, respiratory problems, and infectious diseases were among the chief killers of the very young. Older youths, especially those younger than 15, fell victim to diphtheria, typhoid fever, whooping cough, respiratory diseases, and complications stemming from normal childhood illnesses such as measles and mumps. Ironically, seeking ways to have fun caused young children to engage in activities that were hazardous to their health.

In immigrant neighborhoods, which characteristically lacked playgrounds, they frolicked and played team sports in filth-laden streets and back alleys. After rainstorms, youngsters amused themselves by building dams in street gutters or sailing sticks of wood in the dirty, possibly contaminated, water gushing through them.

While the abysmal environment in workplaces and tenement districts put the health of America's foreign born at greater risk, lifestyles grounded in poverty made immigrants physically less able to ward off illnesses. A hand-to-mouth **Cultural Variations** existence characterized by nutritionally deficient diets and poor personal hygiene contributed to the high incidence of diseases. Illness and mortality rates, however, differed among the immigrant groups. Eastern European Jews had lower death rates than southern Italians who inhabited the same squalid urban neighborhoods. These variations reflected, in part, immigrants' different cultures. Religious laws governing diet, hand washing, and bathing made Jews less vulnerable to certain diseases. When southern Italians and other groups that liked fresh fruits and vegetables in their diet washed produce in contaminated water, they turned healthful foods into potentially lethal fare. After investigating water and milk supplies and finding them free of bacteria, the health commissioner in one Minnesota iron-ore district concluded that a 1906 typhoid fever epidemic that struck Scandinavians but not other ethnic and new immigrant groups living in the same area could be traced to the Scandinavians' custom of leaving food on the table between meals. Flies carrying bacteria from infected human excrement in the outdoor privies to the uncovered foods contributed to the spread of the disease. Notable differences among the various nationalities notwithstanding, the disease and mortality rates were higher among new immigrants than among the "native" population and the old immigrant groups.

In immigrant households, women took charge of nursing sick family members as well as lodgers. They kept all-night vigils at bedsides and assumed responsibility **Folk Cures and Rituals** for preparing and administering medications. Because the typical immigrant family seldom called on doctors, the medicines that the sick took were rarely drugs prescribed by a trained physician. Families struggling to survive on scanty incomes shunned doctors because they could not afford to pay the fees. Cost, however, was just one reason why people refused to consult physicians. Many new immigrants, in particular, came from countries where people had more faith in their own cures than in trained physicians. In some immigrant homelands, doctors were actually unpopular figures. Southern Italians represented one group that generally distrusted them. Eastern European Jews did not share that antipathy and were more likely to consult a physician if a family member became ill. It was usually poverty—not hostility—that kept Jews from seeking medical attention.

Just as with other aspects of immigrant life, the folk cures immigrants believed in were rooted in distinct traditions they carried with them. Folk medical practices, therefore, differed among—and even within—the various nationalities. Reflecting the strong regionalisms that characterized Italian society, Italians had a particularly varied range of folk remedies and rituals. Still, because most folk practices were embedded in peasant cultures, they shared common characteristics. Ancient remedies typically included various edible or surface-applied concoctions. Immigrants prepared potions and ointments from a variety of herbs, oils, plants, and minerals indigenous to their homeland regions. In America, a similar substance might be substituted for one not readily available. To ensure a ready supply of the proper ingredients, immigrants grew herbs and plants presumed to have therapeutic value. In addition to time-honored remedies, therapies also included a wide range of superstitious practices, amulets, incantations, prayers, and religious rituals. Catholic immigrants appealed to saints believed to possess powers to heal particular illnesses. When a child came down with whooping cough, parents most likely prayed to a saint legendarily associated with curing throats; an eye problem prompted a plea to a different venerated personage. When a doctor's treatments or Jewish folk medicines failed, Jews also turned to religious rituals and sought divine intervention through esteemed people believed to possess special powers.

Although immigrants fervently believed in the efficacy of their folk remedies, illnesses usually ran their course. People with minor afflictions simply got over them. Individuals with virulent diseases or who developed serious complications from normally curable conditions died. If a person recovered, that reinforced immigrants' faith in ancient methods; if a person expired, the bereaved perhaps sought mystic or supernatural explanations but did not lose faith in their own remedies.

Local, state, and federal health officials compiled data on diseases, death rates, and infant mortality, but reliable figures on the health of America's immigrant population in the late nineteenth and early twentieth centuries are hard to pin down. There is no question, however, that immigrants suffered a wide range of sicknesses. And although no exact statistics are available, it is equally clear that ordinarily treatable ailments turned deadly for adults and children alike. Moreover, there is no doubt that by coming to the United States countless immigrants sacrificed their good health or shortened their lives.

Immigrant Neighborhoods and Popular Images

Immigrants abhorred the ugliness of the neighborhoods where so many began their lives in America. Although scores of the foreign born had lived in urban and even industrialized areas, few had experienced such dismal conditions in their native lands. Memories of pastoral settings, fresh air, and clean water intensified the repulsion and mental anguish that their present circumstances surely caused. One immigrant spoke for millions when he stated that parents regretted that rather than "playing on grass as children did in the Old Country . . . [their sons and daughters] played on cinder-piles" in industrial towns. They wished their young could frolic among trees or wade in creeks instead of running around "among the ash-cans and swill barrels" on filthy thoroughfares or devising games to play in slimy gutters. Even the cobblestone or earthen courtyards in their lands of origin were preferable to the garbage-filled, putrid alleys that now served as playgrounds for youngsters. By emigrating, they had exchanged accustomed lifestyles for an unfamiliar, often harsh, existence in a society that itself was undergoing rapid change.

Conditions in immigrant neighborhoods generated much condemnation by social workers, reformers, and crusading preachers. Aiming, in part, to capture the attention of Americans and stir their consciences, people went into the foreign districts to gather information about what immigrants experienced each day. Investigators, journalists, and crusaders of all ilk roamed through the foreign quarters. They took pictures, knocked on people's doors, asked questions, jotted down notes, snapped more photographs, and then provided firsthand graphic observations and lasting pictorial evidence documenting life in the immigrant slums. At times, their shocking reports spawned legislation aimed at alleviating the squalor and improving conditions in these areas.

The exposés, social surveys, and adverse publicity contributed to a way of thinking that associated immigrant districts not only with dilapidated housing, unhealthy living conditions, and poverty but also with what contemporaries considered "social diseases." Ironically, both well-meaning reformers and hostile nativists helped promote this intensely negative image of the foreign neighborhoods and of the people who lived in them. On one hand, reformers lambasted greedy landlords for exploiting the foreign born while, on the other hand, sympathizers and critics blamed immigrants for the wretched conditions that characterized life in the tenement districts. Critics pointed to boarding as the major reason why immigrants' living quarters were so congested. Worse yet, they accused the foreign born of creating so-called social problems and promoting social instability. Linking moral behavior to living conditions, critics alleged that the immigrants' lifestyles bred immorality and, furthermore, contributed to the breakdown of families. Immigrants were seen as encouraging the exploitation of women and children because they permitted them to work. Child labor and married females engaging in gainful activities, critics alleged, damaged family life. From this standpoint, then, the cultural values and aspirations that significantly shaped immigrants' daily lives were undermining family stability and contributing to social disintegration. As they publicized the terrible conditions in the foreign districts, though, both detractors and well-intentioned reformers often overlooked the rich institutional life that nurtured stability in immigrant neighborhoods. For, amid all the dreadfulness and seeming instability, ethnic communities took root and flourished.

NOTES

Immigrant life stories and quotations were derived from Louis Adamic, *Laughing in the Jungle: The Autobiography of an Immigrant in America* (Harper and Brothers, 1932); John Bodnar, ed., *Workers' World: Kinship, Community, and Protest in an Industrial Society, 1900–1940* (Baltimore: Johns Hopkins University Press, 1982); Marcus E. Ravage, *An American in the Making: The Life Story of an Immigrant* (1917; repr., New York: Dover, 1971); Edward A. Steiner, *From Alien to Citizen: The Story of My Life in America* (New York: Revell, 1914). Immigrant quotations derived from secondary sources are cited separately.

1. As quoted in Alexis Sokoloff, "Mediæval Russia in the Pittsburgh District," in *Wage-Earning Pittsburgh,* ed. Paul Underwood Kellogg (1914; repr., New York: Arno, 1974), 87.

2. As quoted in F. Elisabeth Crowell, "Painter's Row: The Company House," in *The Pittsburgh District: Civic Frontage,* ed. Paul Underwood Kellogg (1914; repr., New York: Arno, 1974), 132.

5

Life in Ethnic Communities: Immigrant Institutions and Businesses

Immigrants searching for a better life in America had to adjust to an often difficult and at times bewildering world. The constant influx of new arrivals, together with the departure of migrant workers, underscored differences between the more settled existence in homeland villages or towns and life in urban-industrial America. Moreover, many immigrants discovered that they had exchanged life in communities where inhabitants knew one another for life in ethnically diverse quarters.

For probably the majority of migrants who chose an urban destination, the unpleasant foreign districts became the only America they knew. But even as they grimaced at the abominable physical conditions, when immigrants looked at their neighborhoods they saw more than impoverished people, dilapidated dwellings, and a filth-laden environment. They saw a place where they could interact with their "own kind." They mingled with people who spoke the same language, had comparable values, said the very same prayers, upheld equivalent customs, had faith in folk cures, enjoyed similar pastimes, liked identical foods, and shared similar—probably idyllic—memories of the homeland. To outsiders, the foreign quarters contained a jumbled mix of alien cultures that was nurturing social chaos on American soil. To the people who lived in them, the immigrant districts contained networks of ethnic churches, schools, newspapers, organizations, and businesses that served their needs, helped them adapt to a strange land, and enlivened an often bleak existence. Immigrants who settled in western and more rural regions of the United States also established institutions but not necessarily the variety that emerged in urban-industrial America.

The emergence of ethnic institutions points to the fact that immigrants lived complicated lives. Besides going to work, seeing to one's familial responsibilities, or coping with miserable living conditions, the foreign born had other matters to attend to. By creating their own churches, organizations, businesses, and social outlets, immigrants became involved in activities that helped them adjust to life in America while at the same time let them cling to the traditions, beliefs, and customs of the world they left behind. The growth of ethnic institutions and businesses also signaled the development of stable ethnic communities. As these communities evolved amid the flux and change that accompanied the migration process, the lives of transient and permanent immigrants continued to intertwine.

BUSINESSES, ORGANIZATIONS, AND
EARLY MIGRANT LIFE

Foreign Enclaves, Colonies, and Communities

As immigrants streamed into America's cities and towns, they transformed entire neighborhoods into foreign districts teeming with diverse nationalities. While it was true that the foreign born moved into inexpensive industrial areas, migration patterns were neither haphazard nor governed only by economic factors. Immigrants chose specific neighborhoods because their "own kind" lived there. Chain migration patterns were so strong that when migrants came from different sections of the same country they went to specific neighborhoods because people from their own villages or neighboring villages had already settled there. Thus, as more immigrants arrived, a single nationality might establish several settlements in separate sections of the same city or town.

When contemporary Americans referred to foreign-born populations, they often used the term "colony." While "colony" was commonly applied to a single nationality, the term was employed in different ways. "Colony" was synonymous with a geographic area that was associated with a single nationality. In Chicago, for instance, there was a "Polish colony" on the city's North Side and a large "Italian colony" in its West Side. "Colony" also embraced all the people of a single nationality irrespective of where they lived. When Chicagoans spoke of the Italian or Polish colony, they were referring to all Poles or Italians who resided in the city, not just those in a specific neighborhood.

Despite identifying areas with certain nationalities, a single immigrant group almost never monopolized a neighborhood. Hence, while a geographic district might be dubbed "Little Italy," "Little Poland," "Little Hungary," or "Chinatown," it was not unusual to find more than twenty different nationalities residing there. Indeed, early twentieth-century foreign districts in most urban areas resembled a crazy quilt of foreign colonies. Even when immigrant groups clustered within a several-block radius, rarely did one nationality dominate an entire street. Single nationalities

"The Foreign Element in New York—The Chinese Colony, Mott Street," 1896. *Harper's Weekly,* February 29, 1896, p. 209.

did take over residential buildings, but it was probably more common for multistory tenements to accommodate several different ones. Often various groups dwelled in tenements flanking each other. The reason some areas were associated with particular nationalities was because they were the first to settle there or they, in fact, made up a plurality—even if not a majority—of the residents. The concentration of ethnic businesses, together with churches and organizations, also imparted a distinctive ethnic identity to particular neighborhoods.

The presence of other nationalities did not prevent people from interacting with their own countrymen and countrywomen who lived in the same neighborhood or a few blocks or even miles away. By maintaining close relationships with relatives, friends, or fellow compatriots, individual immigrant groups were able to create their own ethnic communities within the multiethnic districts. These communities, though, differed from what most immigrants had previously known. In their homelands, communities were often territorially based. People who lived in the same village or, especially in the case of most Russian and eastern European Jews, in particular towns represented a community. In the United States, immigrants had to cultivate a new sense of community that—in addition to being rooted in a common language, history, culture, and origin—was based on mutual concerns. As it turned out, it was a shared interest in as well as a commitment to their particular institutions that formed the foundation of immigrant communities. Creating their own ethnic institutions, and thus building their own communities, was one way immigrants coped with being strangers in a foreign land.

Saloons and Coffeehouses The process of community building actually began during the first stages of a migration movement. While it was true that single males or married men without their families made up a significant portion of the early streams, the necessity to meet the peculiar needs of these working-class migrants gave rise to ethnic businesses and organizations. Ethnic coffeehouses and saloons were among the first to appear. And, over the years, both of these commercial establishments increased in number and importance. At the start of the twentieth century, the foreign quarters in even medium-sized towns could have somewhere between fifty to eighty saloons and twenty or more coffeehouses. The popularity of both businesses stemmed, in part, from the fact that a majority of migrants came from lands where drinking was an important aspect of social life. People naturally carried this cultural tradition with them. The widespread appearance of taverns in pre–Civil War America, and especially beer gardens where families gathered to socialize, attested to German immigrants' partiality for beer. Pubs in settlements populated by Irish immigrants offered evidence of their taste for whiskies and beer. Migrants who later hailed from the Austro-Hungarian and Russian empires drank beer but also liked a variety of hard liquors. Italians typically favored wines. Although they had national liquors, Syrians, Greeks, Bulgarians, Turks, Armenians, and people from the Balkans in general were more partial to coffee than to alcohol.

While social reformers, temperance advocates, and detractors of the new immigrants denounced saloons and coffeehouses as unwholesome centers of evil and corruption, from the immigrants' perspective these places performed vital functions in their communities. During the pioneer stage of migratory streams, if workers wanted to indulge in social drinking they often had no choice but to frequent saloons owned by "Americans" or other nationalities. Anxious to attract new arrivals, American saloonkeepers even employed "foreigners" to tend bar. As the volume and pace of migration increased, an enterprising immigrant usually managed to rent space and open a modest tavern or café that catered to his countrymen. A potential bar owner might be required to get a license to vend liquor; but, because a determined individual needed only to find a place where he could brew coffee, launching coffeehouses was fairly easy. With rooms large enough to hold a few tables and chairs, saloon and café operators were in business. These establishments sold beverages and perhaps some traditional foods or desserts such as baklava in the Greek coffeehouses. They quickly evolved, however, into service as well as recreational centers that met the needs of their largely working-class migrant patrons.

Although the types of services at immigrant-run saloons and coffeehouses varied, they nevertheless shared common features. Coffeehouses and saloons were informal employment agencies. Internal migrants who had perhaps responded to word-of-mouth reports about job possibilities knew that taverns and cafés were reliable sources of information about local opportunities. Recent arrivals or laid-off workers were also aware that immigrants with reputations for securing jobs for countrymen frequented such places. In addition, when they needed workers, employers made their way to these locations. A case in point was the local foreman who, "when short of men," simply went to a local immigrant-run saloon and was able "to yank in the fellows." Saloons and coffeehouses served their mostly male migrant population in other ways. By agreeing to put workers' surplus money in their safes, saloonkeepers, in particular, provided a convenience that offered peace of mind. Because copies of immigrant and occasionally homeland newspapers were available, migrants had access to information important to their lives in America and also kept abreast of what was happening back home. People who were illiterate could always find someone to read these papers to them. Some bartenders personally provided such reading services to their customers. By having a supply of writing paper and pens on hand, operators facilitated migrants' yearning to keep in touch with family and friends.

Beyond meeting the practical needs of a typically male and often transient population, immigrant-run taverns and cafés were social hubs. Although coffeehouses and especially the saloons were usually rather dingy places, they offered relief to men who had spent long hours toiling in the workplace. They became refuges from squalid, congested boardinghouses or the overcrowded living quarters men shared with the families they lodged with. At all hours of the day, people could be seen sitting around tables and drinking coffee, alcohol, or soft drinks; the air was normally heavy with smoke as men puffed on cigars, pipes, or cigarettes. They sang songs, shared news from home, debated a wide range of issues, and handed out useful as well as unsolicited advice. Patrons played cards, threw dice, and engaged in other traditional games of chance. Proprietors of some saloons and coffeehouses managed to acquire a pool table for their customers' use. Within the confines of these crude recreational centers, migrants found camaraderie and the semblance of a social life. They also could find conversation on topics that interested them, advice they needed, and information they required.

Reformers and teetotalers universally expressed indignation that poor working people would spend even a few cents on alcohol or gambling. For the most part, though, the gambling was for petty stakes and the alcohol was cheap. There were undoubtedly too many instances of workers drinking up or gambling away their earnings. The millions of dollars immigrants sent back home, however, suggested that, in general, they neither drank nor gambled away their wages, and, furthermore, they did not lose sight of their familial obligations. From the standpoint of hardworking foreign-born males, they were participating in well-earned leisure-time activities that were socially acceptable. Immigrants had to learn that, in America, overindulging in their favorite pastimes could land them in jail. Drunkenness, which had not been a crime in migrants' homelands, was a frequently recorded reason for arrests in the foreign districts.

Purpose and Development

Mutual Aid Societies

Foreign-born laborers devised ways not only to cope with a lonely existence but also to deal with personal crises. To moderate the potentially devastating effects of illness, disability, or death, immigrants banded together to form mutual aid societies. The first voluntary associations operated on the basic principle that members would lend one another a helping hand in time of need and take care of funeral arrangements should that be necessary. Individuals paid dues to maintain a treasury, which was used to dispense small sickness or unemployment benefits. In the event of a member's death, each person in the society was assessed a larger amount to pay for the burial expenses. By extending assistance in times of need and promising that someone would handle their funerals, these early self-help organizations provided foreign-born people with some of the same security they had known in their homeland villages and towns.

As migratory streams gradually swelled into mass movements, the number of local mutual aid societies not only increased but also sprang up far and wide. Ultimately, most ethnic groups established national religious and secular bodies that drew the scattered local societies into centralized organizations commonly referred to as "fraternals." Designed to serve their own people, the fraternals typically accepted individuals of a particular nationality. The religious bodies limited membership to people professing a specific faith, but the secular associations usually welcomed fellow compatriots regardless of their denominational affiliation. By forming female counterparts to the male mutual benefit societies, women added their strength to the various fraternal organizations.

Despite embracing religious or ideological objectives, fraternals were primarily insurance organizations that served the practical interests of workers in a foreign environment. Most amassed treasuries that enabled them to provide more extensive benefits than the early local self-help groups could afford. Although the amounts varied and changed over time, the male societies paid death benefits ranging from $300 to $1,000. Female organizations offered smaller indemnities. These lesser amounts were due, in part, to the organizations' smaller memberships and, in part, to the attitude that women were not major breadwinners and their deaths were not seen as inflicting the same financial loss as the death of a male head of household. The societies also provided one-time disability payments to workers who lost a limb or an eye or sustained a crippling injury. Members forced by illness to miss work could depend on a small weekly stipend for at least a short period. Besides providing monetary compensation to members or their families, fraternal societies aided immigrants in the quest for jobs. People who left a locale could transfer to one of their organizations' local lodges at their new destinations, and recent arrivals seeking jobs could prevail upon their fraternal brothers for assistance.

Benefits and Activities

Through their local branches, the fraternals touched the lives of ordinary immigrants. They held out the promise of dignified treatment for persons thousands of miles from home. "Committees of the sick" visited lodge members to determine the validity of their claims, but they also provided comfort to fellow countrymen who were suffering. Because chapters maintained control of their modest local treasuries, members needing short-term financial aid could appeal directly to their lodge brothers. If there were sufficient funds in the account, they might receive a small loan to tide them over. Members of fraternals also saw to it that their deceased brothers and sisters received decent burials reminiscent of ceremonies in their homelands. The regulations of both religious and secular organizations stipulated that members, properly adorned with their respective organizations' funeral badge, had to march in a fellow lodge member's funeral. Reflecting on this practice, one man no doubt expressed the inner feelings of many migrants when he asked, unless you belong to a fraternal "do you think that on this foreign soil anyone besides your close family and the undertaker would come to your funeral?" The realization that they could expect to be accorded the dignity of a traditional service complete with a cortege of mourners provided some solace to immigrants who came from cultural traditions that valued a proper burial.

Especially as their numbers grew, local chapters extended their activities beyond looking out for the welfare of their members. The fraternals had their own badges and flags that let them stand out at public affairs. Lodge members wearing elaborate insignias and marching in unison behind colorful banners added pomp to community events. They contributed to the pageantry of dedicating churches and enhanced the dignity of funeral processions. Besides assuming a highly visible role in public happenings, lodges became active in ways that advanced their ethnic communities' broader interests. They sponsored dances and other social events. Through fraternal newspapers, which regularly published the addresses of affiliates, lodges developed contacts with countrymen and countrywomen who lived in various sections of the same city or geographic region but of whose presence they might not otherwise have been aware. Because interlodge affairs involved several colonies, fraternals helped bring immigrants into contact with their compatriots who not only lived in different neighborhoods but who also had emigrated from other regions of the same homeland. By fostering such interaction, fraternal societies contributed to the emergence of stable ethnic communities.

Jewish and Chinese

Jewish immigrants from Russia and eastern Europe banded together into groups commonly called landsmanshaft. These informal associations had the distinguishing characteristic that members were natives of the same town. Some landsmanshaftn were typical mutual aid societies that provided benefits customarily associated with fraternal organizations. Other landsmanshaftn were local groups dedicated to one of a wide variety of religious, political, ideological, or economic activities. By the early twentieth century, large numbers of the landsmanshaftn had opted to affiliate with one of the national Jewish organizations. At the same time, scores of these local associations remained independent and, therefore, upheld the tradition of neighbors working together.

Because they were rooted in kinship ties and shared geographic origins, Chinese mutual aid organizations resembled the Jewish landsmanshaftn. Family members and fellow villagers banded together into *fong*s. People from districts or Chinese provinces formed *huiguan,* which were popularly known as "companies." By extending a helping hand to countrymen, these bodies functioned in ways similar to the European fraternal lodges. They helped newcomers find jobs and housing; they provided medical attention to the sick and buried the dead. Chinese culture, however, placed an additional demand on these associations. Trying to uphold the tradition of being buried in the homeland, they made arrangements to return the bodies or, at least, the bones of the deceased to China. Some companies even maintained their own cemeteries where bodies could be interred until the remains could be sent back. Local associations also sponsored social and cultural activities and established recreational centers.

COMMUNITY INSTITUTIONS: HOUSES OF WORSHIP

Worldly concerns dominated their everyday existence, but religion also played a vital role in the lives of many immigrants. Religion and church-related matters, however, were more complicated in America than what they had been in people's homelands. First of all, immigrants confronted the reality that, in addition to distinctive languages, each nationality came with its own traditions and devotional practices. A determination to reconstruct their traditional religious lives thus prompted ordinary lay people to found separate places of worship instead of joining existing congregations. As a result, by the dawn of the twentieth century an indeterminable but large number of "nationality churches" and synagogues existed in cities, towns, and rural regions. Despite vast differences in backgrounds and experiences, there was enough uniformity in their collective stories to support generalizations about the impact religion had on immigrants and their communities. For, regardless of where they came from, immigrants who sought to re-create the religious dimensions of their lives had to reconcile deep-seated traditions with circumstances they encountered in the United States.

Religious Diversity   In several ways, the mass migration that brought millions of people into the United States during the late nineteenth and early twentieth centuries fundamentally altered the country's religious landscape. Poles, Slovaks, Italians, Hungarians,

Lithuanians, and others added ethnic variety to the Catholic Church's largely Irish and German makeup. Eastern Rite Carpatho-Rusyns further enriched the church's diversity. With people adhering to the Roman and Greek rites pouring into the country, the number of American Catholics under the jurisdiction of the papacy in Rome doubled from approximately 6 million in 1890 to over 12 million in 1906 and reached nearly 16 million in 1916. By affiliating with a few existing churches, newcomers also somewhat enhanced the multiethnic character of Protestant denominations, especially Presbyterian and Reformed bodies. Protestantism became even more diverse as Lutherans from different countries organized separate administrative bodies. Eastern European Jews, who were mostly Conservative and Orthodox, added a significant new dimension to the Reform and principally German Jewish population. The Greek, Bulgarian, Serbian, and Ukrainian migrations contained members of several Orthodox churches that previously had not been part of America's religious makeup. The currents of migration also carried people adhering to a mixture of religious and spiritual beliefs, including Buddhism, Taoism, and Confucianism.

Devotional Practices

Many immigrants had grown up in lands where people practiced religion in different ways. This was particularly true for natives of southern and eastern Europe who, in addition to regular weekly devotions, boasted rich cycles of **Religious Cultures** religious holidays and festivals. On one level, individuals participated in public worship and observed feasts decreed by either religious law or the secular government. The important events in people's lives, beginning with their christenings, took place at least partially in the church. Wedding celebrations commenced only after family and friends had witnessed the solemnization of marriage vows in the church or synagogue. A house of worship was the unavoidable stopover in a funeral procession's march from the deceased's home to the cemetery. Because public devotions often involved nearly an entire village population, religiously based activities constituted part of community life.

On another level, religion involved more than observing the Sabbath, celebrating feast days, or solemnizing rites of passages; it was an integral part of people's daily existence. But, rather than being grounded in an understanding of theological doctrines, religion—especially in peasant cultures—was a system of rituals rooted primarily in an agrarian past. Believing in supernatural intervention in human affairs, people regularly appealed to the deity to see to their practical concerns. Prayer books contained invocations for entreating the Lord to change the weather, to improve the harvest, to cure sick animals, or to help individuals or communities in some way.

Folk Beliefs

People also venerated particular saints who, it was commonly thought, could grant special favors. Pious devotion to the Madonna and canonized individuals was commonplace in southern and eastern Europe, but the "cult of the saints" was particularly strong in the rural regions of southern Italy. Each Italian village had its own patron saint who, residents believed, watched over them and could be prevailed upon to act as an intermediary between them and God. Besides the routine veneration of their saintly patrons, villagers paid homage in grand style on the saint's annual feast day. The yearly *festa* began with villagers packing the church to hear Mass and a tribute to the patron saint. The religious services over, people joined in a massive procession that included brass bands and an enormous statue of the saint. Crowds chanted as the figure was ceremoniously carried through village streets. The annual daylong *festa* characteristically took on a festival atmosphere. Vendors' stands lined the streets; people ate, drank, danced, sang, gambled, and joined in various other entertainments. Fireworks displays drew the days' celebrations to a close. Every village had a patron; consequently, competition among villages to outdo one another's public adulation of their saints contributed to the spectacular, even ostentatious, nature of the *feste.* Italian immigrants naturally brought the cherished tradition of the annual *festa* with them to the United States.

Southern Italians were not the only people with a vibrant folk religion. Religious cultures throughout southern and eastern Europe were marked by a blend of folklore and superstition. At times, individuals prevailed upon clergymen to bless items thought to bring good fortune or good health. Inhabitants engaged in private and communal rituals aimed at protecting a village. For instance, residents conducted ceremonies thought to rid their communities of witches and demons or prevent them from entering the confines. Believing in the "evil eye," Italians and Greeks wore amulets to protect themselves against people who might have the ability to cast curses. Slavic peoples had similar superstitions as well as comparable charms and rituals believed to possess the power to counter evil. Although Americans often expressed disdain for what they regarded as the peculiar religious habits of immigrants, these deeply ingrained beliefs provided the foreign born with some comfort and a sense of security in a strange, often hostile world.

Rural Churches

Founding Houses of Worship
Reconstructing their religious lives could prove difficult for immigrants who lived in rural America or in farming districts with widely scattered households. Besides identifying a convenient church site, farm families, who were already surviving on uncertain and meager resources, had to find ways to support a pastor. Given the chronic shortage of clergymen, convincing someone to endure the hardships of ministering to a poor, rural

community was no mean feat. This was especially true during the initial stages of most migrations into the Midwest and Great Plains. After building and furnishing a church, financially strapped congregations might be unable to scrape together the resources to provide clergymen a decent standard of living. A Lutheran pastor serving a rural Illinois congregation offered an illustrative example of the deprived existence clergymen might expect. Having accepted the call by a congregation that did not have the wherewithal to afford both a parsonage and a church, this pastor found that, with the added expense of securing his own housing, his paltry salary of $200 a year did not even "cover the necessities of life."

With clergymen in short supply, many rural communities had to reconcile themselves to periodic visits by itinerants who might have erratic schedules. Traveling ministers could show up each month or, perhaps, every two to three months to conduct religious services, perform weddings, or administer sacraments. Sometimes, as a German community in rural upper Michigan learned in 1882, the interim between visits could be much longer. After administering first Holy Communion to the children, the priest, who normally had made monthly visits, did not return to this out-of-the-way farming community for six months. In the absence of permanent pastors, immigrants devised alternatives to the traditional clergy-led services. They gathered together on Sundays at someone's home and sang religious songs, read from the Bible, and prayed. For individuals who longed to partake in communal worship, such efforts filled a need; for others, itinerant ministers and impromptu services fell short of fulfilling their longings. Evaluating her own experience, one worshipper, no doubt, expressed the mixed emotions of many immigrants when she judged a recent improvised service "quite fun and good" but regretted that an "uneducated man" had led it. "If only I could . . . hear a good sermon" like the ones pastors preached in her homeland, this woman wrote.

Although people lived on farms several miles apart, as the number of families increased the various nationalities took the initiative and formed their own congregations, built churches, and acquired pastors. The first churches, and especially the Protestant ones, in many rural communities matched the simplicity of the congregants' homes. Sod and log churches dotted the landscape of farm settlements and towns in the West. Over time, as memberships grew larger and finances improved, congregations replaced these crude structures or small chapels with more spacious, nicely painted frame buildings. Some initiated ambitious, costly projects. A rural German Catholic parish demonstrated that tendency when members decided to construct their permanent church. A particularly zealous member reported that, although the parish did not yet have a regular pastor, it already had 40,000 feet of lumber "to build a worthy house." Admitting that "it will cost us every cent we can raise" to finish it, the man seemed optimistic that parishioners would make the necessary sacrifices to erect a building that conformed to their perceptions of what a house of worship should be.

Pioneers in Urban America

In urban areas, attending religious services presented a challenge for lone males and the first families that arrived. They usually turned to an existing church and, if possible, chose one whose pastor spoke a language closely related to their own. For example, Slavic Catholics who moved into Pittsburgh in the 1880s and 1890s attended the area's Czech church, which had been erected by first-wave immigrants. When, as often might be the case, no similar-language parish was available, the devout simply made do by going to the Catholic church located closest to where they lived. Because religious services were universally conducted in Latin, Catholic immigrants theoretically could attend any Roman Catholic church in the United States. Language barriers, however, not only prevented them from understanding the sermon but, more important, thwarted their ability to go to confession or obtain a priest's services should they be needed. When newcomers managed to secure their own priest or, perhaps, the occasional services of an out-of-town clergyman, pastors of existing churches often let them hold services in the basements. Protestants similarly accommodated the foreign-born adherents of their faith. Although grateful to have a place to worship, the fledgling congregations smarted from the humiliation of being relegated to cellars. If they wanted to participate in familiar rituals, the pioneers from lands dominated by Orthodox denominations usually had little alternative but to await the arrival of their own clergymen and lay preachers. The situation changed for immigrants of all faiths as more families moved in and ordinary laypeople organized their own churches.

Lay Initiative

Although immigrants established countless houses of worship throughout the United States, founding them was a new experience for most people. In their homelands, people typically attended churches that were likely a few centuries old by the time mass emigration got under way. But in America, if immigrants wanted to worship in a familiar style, they usually had to acquire or put up their own buildings. Even though every house of worship was not founded in exactly the same way, in the overwhelming majority of cases ordinary laypeople initiated the undertakings and oversaw their subsequent progress. Often Catholic and Protestant lodges launched the efforts. The Slovak branch of one Catholic fraternal that determined "enough Slovaks" finally lived in Pittsburgh so that "it would be good if there were a Slovak church" represented the typical pattern. Following this decision in February 1894, members initiated a vigorous organizing campaign. Promoters formed planning committees, called meetings, collected start-up money from potential parishioners, found a suitable building, petitioned the bishop for permission to establish a church in the diocese, and looked into finding a pastor they hoped would be approved by the bishop.

Time and again, Catholic laypeople made the same decision and trod the same path to organizing a church. Sometimes congregations erected a new building; sometimes they purchased an existing structure. Regardless, the formation of an ethnic church was a clear sign of changes taking place in the district. When an immigrant congregation purchased an abandoned church, this was more demonstrative evidence that a new ethnic group had displaced a district's older settlers. For example, in 1899, when a Norwegian Protestant church was deeded over to an Italian Catholic congregation, the transfer symbolized the flight of old immigrants from Chicago's West Side in the face of what they considered an invasion by undesirable "foreigners." What happened in this midwestern city was illustrative of changes sweeping over urban America as the nineteenth century gave way to the twentieth century.

Although Jews and most Protestants did not need hierarchical permission to found a synagogue or church, they nevertheless followed a course similar to that of Catholic parishes. In the vast majority of cases, ordinary laypeople initiated the efforts and guided the projects to completion. Russian and eastern European Jews usually established congregations, which, like their mutual aid societies, were composed of people from the same town. According to one count, in 1905 there were 60 synagogues and 350 separate landsmanshaft congregations in New York's Lower East Side. Instead of constructing buildings, the often small landsmanshaft congregations rented space somewhere in the neighborhood and held religious services there. The zeal to organize churches and synagogues added to the already unique character of America's immigrant neighborhoods. Steeples jutting into the sky over ramshackle structures, eye-catching cupolas among shabby dwellings, and simple buildings with distinctive signs were clear indications that one had entered a foreign district.

Separation of Church and State

Even as immigrants transplanted a cherished institution and clung to their traditional faiths, they had to adapt to circumstances unlike those they had known in their homelands. Specifically, immigrants had to adjust to America's system of separation of **Maintaining and Administering Houses of Worship** church and state. In many countries, congregants were not the chief financial backers of local churches. Instead, governments imposed church taxes and used the revenues to pay clerical salaries, medical costs, and pensions. Ordinary upkeep often rested with a nobleman or local gentry. The situation was fundamentally different in the United States, where individual flocks had to accept financial responsibility for their churches. This meant that laypeople had to bear the burden of acquiring a suitable building or constructing one. They were responsible for all maintenance costs and for any additional structures such as a parsonage or school that the parish decided to erect. Besides paying their salaries, they also provided a place for pastors to live. Given these obligations and usually starting life in debt, congregations devised several methods to defray loans and to obtain necessary day-to-day operating funds. They instituted monthly assessments, charged pew rents, and inaugurated special collections to acquire money to purchase statues, bells, and other items.

Many immigrants took their financial responsibility seriously and contributed regularly to their churches. In their struggle to survive, however, churches could escape neither the influence of large transient populations nor premigration experiences that did not require regular lay support. Being unaccustomed to contributing to churches in their homelands, some immigrants balked at parting with even small amounts of their hard-earned money. Reasoning that they belonged to a church in the Old Country, men planning to return home were reluctant to hand over any of their wages to one in the United States. Attitudes toward financially supporting churches also varied among immigrant groups. Anticlericalism and religious indifference made Italians less inclined to donate money, while cultural traditions made eastern European and Balkan peoples more likely to be generous. At times, giving proved difficult even for those inclined to do so. During strikes or recessions, families could not afford additional drains on already subsistence incomes.

No matter what faith they professed, the need to provide financial support for houses of worship affected immigrants' quality of life. Contributions drained precious bits of money from already tight family budgets and siphoned cash from migrant workers trying to build a savings. Maintaining a house of worship thus called on immigrants to make sacrifices that further increased the hardships and aggravated the deprivation that so many coped with each day. The fact that people made such sacrifices was testimony to the important role religious institutions played in their lives.

Lay-Hierarchy Conflicts

Nationality churches bound people together but could also tear them apart. Despite a shared commitment to their churches—and at times because of it—congregations found themselves embroiled in bitter conflicts. Members, for instance, clashed with their respective hierarchies. Its administrative system made the Roman Catholic Church particularly prone to struggles between the laity and clergy. Many new immigrant as well as French Canadian Catholics resented the American Catholic Church's domination by old immigrants and, more specifically, by Irish clergymen. Given the fact that in the early 1900s, 62 percent of U.S. bishops were either born in Ireland or of Irish heritage, it was little wonder that other nationalities viewed the Catholic Church in the United States as "Irish" controlled. Ethnic animosities aside, the fact that they had founded and then assumed financial responsibility for their churches caused foreign-born laities to assert that they, instead of the clergy, should administer church affairs. Lay members sometimes went so far as to challenge long-standing Catholic Church policy by insisting that the congregation owned church properties. The American hierarchy held fast to the principle that deeds for church lands in a diocese must be put in the bishop's name.

Differing convictions regarding lay involvement in parish government could cause festering antagonisms, especially toward "Irish" bishops, to erupt into open conflict. This happened in 1896 when what started as a local parish dispute in eastern Pennsylvania ultimately turned into a full-blown schism. Approximately a decade later in 1904, the disaffected congregations formed the Polish National Catholic Church in America. By 1916, 30 congregations with an aggregate membership of approximately 30,000 belonged to this schismatic body, which remained independent of America's Catholic Church. Issues involving a married clergy also produced friction. By refusing to accept their married clergymen, U.S. bishops infuriated immigrants belonging to the Eastern Rite, popularly known as Greek Catholics. Discontented Eastern Rite congregations abandoned Catholicism for an Orthodox body.

A clash of cultural traditions contributed to extraordinarily bitter relations between Italian immigrants and the American Catholic Church hierarchy. While Italians considered themselves Catholic, in the view of the American clergy these immigrants were not "real" Catholics. Italian men in particular shunned traditional religious observances and Italians in general engaged in folk practices the Catholic Church establishment deemed "pagan." The immigrants' determination to replicate their village *feste* rankled bishops. American clergymen were appalled at the spectacle of Catholics parading through the streets and pinning money to the robes of a huge statue, which was the centerpiece of massive public processions. Overall, the carnival-like atmosphere of these religious festivals embarrassed the Catholic clergy, horrified Protestant ministers, and shocked Americans. But from the immigrants' perspective, the annual *festa* was a cherished part of their traditional culture and the high point of the year for Italian communities. It was no surprise, then, that the bishops' failed attempts to do away with the *feste* only aggravated Italian immigrants and intensified their animosity toward the American Catholic Church.

Protestant churches also wrestled with divisions and strife. The Evangelical Lutheran Synodical Conference of North America, controlled largely by the German-dominated Missouri Synod, proved too conservative for most Scandinavian Lutherans. Swedish, Norwegian, Danish, and Finnish Lutherans also discovered that even though they all professed adherence to the same theological precepts, in reality they practiced different religions. Unable to set aside doctrinal, cultural, and language differences, these immigrant groups either formed their own national religious organizations—synods—or remained allied to synods in their respective homelands. In 1908, there were 24 Lutheran synods in the United States, and nearly every one was ethnically based.

Congregation Disputes

Church-related battles generated tensions that rippled through immigrant communities. Since immigrants brought their religious differences with them, disagreements linked to dissident movements in their homelands fractured some congregations. However, the discord that troubled churches was more likely due to the greater role that laypeople had in administrative affairs. Stormy debates over whether to challenge a bishop's authority or affiliate with a synod produced deep ruptures within individual parishes. Disputes concerning an unpopular or controversial clergyman could wreak havoc on church communities. Relieved that, at last, "a notable outward unity" now prevailed, an Illinois preacher detailed what could precipitate seemingly "unending conflicts" among congregants. For nearly five years, the members of this particular flock had warred "partly over the building plan" and "partly over the provision of the congregation with pastoral care." In this clergyman's opinion, the continual infighting had caused some people to stay away from religious services.

As coreligionists lined up on opposing sides of controversies, church matters could escalate into open confrontations and even lead to the creation of rival churches. Conflicts involving churches also spilled out into the neighborhoods and affected social relationships within immigrant communities and among family members. The battle that took place between Polish nationalists, who formed a splinter congregation in Chicago, and their compatriots, who had backed the clergy in a dispute over control of parish affairs, is a case in point. During what turned into a twenty-year conflict, one clergyman reportedly carried a pistol when he ventured out into the neighborhood. Besides riotous public behavior, people entered the breakaway church and protested by flinging hymnbooks, hollering, and pounding their feet. This was by no means an isolated case. In addition to verbal and sometimes physical encounters between church members, there were numerous examples of clergymen and rabbis being accosted by irate congregants, being forced to barricade themselves against an onrushing crowd, or being chased out of town.

Social and Community Life

Although certainly dramatic and definitely important, the clashes with the clergy and the infighting that plagued some immigrant congregations represented only one aspect of a complicated picture. Many immigrant churches did not become battlegrounds pitting church leaders against communicants or turning congregations into rival factions. While Italian and Polish parishes, in particular, could have tumultuous relationships with church officials, scores of immigrant congregations enjoyed relatively—if not completely—harmonious relationships with their respective hierarchies. In addition, individual congregations peacefully resolved minor squabbles as well as contentious issues. Moreover, even amid turmoil, nationality churches provided opportunities for immigrants to combine religious ceremonies with socializing. Indeed, after regularly scheduled religious services, it was common for people to assemble in groups to chat, gossip, or share letters from the Old Country. Families and friends came together to celebrate baptisms, marriages, and bar mitzvahs. So, in spite of the discord spawned by congregational politics, churches and synagogues helped strengthen family and friendship ties within immigrant communities.

Additionally, the need for congregations to raise their own operating funds caused members to work together in ways that enhanced their social lives. In order to garner money, congregations arranged fund-raising events such as dances, picnics, and bazaars. By encouraging social mingling, these affairs functioned as more than moneymaking ventures. Arranging festivities typically required individual members to donate their time, especially women who prepared the food. With arrangements made, parishioners could look forward to an afternoon or evening of chatting, dancing, eating, and drinking. By issuing invitations to fellow congregations, the events helped promote goodwill among an ethnic group's several colonies. Besides being occasions for countrymen and country-women who lived throughout an area to come together, church socials were popular among couples who were courting. Because children normally accompanied their parents, parish events were family affairs.

Exceptionally conservative Protestant pastors looked askance at the practice of holding dances to raise money and refused to accept funds derived from such activities. In these instances, besides relying on voluntary contributions, congregations organized bazaars that featured hand-crafted items and homemade foods for sale. Although religious restrictions prevented some congregations from promoting fund-raising socials, with the passage of time church-sponsored events played a vital role in the financial solvency of nationality churches and became an important aspect of immigrant community life.

Immigrants established houses of worship primarily because they wanted to continue practicing their homeland religions. Besides attending weekly services, many hoped to uphold traditions and observe feasts that had been holy days in their homelands. In the United States, however, many religious customs were preserved, some died, and yet others were born. Immigrants discovered that circumstances in America could not easily accommodate the array of feast days, collective rituals, and, especially, processions possible in villages and towns. Work disrupted people's religious lives. Twelve-hour shifts seven days a week meant that even the most pious had to forgo religious services on the Sabbath. Whether the foreign born labored in the industrial workplace or toiled at home, their lives operated on schedules that could rarely come to a standstill for religious observances that were out of the ordinary in America. So, even with their own nationality churches and synagogues, immigrants had no choice but to modify some religious practices and adjust to new lay responsibilities. Still, one man perhaps gave voice to the inner thoughts of immigrants when he revealed that a combination of religious and fund-raising events involving his church had evoked fond memories. There were so many activities during a single month that he and others "felt as if we were in the old country." Ironically, by stirring such sentiments, ethnic churches helped immigrants feel more at home in America.

COMMUNITY INSTITUTIONS: NATIONALITY SCHOOLS

Cultural Attitudes

Education and Schools

A variety of nationality schools enriched the web of stable institutions that emerged in immigrant communities. Because, by the early twentieth century, most states had enacted compulsory education laws requiring boys and girls to remain in school usually until 14 years of age, foreign-born parents had to grapple with educational issues in one way or another. It was a mix of ingrained attitudes, economic considerations, and parental aspirations, though, that often determined whether youths went to school, what type of school they attended, and how long they remained in school. For just as immigrants had cultural traditions that shaped their religious and home lives, they also arrived with well-cultivated points of view about education. Jews, Scandinavians, and Germans came from cultures that fostered respect for learning, whereas southern Italians were from backgrounds that placed minimal value on formal education. By and large, Slavic groups and peoples from the Balkans shared the Italians' attitudes. Their values had been molded in peasant societies that emphasized putting the family's interests first. In addition, these were cultures in which the idea that children should not be better educated than their parents held popular sway. Generally speaking, in the countries that sent millions of people to the United States in five decades between 1870 and 1920, the formal education of females was deemed particularly unnecessary.

Their cultural backgrounds meant that most new immigrants were not predisposed to establish schools purely to advance the intellectual development of their children. Nevertheless, immigrants were practical people who understood that their sons and daughters needed to become proficient in English. Even as parents realized this fact, they wanted their children to learn their "mother tongue"—the language that they, the parents, spoke—and also to gain knowledge of their ancestral culture. As a result of these dual desires, immigrants devised different types of schools to promote language, culture, and religion.

For immigrant parents, the educating of their young was a perplexing matter. In addition to weighing what was in the best interests of their families, parents pondering how to handle their children's education had to wrestle with the popularly held belief that, when it came to the children of immigrants, the public schools' mission was to create loyal citizens and to instill "American" values. Given these aims, from the immigrants' standpoint, attending such institutions carried the inherent threat that youths might reject their parents' culture and ancestral heritage. In the midst of the anti-Catholicism that pervaded American society in the nineteenth and early twentieth centuries, Catholics were especially leery of public schools. They saw them as a proselytizing force dedicated to converting young Catholics to Protestantism. Fearing that if children became "Americanized" they might shed their parents' Catholicism along with their mother tongue, clergymen and zealous laypeople pushed for nationality schools that would emphasize religion in combination with language and culture.

Religious values and Old World experiences also influenced Protestant views of public education. For example, Scandinavian Lutherans had a generally positive attitude toward public education. In their judgment, religious and moral training should be left to parents and the church. German Lutherans, however, disliked public schools because they wanted their children to be taught morality and protected from what parents believed were society's dangerous, corrupt influences. Accordingly, these German Protestants tended to prefer sectarian schools in which subjects were taught in German.

Parochial Schools

Although figures on private schools during the half century between 1870 and 1920 are imprecise, there is no doubt that immigrants established fewer schools than churches. The smaller number of schools was due, in part, to the fact that unattached adults rather than families predominated in the early stages of the new immigration wave. It also reflected parental indifference as well as an unwillingness to donate money toward schools. Be that as it may, immigrants founded thousands of parochial schools, which was the term applied to all religiously based and private nationality schools. According to one estimate, in the early 1900s between one-third and half of German Lutheran youngsters attended a church-affiliated institution. The more than 2,100 parochial schools allied with the conservative Missouri Synod claimed a total enrollment of nearly 100,000 German Lutheran children. Catholics, though, boasted the largest number of elementary schools. In 1910, there were at least 4,845 Catholic schools in the United States, and the preponderance were ethnically based.

Rural communities supported nationality schools, but the most striking expansion naturally occurred in cities. In its 1908–1909 survey of 37 cities located on both coasts of the United States as well as in the country's midsection, the Dillingham Commission estimated that the children of foreign households accounted for nearly two-thirds of the parochial school population. Given the tendency for Irish immigrants to settle in urban areas, the sons and daughters of Irish Catholics claimed a significant segment of these youngsters; however, as time passed new immigrants contributed to the parochial schools' continued growth. During the five years from 1910 to 1915, the number of children attending Catholic institutions increased more dramatically than did the number registering in the public schools. While the public institutions experienced nearly an 11 percent increase in enrollment during this period, the total population of parochial schools escalated almost 18 percent. One survey found that by 1919 the number of Catholic schools had risen to 5,788, which meant that, on average, 105 new schools had been started each year since 1910.

When it came to establishing schools, immigrants were not of one mind. Factions battled over whether advancing religious loyalty or cultivating an ethnic identity should be the schools' primary objective. Despite sharp differences between the more religiously and secularly oriented groups, parents usually wanted to ensure that their children received basic religious instructions. For Catholic youths, this normally entailed going to school until they had taken their first Holy Communion, which might occur in the third or fourth grade. Some children attended a few years longer until they received confirmation. Similarly, children enrolled in Lutheran elementary schools stayed, at least, through their confirmation. For youngsters in many immigrant households, reaching these religious milestones signaled the end of their parochial education. Concluding that their sons and daughters no longer required catechism lessons, parents transferred them to public schools, sent them into the workplace, or—especially in the case of females—kept them at home so they could help with domestic chores.

Language and Religious Schools

Some nationalities showed a marked preference for public institutions. Greeks and eastern European Jews ranked highest among the new immigrants while Swedes and Danes were among the most likely old immigrants to enroll children in public schools. Choosing a public over a parochial education for youngsters did not mean, however, that parents were uninterested in cultivating an ethnic identity. By the 1880s, at least nine states had enacted laws providing for foreign-language training in pubic schools. Cities in other states had provisions allowing the teaching of foreign languages. Local boards in rural areas dominated by a single ethnic group simply permitted schools to offer classes in a foreign language. In public institutions that gave children such easy access to language courses, educators developed curricula designed to make students bilingual. Specifically, they encouraged children to learn English as well as the mother tongue.

Even when school districts did not introduce language classes, immigrants who sent their children to public institutions still saw to their religious and cultural training. Youngsters in Christian households attended Sunday school classes; Jewish males went to Hebrew schools, where they studied religion, Yiddish, and Jewish culture. The U.S. Board of Education reported that in New York alone, there were at least five hundred of these Talmud-Torah schools in 1913. Greek schools, where many children could expect to spend their afternoons studying the Greek language and culture, were commonplace. Czech freethinkers and Finnish socialists also supplemented the regular elementary education in their communities by offering basic language and cultural training in conjunction with a heavy dose of ideology. Their designation notwithstanding, the various language and religious schools in immigrant communities were usually no more than classes taught by a clergyman, rabbi, or learned person.

Parochial Schools

There was no typical school day for the thousands of boys and girls living in America's immigrant communities. Some youngsters went directly to school each morning while others, especially boys, peddled newspapers before heading off to the classroom. Youths with jobs might spend their after-school hours selling papers, working as pin boys in bowling alleys, or laboring in a local industry. Children whose families owned a business helped out in the afternoon; domestic chores usually awaited young schoolgirls. A few times a week, the school day was much longer for youths whose parents required them to attend religious or language instructions. Following a full day of classes, they could anticipate spending additional hours with a teacher before heading home.

Schools and Curriculum

A nine-year old Italian "newsie" who had been selling newspapers in Hartford, Connecticut for two years, 1909. Courtesy of Library of Congress.

Children who went to parochial schools often passed their days in drab, uncomfortable surroundings. In some instances, clergymen, eager to provide an alternative to public education, turned church basements into makeshift classrooms. If, as happened in one Pittsburgh congregation, the pastor was able to secure several instructors before there was a school building, the staff had to find ways to teach several grade levels in the church cellar. Even in multiple-room buildings, individual class sizes could exceed fifty. In rural areas, buildings might be no more than dreary one-room, poorly insulated wood or sod shacks in which a lone teacher taught children who had attained different levels of achievement.

Whether they attended a parochial school or received special instructions, young students could expect the curriculum to be heavily religious, the learning to be rote, and the teachers to be stern disciplinarians. And especially during the pre–World War I era, many children enrolled in primary schools could anticipate being taught in a foreign language. Due to their migration patterns and the recentness of their arrival, new immigrant groups either lacked their own American-based teaching orders or the newly formed ones were as yet too small to fill the demand. This shortage of their own American-born teachers prompted ethnic congregations to import nuns from the homeland. Catholic parishes pleaded with teaching orders in the Old Country to send sisters to train their children. Women who came in response to these pleas usually could not speak English. Besides religion and language instructions, the nuns provided the children with a cultural education that placed strong emphasis on the literature and history of their ancestral homelands. By and large, though, children who attended parochial schools did receive English-language training. Individuals overseeing these schools usually attempted to make certain that, in addition to language classes for children who could not speak English, at least part of the day's instruction was conducted in English.

Public Schools

Although public schools did not belong to the broad network of institutions that immigrants created, they naturally made up an important aspect of daily life for the children who attended them. Depending on where they lived, boys and girls who spent their days in the public schools encountered situations ranging from good to terrible. Just as throngs of immigrants flooding into the country put severe pressure on available housing, the influx of thousands of children strained existing educational facilities. Until new buildings could be constructed, officials had no alternative but to squeeze rapidly mounting numbers of students into limited amounts of space. During the 1880s, New York school officials solved the problem of inadequate accommodations by dividing the school day in half in some immigrant quarters. Still, children assigned to either the morning or afternoon session in the city's heavily populated Lower East Side found themselves seated in classes of a hundred. Dirt, poor lighting, and inadequate ventilation made the cramped conditions even worse. By the onset of the twentieth century, officials in New York and other districts with large immigrant populations had taken steps to better their public school systems, but the type and quality of improvements varied considerably.

"Retardation"

The physical environment in public schools probably had a less adverse affect on immigrant children than the treatment many endured. Being instructed by teachers who were ill prepared to deal with huge classes of non-English-speaking individuals added confusion to already trying circumstances. Additionally, more than a few boys and girls discovered that their experience could be a humiliating one. Either because their previous education was deemed deficient or their English was considered substandard, children in public schools might well be placed in classes with younger pupils. These youngsters were labeled "retarded," which meant they were older than the normal age of students in their grade. In its survey, the Dillingham Commission discovered that more than 43 percent of non-English-speaking pupils were considered retarded. A breakdown by

Essex Market Public School on the East Side of New York City, ca. 1890. Courtesy of Library of Congress.

nationalities revealed that nearly 67 percent of Polish and Jewish pupils and about 64 percent of southern Italians had been placed in the "retarded" category. As a result of the school systems' "retardation" policies, young people found themselves forced into classes with children who might be about two-thirds their size and perhaps half their age. Recently arrived older boys and girls who could speak no English met the same fate.

Attendance and Completion

Whether their parents chose to send them to a public or parochial institution, a significant number of children in foreign-born households did not complete their primary education. And only a comparatively small percentage of youths who did finish eight years of elementary school went on to get a high school diploma. According to the 1910 U.S. census, nearly 70 percent of the children between the ages of 14 and 15 in immigrant households were in school. As they got slightly older and reached the legal working age, however, the children of immigrant parents were less likely to continue their education. In 1910, fewer than one-third of these youths between 16 and 17 years old were attending school. Compared to other new immigrant groups, the children in Jewish households were more likely to get a full primary education and also move on to the secondary level. The Dillingham Commission concluded that children of English-speaking Canadians had the highest rate of attendance in secondary schools. These two groups were followed, in order, by Scottish, Welsh, and English youths.

An Assessment

Critics maligned them, but nationality schools gave the children of immigrants a basic education. The overwhelming majority of youths who either emigrated at young ages as part of a family unit or were born in the United States learned to speak English. Based on its samples, the 1910 census estimated that 99.4 percent of the children between the ages of 10 and 14 years who had either one or two foreign-born parents were literate. Some of these youngsters were possibly literate in a foreign language instead of English; nevertheless, it is probable that the majority were reasonably competent in English. It is not possible to gauge how successful they were, but the nationality schools did try to impart at least a basic knowledge of American history and geography. Overall, it is impossible to measure the cultural impact that the various ethnic educational undertakings had. All the same, by controlling the education of young children during their formative years, the various nationality schools instilled religious and ethnic cultural values in them.

ETHNIC INSTITUTIONS: THE PRESS

Statistics and Kinds From 1884 to 1920, at least 3,444 new foreign-language papers were added to the uncounted number of existing immigrant publications. Although, by one tally, 3,186 shut down during this thirty-six-year period, at the end of World

War I there were at least 1,052 foreign-language newspapers still being published in the United States. While some immigrant newspapers were short lived and longer-lasting ones ultimately died, neither the duration nor raw statistics adequately reveal the importance of the ethnic press. From their formative years onward, newspapers served the needs both of ordinary immigrants and of ethnic communities.

Large communities were occasionally able to sustain foreign-language dailies or weeklies that were not identical but, nevertheless, comparable to the local English-language papers. With varying degrees of success, some immigrants also managed to establish commercial papers that reached a nationwide readership. In general, however, instead of commercial or local ventures, the majority were organizationally based and came out either monthly or semimonthly. A wide array of fraternal societies, church bodies, literary organizations, politically oriented associations, and advocacy groups put out publications. For instance, Italian and Finnish immigrants each had a vibrant socialist press. Regardless of their affiliation, most immigrant papers included national and foreign news, but in covering these topics they focused on issues relevant to their respective ethnic groups. Publishers usually gave front-page coverage to international matters and regularly devoted at least one page to news from the Old Country. Besides reports concerning the homeland, subscribers to immigrant publications could count on learning about happenings in their ethnic communities elsewhere in North America.

Culture, Ideology, Information

Because a paper's contents reflected its publisher's objectives, every imaginable type of information and shade of opinion could be found in the immigrant press. Groups were not averse to slanting the news to suit their agendas. Additionally, papers issued by rival groups often carried on bitter editorial exchanges. To cultivate an ethnic identity among compatriots in America, editors included features that highlighted a nationality's unique literature or history. Sectarian bodies brought out materials laden with religiously oriented items. In spite of their ideological or religious objectives, ethnic newspapers also served practical purposes. This was especially true of the official organs, whose chief goals were to promote their organizations' agendas and facilitate ordinary business operations. Although only members of mutual benefit societies received them, fraternal papers had an impact that went beyond local memberships. Besides saloonkeepers who made copies available to customers, individuals shared their papers with family, friends, and boarders.

The immigrant press accommodated the peculiar needs of a huge foreign-born population. Since the vast majority of immigrants could not read English, publications in their languages contained information that immigrants might otherwise not obtain. Unless reported in the immigrant press, foreign-born peoples in America would have remained ignorant of important current events or legislation relevant to them. Foreign-language publications met the special needs of the country's mobile migrant population. To help people locate someone, papers published requests for information on the whereabouts of individuals. The appeals led to the reuniting of family members who somehow had lost contact. They also resulted in people receiving the sad tidings that the missing person had died—all too often in a work-related accident.

Community Activities

In terms of everyday life in pre–World War I America, immigrant newspapers benefited communities in ways not envisioned by their founders. By focusing on activities or matters important to their members, fraternal newspapers actually served the broader interests of local colonies. For instance, lodges used the fraternal press to publicize social events and to extend invitations to countrymen and countrywomen who lived in different sections of the city or in nearby towns. Time and again, readers of the immigrant press came across the type of information that Slovaks living in a section of western Pennsylvania got when they perused their June 1898 papers. Residents from throughout the region discovered that they were invited to an all-day social sponsored by a Homestead lodge on the Fourth of July. During the founding stages of churches, papers performed important functions by carrying notices of planning meetings and providing progress reports on the undertakings. Before communities had their own regular pastor, the immigrant press sometimes informed the local community when an itinerant clergymen would be in the area. In addition to notices inviting people far and wide to participate in the fanfare that accompanied church dedications or special feasts, foreign-language papers printed notices about rallies to support striking workers or to stage protests.

Advertisements

The foreign-language press was filled with advertisements for goods and services. Immigrants or their children who were independent craftsmen and professionals regularly placed ads in their nationality newspapers. Usually for a reasonably small fee, doctors, dentists, bankers, lawyers, undertakers, and real estate agents listed their addresses. By purchasing ads, immigrant owners of shops took advantage of the opportunity to spread the word about what they had to offer. American businesspeople who wanted to attract an immigrant clientele bought space in the print media. Savvy retailers had their ads translated into foreign languages. Mail-order operations also targeted the immigrant press. Besides artificial limbs, advertisements for medicinal products were among the most common to appear in foreign-language publications. Companies offering effective medications as well as quacks hawking preparations that, in truth, should have been labeled "snake oil" made use of the immigrant print media. Some advertisers actually provided information useful to migrant populations. Seeking to capitalize on the immigrant trade and gain the edge in a competitive market, steamship companies took out ads that gave ticket prices and, often, departure schedules from major U.S. ports to overseas destinations. By glancing through their foreign-language papers, immigrants remained informed about the costs and details of any trips they might be planning.

American Oriented

The immigrant press also served as an educational medium that helped immigrants become informed about American society. They carried a wide array of items on U.S. history and published short biographies of important historical persons. Readers could expect the February issues of many papers to feature the lives of George Washington and Abraham Lincoln. In articles designed to educate them about the historical origins of Thanksgiving and the Fourth of July, immigrants got pointers on how to celebrate these "American" holidays in appropriate style. Short feature articles highlighted the life and works of prominent literary figures. Thus, by being published in foreign languages and serving largely alien populations, the ethnic press helped both temporary migrants and permanent immigrants adjust to life in a strange land.

IMMIGRANT BUSINESSES

Saving money ranked high among the objectives of both sojourners and permanent immigrants. This particular goal led southern and eastern European immigrants, in particular, to rely on a distinctive system of banking. Differing **Immigrant Banks** from legally incorporated financial institutions, "immigrant banks" that the foreign born patronized concentrated on the safekeeping of money and the handling of overseas remittances. Many of the banks also sold steamship and railroad tickets or arranged for individuals to send prepaid tickets to people abroad. Because they routinely appeared in areas that attracted new immigrants, the majority of these businesses could be found in cities, towns, and mining patches of industrialized states east of the Mississippi River. Based on its 1908–1909 study, the Dillingham Commission estimated that there were at least 2,625 immigrant banks in the United States. It could not determine the precise number, in part, because immigrant banks were informal operations not subject to the legal controls governing standard banking facilities. In addition, rather than being independent institutions, banks were often linked to immigrant-owned enterprises such as saloons, coffeehouses, and shops.

Origin and Functions

The origin of immigrant banks lay in the desire of foreign workers to find a secure place for their savings. Rather than handing over their money to American banks, migrants chose to entrust a countryman with its temporary safekeeping. Some immigrant banks thus got their start when newcomers prevailed upon saloonkeepers or coffeehouse owners to take short-term custody of their money. The tendency for immigrants to maintain close ties with their homelands let these businessmen broaden their services. They started selling steamship tickets or facilitating the sending of money back home. Seizing on their countrymen's financial and travel needs, enterprising immigrants who opened butcher shops, groceries, and other small businesses engaged in various banking activities as well. Inside these shops, immigrants could secure a transportation ticket for themselves, get a prepaid ticket for someone planning to emigrate, or arrange an international money transfer. As a consequence, a bank was sometimes merely a desk and a safe located in a section of a saloon or grocery store. Although immigrant banks usually catered to a particular nationality, some served a multiethnic clientele. Because their activities involved transactions with the homeland, operations run by immigrants from the Austro-Hungarian Empire could accommodate several ethnic groups.

Steamship ticket offices managed by foreign-born agents also evolved into immigrant banks. These representatives started out by selling over-

Italian store and bank in Stamford, Connecticut, 1892. Courtesy Immigration History Research Center, University of Minnesota.

seas tickets for companies and then expanded their operations to meet the interrelated financial demands of a steadily growing clientele of labor migrants. Workers who wanted to send money orders home or buy ship or railroad tickets found it convenient to leave their money in safes at the steamship offices until they had accumulated sufficient amounts to carry out their desired transactions. In a manner of speaking, these combination ticket agencies-banks became single-stop service centers for migrants' financial and travel needs. Newcomers to a neighborhood had only to look for steamship posters and advertisements in the windows to know they had found a business that could accommodate their particular wants.

Day-to-Day Operations

The immigrant banks offered conveniences that suited the distinctive lifestyles of their foreign-born and migrant clientele. Non-English-speaking customers could confidently transact what they considered important business in a language they understood and with countrymen they trusted. In addition, immigrant banks had flexible opening and closing times that accommodated their patrons' work schedules. Bank managers made services conveniently available in the evenings and for at least part of the day on Sundays. When the banks were closed, some proprietors took deposits from customers they encountered on the street. Adopting a pay-on-demand mentality, bankers acquiesced even when immigrants made unreasonable requests. Take, for instance, the man who told of being awakened after midnight by a bank patron who suddenly decided to leave town and wanted his money immediately.

Migrants did not usually keep large sums in their savings accounts. Normally, after they had accumulated a specified amount, they either sent it to family overseas or purchased passage to bring wives and children to the United States. According to the Dillingham Commissions inquiry into saving patterns, this strategy meant that the average account in immigrant banks contained $65.45. People planning to return to the Old Country no doubt built up larger reserves and then personally took their money back home.

By and large, immigrant banks were temporary depositories rather than income-producing or lending institutions. New immigrants in New York and a few other cities did establish bona fide financial institutions that performed normal banking activities and generated profits; a small number even provided loans for houses or business ventures. With notable exceptions, though, immigrant banks were not sophisticated operations. People who ran them received commissions from ticket sales, but they typically derived their livelihoods from the businesses they owned. For their part, depositors did not gain financially because, as a rule, immigrant bankers were merely custodians of money and did not pay interest on savings accounts. The importance of immigrant banks was perhaps best demonstrated by what immigrants did when no bank was available.

Men living in mine patches, for example, hid money in mine chambers or looked for secure hiding places in their boardinghouses. By putting cash in their boots, stuffing it in money belts, or sewing it into their clothes, many simply kept their money on their person.

Immigrant banks did not always serve their clients well. A few scoundrels engaged in fraudulent activities or absconded with money left in their safekeeping. Depositors also lost their meager savings when, unbeknownst to them, a banker used funds to make what turned out to be risky loans. Savers saw their money vanish when economic downturns, such as the panic of 1907, forced even some of America's chartered banks out of business. In general, however, people who operated immigrant banks were trustworthy individuals. Nevertheless, they could not withstand the growing pressure to standardize banking practices in the United States and ostensibly protect depositors. Following the investigation by the Dillingham Commission, some states enacted regulatory legislation that severely restricted unincorporated immigrant banks and, in some instances, put them out of business. Although the number of immigrant banks declined, these casual operations were still serving many of America's immigrant communities as late as 1914 when the outbreak of war suddenly interrupted transatlantic communications.

Skilled Trades

Premigration Skills and Independent Livelihoods

While most immigrants who flocked to the United States in the half century between 1870 and 1920 spent their entire working lives doing manual labor, some entered business for themselves. Immigrants who successfully used their expertise to turn uncultivated lands into income-producing farms arguably belonged to the category of self-employed. For these immigrants, America provided the means to secure an independent living for themselves and their families. Other immigrants came with skills or knowledge that paved the way to becoming self-sufficient tradesmen. This was especially true for the people belonging to the wave of old immigrants as well as northern Italians. Their early migration streams included a wide range of skilled people such as carpenters, cabinetmakers, blacksmiths, barbers, tailors, jewelers, clockmakers, butchers, bakers, sculptors, artists, and musicians. Craftsmen operating on their own, together with all types of immigrant-run businesses and workshops, could be found in places where old immigrants settled. Some immigrants also used expertise or past experience to gain a foothold in particular trades. Germans, for example, used their know-how to move into—and in some areas take over—the brewing and distilling industries.

Coming to America with even well-honed or specialized skills was no guarantee that an immigrant would achieve an independent existence. Many craftsmen discovered that they lacked the capital necessary to establish themselves. Artisans lost out to competition in small markets that could absorb only a limited number of people. Moreover, America's rapid industrialization during the latter decades of the nineteenth century significantly reduced the chances for becoming an independent tradesman. Many skilled immigrants who had originally aspired to be their own bosses found they had to turn to the soil or, more likely, to the factory to earn a living. Some ambitious immigrants, however, were able to do what a cabinetmaker from northern Hungary did when his "business gave way to modern development." In telling his story, he recounted that, instead of seeking employment in one of the emerging mass production plants, he completely abandoned his trade. Taking advantage of the fact that so many "immigrants were going back and forth," he opened an office that specialized in remitting money overseas. Then, by becoming an agent for steamship companies, he expanded his business to include selling tickets for travel by land and by water.

Commerce

Some immigrants intended to enter commerce. Italians from Genoa and the surrounding area in northern Italy apparently had that goal in mind. Reflecting their origins in a region with a venerable tradition in the commercial trades, the Genoese opened saloons and restaurants; they also went into confectionary and fresh fruit businesses. Their premigration experiences as well as cultural traditions also equipped eastern European Jews and Armenians with abilities suitable to the retail and professional undertakings. Seeking to avoid or, perhaps, escape life as industrial workers, other immigrants took advantage of commercial opportunities that appeared as their ethnic enclaves grew larger and more stable. Regardless of why they did it, going into business let immigrants avoid the inflexible work schedules that played havoc with family life and people's religious customs. For some families, self-employment meant less annual income than what a breadwinner could earn doing unskilled labor, but choosing the commercial route gave immigrants more control over their lives.

Peddling and Street Vending

Peddling offered one way for immigrants to become their own bosses. The vending of goods was also a logical start- **Retail Trades** ing point for ambitious people who hoped one day to operate their own stores. Cities often required street vendors to obtain a special license and, moreover, charged a fee for it; nevertheless, with minimal cash, a person could usually purchase or rent a cart, fill it with goods, and begin selling. Small-scale merchants with their peddlers' wagons roved through the immigrant neighborhoods and sometimes crossed into areas outside them. While certainly a safer undertaking than industrial labor, peddling had its own peculiar risks. Peddlers fell victim to the senseless hostility toward "foreigners," especially by young hooligans. A commentator on immigrant life in Chicago reported that children singled out the "most foreign-looking" for harassment. Using the contemporary derogatory term to express their prejudice toward Italians, youngsters upset their fruit carts "simply because they are 'dagoes.'" Jewish peddlers were "stoned and sometimes badly injured," she recounted, "because it has become a code of honor in a gang of boys" to show their contempt. Chicago was not unique. Such malicious behavior occurred wherever immigrants lived.

On certain days, streets in the foreign districts were transformed into large open-air markets as peddlers with loaded pushcarts descended on an area and set up shop. In 1901, for example, an estimated 1,500 peddlers vended goods along Hester Street and the streets adjoining it in New York City's Lower East Side. Although it was located in New York's largely Jewish sector, it became synonymous with the open-air markets that regularly cropped up in immigrant neighborhoods. Even when a single ethnic group made up a disproportionately large percentage of a neighborhood's residents, all the nationalities shopped at these markets. On market days, two-wheel wooden carts that peddlers had pushed around by hand became temporary sales counters. Carts and crude booths lined both sides of a street; sometimes, they snaked along several adjacent streets. From early morning, when the buying began, the market districts swarmed with people trying to get through places made nearly impassable by stalls, pushcarts, and buyers carrying baskets. Friday mornings were particularly busy at markets in Jewish neighborhoods. Shoppers bent on acquiring everything they needed for the Sabbath meal and laying in provisions for the weekend moved busily about carts piled with salable goods. Dur-

Italian immigrants selling bananas from a pushcart, ca. 1905. Courtesy of Library of Congress.

ing the days leading up to Jewish as well as Christian holidays, the markets teemed with people seeking specialty items and foods.

Although nearly every conceivable type of product could be found in the markets, each stall had its own specialty. Side by side were pushcarts laden with dried fruits, fresh fruits, vegetables, meats, fish, pickles, preserves, breads, or sundry baked items. Sellers specialized in small furniture items, household utensils, crockery, glassware, pots, pans, boots, shoes, jewelry, books, stationery, or candles. There were carts stuffed with rolls of wallpaper or oilcloth. Clothing vendors offered outerwear, underwear, children's clothes, women's garments, or men's apparel. Buyers wanting to make their own clothes, curtains, or rugs could find cloth remnants and samples from wholesale houses and, sometimes, even fine lace.

Hester Street in New York City, ca. 1903. National Archives and Records Administration 196-GS-369.

On any given day, an onlooker could witness people hawking goods, haggling over prices, and striking bargains in the markets and on the streets of the foreign districts. Customers often walked away with only subsistence purchases. Vendors were always hoping the day's sales would yield a reasonable profit, but there is no way to know how much money they made. Depending on the season and what they sold, peddlers' revenues not only varied but also fluctuated. Contemporaries estimated that in the early 1900s a peddler with a cart could realize as little as $5 a week, which was only about half of what full-time industrial laborers and garment workers could expect. Peddlers themselves reported more handsome profits. If, as one New York vendor explained, they managed to get a good site, individual sellers might net more than $10 in a single day. Moreover, as with so many other immigrant endeavors, peddling could be a family undertaking. A household's net earnings obviously rose when women helped out by operating a second pushcart. Parents also enlisted their children's services by renting peddlers' wagons and putting them to work.

Although the vast majority of street vendors were striving to achieve economic independence and earn enough for their families to live on, immigrants took up peddling for different reasons. A blend of cultural and religious factors prompted Russian and eastern European Jews, in particular, to peddle. Having emigrated from lands where discriminatory laws forced them to live in cities and, hence, engage in various types of retailing, their premigration experience pointed Jews to merchant-style activities. In addition, by becoming their own bosses, Conservative and Orthodox Jews could set work schedules that let them keep the Sabbath by abstaining from work on Friday evenings and on Saturdays. Thus, instead of being rebuffed by unsympathetic employers who refused to acknowledge religious holidays that did not conform to the Christian calendar, pious Jews could observe holy seasons in traditional fashion. Immigrants might turn to peddling out of necessity. It became a temporary fallback for people thrown out of work; recent arrivals resorted to peddling to tide them over until they found employment. From the outset, though, many street vendors were aspiring businesspeople who hoped they could accumulate sufficient money to open their own shops. It is impossible to know how many ultimately achieved this goal. Many peddlers did manage to build profitable independent businesses, but far more probably spent their lives eking out a living on the street or gave up and turned to wage labor.

Neighborhood Stores

Just as immigrants opened saloons and coffeehouses to capitalize on the needs of a largely male migrant population, the changing character of migratory movements created additional opportunities for enterprising individuals. As families made up a larger percentage of the foreign influx, resourceful persons took advantage of the fact that people were setting up house. Immigrant women obviously needed ingredients to prepare

Eleven-year-old peanut vender in Wilmington, Delaware, 1910. Courtesy of the Library of Congress.

everyday meals for their families. And because most females preferred to continue cooking customary foods in traditional ways, there was a demand for specialty items as well as cheap ingredients. So, in addition to saloons and cafés, butcher shops and grocery stores were among the first retail establishments to emerge in the foreign colonies. Their ability to accommodate the preferences of customers on tight budgets let them build a solid customer base. Jewish butchers, for example, sold kosher meats that conformed to dietary laws while the Slavic shops offered pork, sausages, poultry, cheap cuts of beef, and soup bones. Depending on what it offered, an ethnic store could attract a multiethnic range of patrons. Take, for instance, Hungarian butchers who gained popularity based on the fact they employed traditional methods that entailed burning off the hair of slaughtered pigs. People preferred this process because they believed it made the meat tender and sweeter.

As the volume of individual mass movements picked up and emigration from other countries got under way, the number and variety of immigrant-run businesses increased. Tobacco shops, candy stores, ice-cream parlors, bakeries, and pastry shops were among the most common businesses found along the major thoroughfares and streets in the foreign districts. Immigrants also opened restaurants, drug stores, and barbershops. The mushrooming of foreign-owned businesses in just one industrial town typified the kind of expansion that took place. In 1900, eastern European groups in Johnstown, Pennsylvania, operated at least 30 businesses; by 1915, the number had increased more than sixfold to 190. Greeks in Lowell, Massachusetts, offered a representative example of a single group's extensive involvement in retailing. According to one count, in 1912 Greeks owned 61 small businesses in this New England town.

Beyond the Foreign Districts

Immigrant-run establishments relied heavily on patrons in the foreign districts, but immigrants also engaged in commercial activities that reached well beyond these quarters. The dusty, filthy streets that made life unpleasant for both native- and foreign-born residents helped nurture a profitable immigrant business: shoe shining. Relying primarily on child labor to get started, Greeks and Italians, in particular, became heavily involved in this enterprise, which required a minimal outlay of start-up money. Benefiting from cultural traditions that encouraged the hiring out of children as a way to increase household income, padrones or their agents convinced parents to send their children to America to work. With this cheap labor force, immigrant operators set up stations outside saloons, barbershops, department stores, hotels, restaurants, train stations, and various entertainment sites in the cities. Some entrepreneurs garnered sufficient capital to establish shoeshine parlors that added shoe repair and hat cleaning to their regular services.

Profiting both from their premigration experience and ongoing ties with people in the homeland, Armenians became heavily involved in the importing of rugs. In cities where they settled, Armenians not only dominated the rug businesses but also expanded their operations to include rug cleaning. Owners of ethnic restaurants attracted patrons from beyond the confines of the foreign districts. Marketers of fresh flowers as well as fresh fruits and vegetables supplied items that also let them develop a clientele outside immigrant neighborhoods. For instance, in cities and towns where they settled, Italians and Greeks established a particularly strong presence in the fresh produce and flower businesses.

Building on what was considered a cultural trait, Greek immigrants turned a traditional liking for sweets into profitable undertakings. Instead of wage labor, some Greeks engaged in candy making and either ped-dled what they produced or opened small stores where they vended their own homemade confectioneries. These candy stores could be found in the foreign districts, but they also became commonplace elsewhere as Greek candy makers established shops throughout downtown areas. According to one estimate, Chicago, which by the early twentieth century was the center of the Greek candy-making trade in America, boasted 925 Greek confectioners in 1906. Chinese immigrants also entered the retail and service trades. It was, however, discrimination rather than cultural traditions that fostered the rise of laundries and restaurants, which were commonly identified with this ethnic group. Doing laundry was not something men had done in China. Excluded from many jobs in the United States, however, Chinese males took advantage of the need for clothes washing and food services, especially in remote towns and isolated labor camps, to build profitable businesses. In the late nineteenth century, as America's Chinese population began shifting, migrants opened Chinese laundries in western cities as well as in rapidly growing metropolitan areas of the Midwest and East.

Start-up Capital

Immigrants determined to go into business for themselves might acquire the necessary capital in several ways. Some newcomers arrived with enough money to take up peddling or open a modest coffeehouse or **Operating Ethnic Businesses** shop. This was particularly true for families who left intending never to return and, therefore, sold any property they owned. "Birds of passage" who, after several back-and-forth trips, decided to remain permanently obtained cash by disposing of possessions in the Old County or redirecting funds they had originally set aside for homeland use. Some aspiring entrepreneurs acquired loans from immigrant-run banks, especially the legally incorporated ones that offered a full range of standard services. A few received financial assistance from American institutions. These borrowers, though, were atypical. It was often difficult for immigrants to get commercial loans to start up businesses; moreover, their cultural values caused many to shy away from going into debt. Cultural traditions, however, benefited Chinese entrepreneurs. Duplicating a practice developed in their homeland, Chinese immigrants who wanted to invest in a business formed a unique credit association known as *hui*. The rules of operation were fairly simple. The several people who made up the *hui* put a stipulated amount of money into a pool, and by some agreed-upon method one of the members won it all. Members met each month and repeated the process until every individual had received a one-time lump sum. A member could win the pool only once. Traditions rooted in the landsman-shaft principle influenced borrowing and lending practices among eastern European Jewish immigrants. They did not establish lottery systems but some Jewish landsmanshaft societies created funds that granted start-up loans. The money, though, had to be repaid.

Although there was no single path to establishing oneself in the retail trades, immigrants who wanted to start a business more often than not had to rely on their own resources. Indeed, the roots of many businesses lay in the scrimping and saving so characteristic of immigrants. While some families created nest eggs as a safety net to weather emergencies or to buy a house someday, others fully intended to start a business with their accumulated funds. Then there were people like John Kroupa who became fed up with the uncertainties of industrial life and decided to become his own employer. Recounting his experience, Kroupa offered but one example of how immigrants moved from worker to business owner. A man "has to be pretty quick in . . . [the] mills, and it isn't a job for a man like me," he explained. So, after losing his job as a steelworker, Kroupa become a watchman. Already piqued that he had been passed over for earlier promotions, he turned down a lesser position when his watchman's job was abolished. His experiences in the workplace convinced Kroupa to go into business for himself. He took the family's savings and, with his children's help, opened a small store that sold hardware, candy, crackers, bacon, eggs, and molasses.[1]

Family Involvement

As with so many other aspects of immigrant life in America, running a business was a family matter. And, as happened in homes with boarders and on farms, all members of the household were expected to contribute. Women were actively involved in the day-to-day operations. While still responsible for child rearing and everyday domestic chores, women served as clerks, perhaps managed the accounts, or took charge of keeping the shop area clean. Depending on the type of business, they helped with the cooking, baking, and processing of salable foods or assisted in the shelving of dry goods and other items marketed in the family's shop. Business owners also viewed their children in much the same way as farm and working-class families. Sons and daughters either had assigned chores or were required to pitch in whenever necessary.

Impact on Communities

Compared to foreign-born wage earners, the number of immigrant business owners was minuscule. Their small numbers, however, obscure the impact that entrepreneurs and their establishments had on immigrant communities. People in the retail trades created a network of interrelated activities that benefited a wide range of businesses in the foreign colonies. The demand for specialized goods as well as hard-to-get foods, spices, and exotic ingredients nurtured robust import businesses that served not only the commercial trades but also boardinghouse keepers and ordinary residents. Saloons, coffeehouses, and restaurants got supplies from bakeries, butcher shops, groceries, pastry stores, confectionaries, and fresh produce vendors. Grocers marketed specialty items obtained from a local baker, pastry maker, or confectioner.

Because proprietors employed relatives or fellow countrymen, both small and large immigrant businesses were sources of jobs in their communities. The life story of one Greek male who arrived in New York in the 1890s illustrates how entrepreneurs and small-business owners smoothed the way for newcomers. Immediately after his arrival, the young man found employment with a "push-cart man" who already had five men in his service. He left his life as a peddler in New York and headed to Chicago, where a countryman gave him a job. After working in his compatriot's fresh produce store for a while, the man had saved enough money and, equally important, had gained enough experience to open his own "little fruit store." Immigrants could be found employed in foreign-owned workshops and establishments located outside as well as inside the foreign districts. For instance, Armenians primarily hired relatives and fellow countrymen to work in their rug import and cleaning industries. Chinese restaurant and laundry owners relied almost exclusively on Chinese help. According to one survey, in 1908 a hundred Chinese-run laundries in the San Francisco area employed an estimated thousand Chinese workers.

Immigrants found that working for a countryman sometimes could be an exploitative rather than a beneficial experience. Young boys imported to work as bootblacks in shoe parlors, for instance, endured long hours for very little pay. The boys began each day of their seven-day workweek between 6:00 A.M. and 6:30 A.M. and toiled for the next 15 hours or more. After the shops closed, the young workers cleaned the premises and washed shoe-shining cloths and hung them to dry. In return for their labor, youths earned between 12 cents and 15 cents a day. The young workers' yearly earnings of $110 to $180 would have been higher if grasping parlor operators had not kept the boys' tips. By the eve of World War I, pressure from critics had led to better treatment and working conditions for young bootblacks in some areas. It was a change in American lifestyles, however, that finally brought an end to the deplorable system. Improved mass transit, together with the introduction of new fashions in footwear, undermined the shoe-shining business. Notwithstanding the countless examples of shameless exploitation, by and large the evidence suggests that, especially over time, the benefits stemming from the wide array of immigrant businesses probably outweighed the misery caused by the dishonesty and greed of unscrupulous entrepreneurs.

Successes and Failures

Despite the financial independence immigrants gained from managing their own businesses, they were at the mercy of the same misfortunes that menaced wage earners and farm families. Economic slumps, layoffs in local industries, or strikes that deprived immigrant families of their incomes had a ripple effect that left store owners with fewer customers able to purchase goods or pay bills. Out of compassion or, perhaps, trying to maintain friendly relations that would pay off when good times returned, grocers and butchers, in particular, often had no choice but to extend credit to patrons in dire straits. Even during good times, the proprietors of modest shops often struggled to survive. Some immigrants simply lacked the experience, savvy, or sufficient capital to sustain their bid to become independent business owners. Whether due to customers' reduced spending capacity, bad management, or, perhaps, bad luck, an untold number of immigrant-owned businesses failed. At the same time, an indeterminable number thrived into the 1920s; indeed, many prosperous businesses would later trace their origins to the first-generation immigrants.

INFORMAL INSTITUTIONS: ENTERTAINMENT

Immigrants, who spent what must have seemed to them endless days working, still found time to have fun. When they decided occasionally to step out in search of a diversion from everyday life, they usually went no farther than a saloon, café, hall, auditorium, or theater in their own neighborhoods or, perhaps, in foreign districts where fellow countrymen and countrywomen lived. For, just as they established their own churches, organizations, schools, newspapers, and businesses, immigrants developed their own entertainment. Besides engaging in activities rooted in homeland cultures, immigrants created new forms of entertainment that were products of their American experiences.

Athletic and Gymnastic Societies
Immigrants transplanted traditional kinds of recreation. This was particularly true for people from lands where athletic societies had enjoyed wide popularity. Since the first waves arrived in the mid-nineteenth century, German immigrants formed a local turnverein, which was a society that stressed physical exercise. By the late nineteenth century, turner halls with exercise and recreational facilities could be found in areas where Germans settled. Athletic and gymnastic societies fashioned after homeland organizations were especially popular among Slavic and Lithuanian immigrants. As with fraternals, chapters of these national athletic organizations emerged in immigrant neighborhoods throughout the country. Initially, memberships were exclusively male, but as more immigrants came the nationals either modified their regulations and accepted girls and women or established female counterparts. At the community level, groups such as the Polish Falcons and the Czech and Slovak sokols promoted physical training by getting together on a regular basis for calisthenics and also by forming drill teams. When their numbers increased,

the locals sponsored gymnastic exhibitions as well as interbranch competitions. They organized various sports teams that played one another. Besides arranging rival events, the branches participated in parades and gave drill exhibitions at church and other ethnic community happenings. In these ways, athletic activities that served a recreational purpose for some people became a form of entertainment for a broad cross-section of immigrant communities.

The ongoing influx of migrants, together with the arrival of more married couples, prompted immigrants to find ways to accommodate a desire for more social diversions. Coffeehouses and saloons, which had traditionally catered to **Amateur Performers** migrant males, added more varied and occasionally more family-oriented styles of entertainment. In Greek establishments, people needed only a small platform, a large thin white sheet, and some candles or other bright light to stage silhouette performances. With the crude stage in place, operators charmed audiences as they skillfully manipulated figures that told a story in shadowy reflections on gauzy screens. Italian cafés offered puppet shows and plays. Sometimes these places featured individuals or groups from the local community, but they also accommodated traveling troupes that, in return for food and lodging, entertained paying customers. Performers received their compensation by passing through the audience during intermission and asking for contributions.

Immigrants with musical training combined personal enjoyment with entertaining others. They formed bands that, in addition to financially benefiting the members, served the broader community. By playing traditional music at weddings, dances, picnics, and other socials, amateur musicians helped their countrymen and countrywomen celebrate important feasts in traditional style. When local bands or choral groups accepted public engagements or, better yet, staged street performances, residents of the foreign districts could escape their dreary tenements and spend relaxing moments listening to familiar music.

The desire to entertain as well as be entertained gave rise to all kinds of theatrical productions in immigrant communities. For admission charges ranging from 10 cents to 50 cents, each **Immigrant Theater** year thousands of immigrants enjoyed performances put on by touring companies or by amateur drama clubs. Churches and parochial schools arranged religious dramas or plays that drew capacity crowds. And throughout the year, immigrants could count on having the opportunity to attend a variety of theatrical and musical events sponsored by the fraternal lodges and sokols in their communities.

Nationalities developed distinctive styles of ethnic theater that reflected the immigrants' cultural roots. For instance, whether educated or from illiterate peasant stock, Italians characteristically came with an appreciation for opera. Danes arrived with a fondness for comedy, and Finns had a liking for amateur theater. By and large, however, most any type of inexpensive production staged at a convenient site in an immigrant neighborhood attracted numbers of people. In halls or makeshift theaters throughout the foreign districts, people were treated to comedies, heroic tragedies, and musicals. Small ensembles chose to present classics that were revered as part of their nationality's cultural or national history. Indeed, it was in theaters in immigrant neighborhoods that many individuals were first exposed to some of their nationalities' great literary achievements.

Irrespective of cultural differences, immigrant productions contained common themes. Specifically, amateur theatrical groups and professional persons gave performances that poked fun at immigrants or sometimes exposed tragic cores of the immigrant experience. Audiences saw comedies built around befuddled "greenhorns"—the contemptuous term for newly arrived immigrants—dealing with unfamiliar situations. Through the comic character Farfariello, whom he created and portrayed on stage, Eduardo Migliacco, an immigrant himself, entertained Italian communities. Untold numbers of Italians laughed at the humorous exploits and listened to the mangled English and Italian of this sometimes clownish, stereotypical "Italian" figure. Audiences reveled in the satire and parodies as the buffoonish Farfariello cleverly managed to prevail over his betters. Performers staged dramas portraying immigrants confronting adversity or coping with loneliness and despair. The more serious dramas of playwright Jacob Gordin, a Russian immigrant who adapted classic works to address modern problems of Jewish life, drew large audiences. Regardless of whether people laughed or cried, theatrical productions appealed to immigrants because they could relate to both the comedy and tragedy of the experiences being depicted on stage.

As individual ethnic communities grew in size, both the range and quality of entertainment they could support increased as well. No ethnic group, however, exceeded the excellence and accomplishments of New York's Jewish population, which by the start of the twentieth century had developed a vibrant, sophisticated theater. According to one estimate, each year more than 2 million people paid between 25 cents and a $1 to gain entrance to theaters in the city's Lower East Side. The performances were in Yiddish, the principal language of the Russians and eastern Europeans who made up the majority of foreign-born Jews in New York. The Yiddish theater that captivated local audiences also received positive reviews from the city's uptown American critics. Despite any widespread acclaim, ethnic theater in New York's Jewish quarters as well as in other immigrant enclaves aimed to appeal to ethnic communities and accommodate their interests.

Beyond their own enjoyment, immigrants hoped foreign-language productions would help instill in their children an appreciation for their ethnic heritage and sharpen their fluency in the mother tongue. Immigrant parents, who often took a dim view of vaudeville, movies, and other types of "American" amusements, also tried to make ethnic entertainment an alternative to what they deemed immoral or decadent activities. In spite of efforts to counter its appeal, the rising popularity of American-style entertainment caused promoters of immigrant productions to make adjustments. The appearance of ten-cent vaudeville and ten-cent movie houses in the foreign districts or close enough to influence the tastes of at least the younger generation encouraged some theater owners to develop ethnic versions of these genres. By 1910, "Yiddish vaudeville" was being featured on stages in the Lower East Side.

Ethnic entertainment had broad-based appeal. People of all classes and ages attended the wide array of performances put on in their communities. Whether a play, musical presentation, or performance by a traveling troupe at a local café or saloon, these events brought together wage laborers, tradesmen, professionals, and retailers of every sort. Besides all social classes, the audiences were made up of married men and women, children, single females, bachelors, and married men on their own in America. The popularity of ethnic entertainment—in all its forms—was due in part to cultural preferences and in part to language barriers. When they spent even a few cents for any type of amusement, in return immigrants wanted something they could enjoy, could relate to, and, of course, understand. The fact that people hard-pressed for time and money managed occasionally to indulge themselves was an indication of how important ethnically derived entertainment was to immigrant families and communities. They might have paid a slight admission fee or felt pressured to make a donation as the entertainers moved, with collection tray in hand, through the crowd, but many likely considered it a small price to pay for a pleasant diversion from the harsh everyday existence of immigrant life.

Many immigrants seldom went beyond their neighborhoods. When they did go outside their own quarters, they likely went to an area where fellow countrymen and countrywomen resided. Because ethnic groups often established several settlements within a city or geographic region but might have found only one or two nationality churches, some immigrants traveled regularly from their residences to other neighborhoods or even nearby towns to attend religious services or congregational meetings. The same was true if they wanted to participate in ethnic social events or entertainment. Still, regardless of where they worked, temporary migrants as well as settled immigrants typically spent their nonworking hours somewhere in the foreign quarters. Because most everything people needed in their daily lives could be found in these areas, there was little reason to leave them. Often, without stepping foot outside their neighborhoods, the foreign born could shop, go to church, educate their children, socialize, be entertained, and keep informed about events both in the United States and abroad. Whether they were sick, unemployed, hunting for a job, needed financial help, or simply wanted some kind of advice, newcomers and longtime residents could likely find assistance in

Ethnic Communities and Identity

times of need. Especially for adults who could not speak English, immigrant neighborhoods were comfortable places where, in a foreign land, they found a familiarity that made life a little easier. Thus, many immigrants were only vaguely, if at all, aware of the world beyond their neighborhoods and had little interaction with people outside their own ethnic communities.

The ethnic communities, which constituted the immigrants' world, however, had neither well-defined nor fixed boundaries. Instead, these communities were made up of a network of institutions supported by people who spoke a common language, came from the same background, and had shared interests. These collective concerns were grounded largely in a desire to have their own churches, organizations, and businesses; consequently, over time, ethnic institutions had a far-reaching impact that went beyond satisfying the needs of specific populations. They encouraged immigrants to develop a stronger sense of peoplehood or ethnic identity than they had felt in their homelands. Indeed, when many immigrants first arrived in the United States, they did not identify themselves by nationality; rather, they considered themselves natives of a particular village or region, not of a country or empire. Having their own separate churches, schools, recreational groups, newspapers, and assorted businesses encouraged immigrants to view themselves as distinct from other nationalities. Even as regionalisms persisted and internal divisions plagued ethnic communities, immigrants, living as they did in a foreign land, were drawn together by a common nationality. It was an irony of the migration experience that people from different parts of the same homeland became, for instance, Italians, Slovaks, or Carpatho-Rusyns in the United States. The identities they forged and the communities they created nurtured a friendly environment in an often unfriendly world. It was not until the onset of World War I that many immigrants from Europe realized just how hostile U.S. society could be.

NOTES

Immigrant life stories and quotations were derived from H. Arnold Barton, ed., *Letters from the Promised Land: Swedes in America, 1840–1914* (Minneapolis: University of Minnesota Press, 1975); Hamilton Holt, ed., *The Life Stories of Undistinguished Americans as Told by Themselves*, 2nd ed., with new introduction by Wernor Sollors (1906; New York: Routledge, 1990); Walter D. Kamphoefner, Wolfgang Helbich, and Ulrike Sommer, eds., *News from the Land of Freedom: German Immigrants Write Home*, trans. Susan Carter Vogel (Ithaca, NY: Cornell University Press, 1991). Immigrant life stories, quotations, and translations from original documents were also derived from June Granatir Alexander, *The Immigrant Church and Community: Pittsburgh's Slovak Catholics and Lutherans, 1880–1915* (Pittsburgh: University of

Pittsburgh Press, 1987). Life stories and quotations derived from other secondary sources are cited separately.

1. As described and quoted in Alois B. Koukol, "A Slav's a Man for A' That," in *Wage-Earning Pittsburgh,* ed. Paul Underwood Kellogg (1914; repr., New York: Arno, 1974), 68–69.

6

Life in a Hostile World: Immigrants in World War I America

In the summer of 1914, war broke out on the European continent. Over the next four years, the Great War, as it became known, claimed millions of casualties and disrupted millions of lives. Although the United States was a neutral nation during the first two-and-a-half years that Europe was mired in bloody conflict, it was a period marked by heightening anxieties in America. The war across the Atlantic jolted Americans into taking a closer look at their own society. As they did, they came face to face with the reality that immigrants had been clustering together in their own ethnic enclaves and, in effect, creating communities unto themselves. The separate nationalities had been attending their own churches, developing their own organizations, sending their children to their own schools, patronizing their own businesses, reading their own newspapers, and creating their own entertainment. In the course of adjusting to life in America, large numbers of immigrants had clung to their cultures and, in the process, had neglected to learn English. By not becoming citizens, too many immigrants had failed, in the view of many Americans, to demonstrate allegiance to the United States. The persistence of ethnic communities, cultures, and languages thus fueled efforts to "Americanize" immigrants. Once the United States went to war, the fear of "divided loyalties," together with a determination to turn immigrants into "good Americans," nurtured a fierce intolerance of the foreign born. At no point in America's history were attempts to eradicate all evidence of ethnic cultures as strident as in the period after the United States became embroiled in World War I.

After the United States entered the war in April 1917, many immigrants had to deal with the fact that not only were they "foreigners" in a country at war but also came from lands now engaged in a brutal conflict with the United States. At the same time, the Great War gave immigrants opportunities to go beyond life in their communities and take part in a national endeavor. In the same spirit as native-born Americans, the foreign born made personal sacrifices, contributed money to help win the war, and served in the military; nevertheless, for immigrants, the pervasive climate of intolerance, suspicion, and coercion that characterized the era inevitably affected ordinary life in their communities. After the international conflict came to an end, the intolerant mentality of wartime America flowed into peacetime and continued to touch the lives of the country's foreign born.

IMMIGRANTS AND AMERICAN SOCIETY ON THE EVE OF WORLD WAR

Citizenship and English-Language Skills When war erupted in Europe in August 1914, it effectively reduced migration from a flood to a trickle. And the two-way migratory streams that had carried individuals back and forth across the Atlantic came to a near halt. Thus, the people residing in the United States in that fateful year essentially made up what, fewer than three years later, would be the civilian population of a nation at war. The last U.S. census before the Great War shed light on what that wartime populace would look like. In particular, the questions the census asked and data officials tabulated offered a profile of the country's nonnative-born population.

Census takers counted more than 13.5 million foreign-born inhabitants in 1910. Among other characteristics, the figures indicated that slightly over 87 percent of America's foreign-born residents claimed a European birthplace. The statistical portrayal also revealed patterns that both friend and foe of immigrants believed had troubling implications for American society. Slightly less than 45 percent of adult males were naturalized citizens and just over 8 percent had taken out "first papers," which was the popular expression for having formally declared one's intention to become a U.S. citizen. All told, in 1910 nearly 2.3 million eligible males expressed no interest in becoming U.S. citizens. Because the citizenship status of married women was the same as for their spouses, census officials did not bother tabulating information on female naturalization patterns.

The 1910 census also showed that a significant portion of the country's foreign-born inhabitants could not speak English. More than one-fifth of immigrants older than 21 stated they could not converse in English. Canvassers did not administer proficiency tests, so it is likely that many foreign-born respondents actually possessed only minimal language skills. With migrants continuing to pour into the country, the number of non-English-speaking people and of noncitizens promised to increase.

From the summer of 1911 to midsummer 1914, an additional 3.2 million individuals passed through immigrant receiving stations, and the vast majority of them hailed from Europe. Although thousands of migrants departed during this three-year period, on the eve of World War I America's foreign-born population probably exceeded 13.7 million. By the time the United States went to war in 1917, therefore, a sizable segment of its civilian population neither spoke English nor claimed U.S. citizenship.

History and Legislation

Citizenship trends exposed by the census reflected migration patterns as well as personal decisions that immigrants had been making during the previous decades.

Naturalization

Since its birth as a nation, the United States followed the tolerant tradition of not requiring or pressuring immigrants into becoming naturalized citizens. Very early in the country's history, however, the U.S. Congress placed restrictions on who would be allowed to make that choice. In 1790, it enacted legislation that limited naturalization to "free white persons." This restriction stayed intact for eight decades until 1870, when the law was changed so that "persons of African descent or nativity" could become naturalized. Other peoples deemed "nonwhite" remained ineligible for U.S. citizenship. Despite attempts to toughen residency requirements, into the early years of the twentieth century it was easy for immigrants to acquire citizenship. During the post–Civil War era, individuals had to file papers declaring their intention to become citizens, wait at least two years, and then submit their final applications. Besides having resided in the United States for five years, applicants were required to have lived at least one year in the state where they filed their final petition. They had to swear they were persons of "good moral character," take an oath of loyalty to the United States, and renounce allegiance to all other countries or foreign sovereigns. Applicants had to supply witnesses who could attest to their moral character.

Although federal laws laid down the basic criteria, throughout the nineteenth century responsibility for carrying out the naturalization process was left to any federal, state, or local court. Without oversight or uniform standards, naturalization laws were poorly enforced and procedures varied from place to place. In addition, there was general confusion about which groups qualified as "white" and, therefore, could be naturalized. In 1882, Congress passed legislation making Chinese aliens definitely ineligible for citizenship, but the eligibility of other Asians remained unclear. Through a series of court decisions over the next two decades, most peoples from Asia were judged ineligible, whereas natives of the Near East and Middle East were typically handled on a case-by-case basis. With no clear guidelines, whether petitioners were deemed "white" and, hence, granted citizenship depended on the perceptions or prejudices of the presiding judges. Indeed, seemingly clear-cut laws were not rigorously followed. For instance, despite the statute denying citizenship to Chinese, the 1900 census recorded 895 naturalized Chinese citizens, and by 1910 the number reached 1,368.

During the opening years of the twentieth century, accusations about corruption sparked demands to change the naturalization process. Reports about operatives for political parties shepherding immigrants through the procedure so they could vote prompted outcries from both reformers and anti-immigrant types. The clamor over alleged manipulation of the so-called foreign vote and complaints about the slipshod enforcement of existing laws prompted Congress to overhaul the naturalization process in 1906. Besides establishing the Bureau of Immigration and Naturalization, it passed legislation designed to eliminate fraud, create uniform procedures, and elevate standards for citizenship. In essence, the new law made it more difficult to obtain U.S. citizenship. Besides now requiring a public hearing at which two witnesses had to testify to the applicant's moral character and "attachment to the principles of the Constitution," would-be citizens had to convince judges they were not anarchists or polygamists. Other newly enacted stipulations marked a greater departure from past policies. The 1906 law required applicants to prove they could speak English and to answer questions that supposedly demonstrated a basic knowledge of U.S. history and government. For the first time in the country's history, U.S. citizenship and English were inextricably linked.

From the immigrants' perspective, the 1906 law made it more difficult and inconvenient to become a U.S. citizen. The new requirements meant that adults who worked ten- or twelve-hour schedules or alternated between day and night shifts not only would have to find the time to study but in all likelihood would also have to locate a facility that offered English-language, history, and civics instructions. After successfully completing the necessary training, applicants, together with their witnesses, would have to miss work—and lose pay—in order to attend the mandated public hearings. By the opening of the twentieth century, then, as the call for immigrants to acquire citizenship began to intensify, the naturalization procedure became more cumbersome and entailed learning English.

Female Citizenship

The more demanding naturalization process potentially disrupted the lives of far more foreign-born men than women. Single women, who met the racial and other criteria, could become naturalized in their own right and through the same process as men. Married women, however, were subject to different rules. Because U.S. law followed the principle that a wife automatically acquired her husband's citizenship, married women could not apply on their own. Without making any formal applications, wives did, however, automatically become citizens at the same time their husbands did. In line with the policy that a woman's citizenship was dependent upon her husband's, foreign-born women who wed U.S. citizens immediately acquired citizenship. In 1907, Congress further expanded the doctrine of male primacy by passing legislation that revoked the U.S. citizenship of women who married noncitizens. Women—both native and foreign born—who chose to marry an alien could not regain their citizenship unless their husbands became naturalized citizens.

"Patriotic" Programs

While most contemporaries showed little interest in how millions of foreign-born peoples were adapting to American society, by the dawn of the twentieth century a core of advocates began championing the **Prewar "Americanization"** idea that immigrants had to be turned into true "Americans." In the view of some people, the shifting origins and changing character of the post-1890 migration posed unprecedented threats to American society and its democratic traditions. Not only did the migration streams carry multitudes of non-English-speaking individuals, they also brought a huge number of males who had reached or were nearing voting age. Both sympathizers and detractors alike were bothered that the new immigrants came largely from nondemocratic countries. They trembled at the thought that non-English-speaking "foreigners," who lacked experience with the electoral process, would be voting in local, state, and national elections. They also feared that, unless immigrants were educated in democratic principles, they would either cling to or fall prey to what some contemporaries considered radical political ideologies. Hereditary societies were the first to take it upon themselves to try to educate the foreign born and promote citizenship. As they carried out their programs, the different "patriotic" groups shared the belief that becoming a U.S. citizen was evidence of one's loyalty.

In the 1890s, the Daughters of the American Revolution launched the first "patriotic" education program for immigrants. Its primary objective was to instill "American principles" into the foreign born and encourage them to become U.S. citizens. The Society of Colonial Dames and the Sons of the American Revolution inaugurated their own efforts in the early 1900s. The organizations' varied activities included sponsoring lectures on American history and government, preparing publications in several languages, and arranging civics classes. The Sons of the American Revolution reportedly spent half of its annual income on promoting good citizenship among the foreign born. Its pamphlet giving immigrants advice and containing information about the United States was translated into 15 languages. All told, employers, teachers, and various organizations distributed 1 million copies of the Sons' publications.

Public Education

While nationalistic organizations thought that promoting citizenship training and indoctrinating immigrants with loyalty fell naturally to them, most contemporaries believed that responsibility for teaching English to

the foreign born rested with the public schools. Because the overwhelming majority of newly arrived immigrants were adults, educators had to
fashion programs to reach out to people who were not required by law to
attend school. In the late 1890s, local systems in a few major cities established evening classes for their ever-increasing foreign populations. By
1901, New York officials were boasting about the program the city had put
in place for adult immigrants. During the next few years, Chicago, Detroit,
Cleveland, Philadelphia, Buffalo, Rochester, and other urban areas established special classes or night schools for the foreign born. In addition
to English-language training, school districts offered courses in civics
and American history. School boards in small towns rarely attempted to
arrange classes for mature immigrants. Overall, despite occasional vigorous efforts, boards of education responded lackadaisically to the rising
tide of immigration. The universally modest response was underscored
by the fact that, in 1914, only 253 "places" in 10 states with large foreign-
born populations had established special instructions for immigrants. In
these areas, the number of classes available could not possibly accommodate all the non-English-speaking people or noncitizens residing in them.
Moreover, when budgets had to be slashed, adult classes were the first to
be eliminated.

The quality of education available in night schools was often poor. Some
terms lasted only three months. Administrators or teachers with little or no
training in the teaching of English to adults routinely handled the evening
classes. The habit of lumping together several nationalities in large classes
led by inexperienced instructors made the situation worse. Besides being
of little practical use to adult immigrants, the content of the lessons could
be demeaning and essentially useless. With a shortage of texts designed
for mature students, older people read children's books and practiced saying silly little rhymes. The physical facilities for night classes did not easily
accommodate adults. When they took their seats, full-grown individuals
often had to squeeze into desks fashioned for young children who made
up the public schools' daytime populations.

During the early years of the twentieth century, local officials attempted
to develop better teaching methods, but the quality of language instructions did not improve substantially. For many immigrants, the classes
remained an affront to their dignity. In 1912, observers reported seeing
grown men reading "Sophia had a little doll" or "I'm a little buttercup."
As late as 1916, entire classes recited rhymes opening with "Little drops
of water, Little grains of sand."[1] The spectacle of a man "six feet tall and
weighing 200 pounds" sitting in a desk suited for a twelve-year-old and
studying a children's textbook was not atypical.

Enrollment and Attendance

Thousands of foreign-born adults took advantage of the public schools'
specially developed English-language instructions and educational pro-

grams. Far more immigrants, however, dropped out of these classes. Critics were quick to point out, and even enthusiasts admitted, that enrollment figures greatly exceeded subsequent participation. By some accounts, only a fraction of the individuals who signed up for language or citizenship classes completed them. School districts that registered 7,000 or more adults at the start of a session admitted that 1,200 or fewer remained to the end. Individuals who completed the courses had erratic attendance records. Many adults felt the material they studied bore no relevance to the everyday lives of ordinary people who needed to develop a practical vocabulary and acquire useful information. After a grueling workday, men were too tired to sit in cramped desks and read children's books or spend the evening repeating an instructor's simple phrases. Immigrants, of course, found other ways to learn English. Those whose businesses or jobs brought them in contact with English-speaking people picked up a basic knowledge. Some immigrants taught themselves or learned from their own school-age children. Still, as the 1910 census revealed, more than one-fifth of adult immigrants could not speak English. The Dillingham Commission discovered that over 59 percent of new immigrants working in manufacturing and mining industries did not understand English.

Private and Employer Programs

Instead of relying on public schools, activists committed to the belief that immigrants had to learn English and become citizens devised other strategies. In 1907, the Young Men's Christian Association (YMCA) launched a language and citizenship program. By developing its own technique, popularly known as the "Roberts method," the YMCA adopted a practical approach to educating adults. Stressing conversation and useful English, the Roberts method tried to provide immigrants with the basic language skills they needed to deal with everyday life. Lessons centered, for example, on clothing, work, shopping, and traveling. Advanced courses focused on civics, history, and naturalization requirements. The YMCA's program was also a subtle attempt to Americanize immigrants by encouraging them to abandon their foreign ways. The idea was to get immigrants out of their enclaves to shop at American stores for American goods and thus to live in what was considered the "American" style. There is no way to unearth how immigrants perceived the YMCA's generally condescending program, but its educational endeavors were probably the most successful of the private undertakings. In 1912, the YMCA reported that 300 of its branches were arranging English-language classes, and an estimated 55,000 immigrants had signed up for them. Still, this was only a fraction of the millions of foreign-born individuals in the country.

Aware that enrolling in night schools was both voluntary and inconvenient, advocates of immigrant education sought to have classes held in the workplace, where so many immigrants spent their days. With instructions readily available in factories, the theory held, immigrants might feel more pressure to attend. It was the YMCA's practical approach that convinced some industrialists to introduce on-site education classes. Industry officials viewed English-language education from the standpoint of their companies' interests and, to some degree, the workers' welfare. So, instead of reading children's books, immigrant workers learned phrases directly related to their factory life. In a lesson on the workday, adult employees in one class recited "I hear the whistle. I must hurry." They also practiced sentences such as "I work until the whistle blows to quit" and "I leave my place nice and clean." Besides lessons dealing with tools and equipment, they learned "The doctor takes care of all accidents that happen in the works."[2] Company owners who established classes during the pre–World War I era did so because they believed that a grasp of English would produce reliable workers. They were more concerned about improving discipline in the workplace than turning immigrants into English-speaking citizens.

Immigrants' Decisions

On the eve of World War I, the obvious fact was that large numbers of the country's foreign-born inhabitants could neither speak English nor had become citizens. There were numerous reasons why. Some immigrants had not lived in the United States long enough to learn English or qualify for citizenship. The low education and citizenship rates also reflected the reality that many immigrants planned to return home. Temporary migrants did not bother learning English because they needed to know just enough to get by. That was also possibly the case for immigrants who planned to stay in the United States. Once they left the workplace, both migrants and permanent immigrants passed their time in the foreign districts with people who spoke their language. Women who spent their days in the home or in ethnic neighborhoods had little need of English. It was also likely that some, perhaps many, adult immigrants simply found studying English too frustrating. As one immigrant put it, by the time they moved to America people had often "passed that age" when "the mind is receptive" to learning a foreign language.

Altogether, the various efforts to educate immigrants during the pre–World War I era marked the initial phase of what by 1915 would evolve into a nationwide "Americanization" movement. In this initial stage, activists typically believed that immigrants should be coaxed—not coerced—into learning English or acquiring citizenship. Thus, during the early years of the Americanization effort, reformers, nativists, and industrialists let immigrants make their own decisions about how best to adapt to their new society. Once the Great War unsettled their world, however, many Americans changed their minds and Americanization became part of a more coercive campaign to turn immigrants into "100 percent Americans."

IMMIGRANT LIFE DURING WARTIME: THE PERIOD OF U.S. NEUTRALITY, 1914–17

When war broke out in Europe, it had a dramatic impact on the lives of foreign-born peoples in the United States. **Homeland** Some immigrants hastened back to join the fight while other **Interests** young men of military of age decided to stay until hostilities in Europe ended. Unable to return to lands now embroiled in conflict, many migrants who had planned to leave were forced to remain in America. Whether they intended only a temporary stay or had already made America their home, immigrants could not ignore the political situations in their motherlands or the havoc that war was wreaking on the lives of friends and relatives they had left behind.

Within days of the outbreak of hostilities, Woodrow Wilson declared the United States a neutral nation and called on Americans to be "impartial in thought as well as in action." But, as the president appealed for all Americans to remain neutral, he acknowledged that the "people of the United States are drawn . . . chiefly from the nations now at war" and it was "natural and inevitable" that sympathies among them would vary widely. Wilson was right. Each of the ethnic groups with origins in Europe responded differently, but each had a particular interest in what was occurring across the Atlantic. Former subjects of Austria-Hungary came to view the war as an opportunity to liberate their motherlands from the Habsburg Empire and to form independent countries. Peoples dominated by the Ottoman Turks saw a chance to escape their control. Irish Americans tried to assess how England's involvement in the conflict might possibly advance the cause of Irish independence. So, as war engulfed the European continent, many immigrants kept close watch on what was happening there.

Throughout the period of U.S. neutrality, immigrants did more than remain informed about happenings in the Old World; the onset of war fueled a surge of political activities in America's foreign colonies. The foreign-language press was filled with information and spirited editorials about immigrants' native lands. In addition, various nationality groups lobbied on behalf of their homelands. Ethnic organizations as well as newspapers in the United States backed independence movements. Immigrants from the Austro-Hungarian Empire cooperated with provisional governments in Europe and gave them financial assistance. Aware that public opinion favored Great Britain and its allies, German immigrants sought to ensure that the United States acted in a neutral fashion. In addition, German Americans worked to counter propaganda that depicted the Germans as vicious "Huns." Ethnic groups attempted to influence U.S. foreign policy by inundating government officials and congressional representatives with letters and telegrams. They held conventions, passed resolutions, and sent memoranda to President Wilson. Seeking to win over American public opinion, nationalities organized rallies and parades.

Anti-
Hyphenism
The interest that ethnic groups showed in European affairs aroused suspicions about their political allegiance. Critics accused the foreign born of having "divided loyalties" and, worse yet, of putting the interests of other countries before those of the United States. In short, they charged immigrants with being "hyphenated Americans." Accusations that the foreign born harbored divided loyalties fueled a fierce attack on "hyphenism." By the summer of 1915, Theodore Roosevelt was openly targeting "the hyphenated American" as "a danger to the country." With the former president leading the offensive, anti-hyphenism quickly invaded the national consciousness. Although Roosevelt saved his most scathing assaults for German Americans, he accused anyone who tried to pressure politicians by using "threats of the foreign vote" of engaging "in treason." Reflecting opinions similar to Roosevelt's, in December 1915 Woodrow Wilson alleged that some citizens "born under other flags" were pouring the "poison of disloyalty into the very arteries of our national life." The comments of these two national leaders reflected the chilling fact that the times were growing increasingly intolerant of the foreign born. Thus, even as the United States stayed out of the European conflict, a growing patriotic ardor fed, in part, by nationalist rhetoric created a climate of distrust that cast suspicion on "foreigners."

Concept

Americanization
Along with denouncing hyphenism, Americans began putting greater emphasis on Americanizing immigrants. In a climate of heightened nationalism, what had been a general indifference about English-language skills or citizenship status gave way to aggressive demands for "Americanization." Although it was not a well-defined concept, Americanization entailed learning English, becoming a naturalized citizen, embracing "American" principles, and adopting "American" standards of living. Being Americanized also meant demonstrating an unqualified allegiance to the United States.

Americanization Day

Americanization gained national attention and filtered into the popular mind during summer of 1915. This awareness started with Americanization Day, a countrywide event scheduled for the Fourth of July. Intending to honor naturalized citizens and individuals who had taken out their first papers, organizers envisioned Americanization Day as a time when both the native and foreign born could jointly and "fittingly express . . . their patriotism and loyalty to America." Preparing for the Fourth of July extravaganza sparked a flurry of activities in cities, towns, and colonies. Posters were plastered in railway stations throughout the country. More than 7,600 placards were displayed in industries employing immigrants, and nearly 6,500 were given to cities for their festivities. When the anticipated day finally arrived, demonstrations took place in at least 107 locations scattered throughout the 48 states. In communities nation-wide, gigantic parades composed of separate nationalities waving American flags, wearing folk costumes, and carrying national banners marched down local streets.

Communities and Workplace

Following the Fourth of July demonstrations, the Americanization movement gained momentum. In cities and towns scattered throughout the United States, the number of agencies involved in Americanizing immigrants mushroomed. Local Americanization groups sponsored classes, lectures, and an array of activities designed to reach out to the foreign born. Attempting to encourage naturalization, "Americanizers" directed tremendous energy toward teaching English and instilling American principles in the foreign born. The Americanization fervor also spilled into the industrial workplace, especially as advocates intensified their efforts to convince industrialists to establish "factory classes" for foreign-born employees.

The program instituted by Henry Ford at his Michigan plant was perhaps the most widely known as well as infamous of the workplace endeavors. Americanization was introduced into the Ford factory as part of the "Five Dollar Day" plan, which Ford announced in January 1914. Despite all the ballyhoo around Ford's five-dollar day workers paid a personal price for such generous wages. To be eligible for the $5 scale, employees had to allow company investigators into their homes to determine whether their lifestyles met specified standards. The company stipulated that only those who demonstrated thrift, honesty, and sobriety and whose home environment was clean and comfortable qualified. Workers whose domestic lives did not measure up were put on probation—at a lower wage rate—for a designated time; if, within a certain period, they failed to make the grade, they were fired. Although native workers were subject to the same rules, because the majority of Ford employees were foreign born the company's heavy-handed policies were aimed directly at them. In trying to force immigrants to adopt what was considered an "American" way of life, the company attempted to root out practices that affected both immigrant families and migrant workers. Specifically, to put an end to boarding of all kinds, guidelines stated that people should not live in congested quarters and that "men who herd themselves into overcrowded boarding houses" were ineligible for the $5 wage.

Besides pressuring workers to change their lifestyles, Ford's Americanization program included trying to force them to learn English. This objective affected about one-third of the plant's foreign-born employees. In 1914, more than 3,200 of the 9,100 immigrants at the factory could not speak English. Thus, along with accepting intrusive investigations into their personal lives, on class days non-English-speaking workers were supposed to go home, wash, change their clothes, and return to the plant for language instructions. The Ford English School's elaborate graduation ceremony, which students were expected to attend, reflected both the symbolic and increasingly coercive nature of the Americanization movement not only in the Ford plant but also in the country as a whole. For commencement, graduates, dressed in gaudy "old world" costumes and carrying signs identifying their native lands, went down into a huge receptacle labeled "melting pot." The school's instructors stirred the pot with huge ladles. Then, the men, wearing identical "American" suits and waving a small American flag, filed out from each side of the huge pot.

Although the Ford Motor Company's English School was probably the most demeaning of the forced Americanization programs carried out in a workplace, industries elsewhere brought pressure on foreign-born employees to Americanize. Instead of intimidation, some companies introduced economic incentives to motivate immigrants. The Electric Hose and Rubber Company in Wilmington, Delaware, informed employees that, after they learned English, the company would increase their wages. Other businesses preferred more coercive policies. In early 1916, the Packard Motor Company in Detroit announced it would not promote noncitizens. The company would continue to employ aliens, but "their only hope for advancement and preferment lies in their speedy adoption

"Immigrants in English class given by Training Service of the Department of Labor in Ford Motor Co., Factory, Detroit, Michigan," post-1908. Courtesy of Library of Congress.

of American citizenship and the forswearing of allegiance to other lands."
One Detroit establishment threatened that foreign employees who did not
attend night school or an English-language class in the factory would be
laid off. Several others announced they would give preferences, including
possible wage increases, to persons attending night classes and, hence,
making an effort to learn English. In the wake of such policies, it is not
surprising that Detroit's night schools reported a 150 percent increase in
enrollment.

IMMIGRANT LIFE DURING WARTIME: THE PERIOD OF U.S. INVOLVEMENT, 1917–1918

Following the U.S declaration of war on Germany in
April 1917, a militant "100 percent" mentality took hold of **"100**
the nation. This 100 percent frame of mind demanded total **Percentism"**
commitment to the U.S. war effort, the government, and the
president. In a drive to create national unity during the crisis, "100 percent
Americanism" became both a popular slogan and a rallying cry. As the
100 percent spirit seeped ever deeper into the national psyche, it nurtured
a zeal for cleansing the country of foreign influences. Immigrants thus
became targets of a more aggressive Americanization campaign that, by
war's end, had evolved into a crusade to make immigrants cast off their
foreign ways and become "good Americans."

U.S. Statutes

The wartime experience of America's immigrants is best
understood against the backdrop of repression that charac- **Wartime**
terized the era. The U.S. Congress contributed to the repres- **Repression**
sive atmosphere by passing legislation designed to quash
criticism of the war. The Espionage Act of 1917 imposed fines of $10,000
and a possible twenty-year prison term for making statements designed to
obstruct military recruitment or operations. The Sedition Act of 1918 went
much further toward suppressing speech. This law made it an offense to
use "disloyal, profane, scurrilous ... abusive" or any type of contemptuous
language when referring to the U.S. Constitution, system of government,
or flag. Statements aimed at slowing down production of war matériel in
American industries were also outlawed. As with the Espionage Act, vio-
lators of this law could spend 20 years in prison.

"Patriotic Groups"

The Justice Department added to the repressive climate by encouraging and, indeed, giving unofficial approval to self-styled patriotic groups.
The American Protective League, one of the most active of these voluntary bodies, developed a working relationship with Attorney General
Thomas W. Gregory. Its reported 250,000 members monitored activities

in communities throughout the country; other secret groups spied on their neighbors as well. A newspaper editor in Iowa reflected the mentality nurturing such clandestine activities when he proclaimed that it was each citizen's duty to join a patriotic society and also "to find out what his neighbor thinks." The maze of local citizens' groups that sprang up prompted Attorney General Gregory to brag that "never in its history has this country been so thoroughly policed." In policing local areas, 100 percenters more often than not administered their own form of justice. The passion to suppress any signs of disloyalty and simultaneously enforce 100 percent Americanism, consequently, gave rise to a spirit of vigilantism. Self-appointed policemen resorted to harassment, intimidation, and illegal activities. People suspected of not supporting the war, making allegedly disloyal statements, or engaging in any type of questionable activities might anticipate a threatening visit from a local "patriotic" society. Those who received unwelcome calls from the these "superpatriots" often had to buy a war bond, donate money, or do something immediately to satisfy their visitors' demand for proof of their patriotism.

Committee on Public Information

The Committee on Public Information, which was created to promote support for the war and for President Wilson, added to the 100 percent fervor sweeping the country. Becoming the government's official propaganda agency, it launched a massive campaign to sell the war. The committee, especially through its Division of Work among the Foreign Born, strove to stir patriotic ardor by bombarding immigrant communities with literature, organizing rallies, and arranging parades. At the same time that the committee was drawing immigrants into the national war effort, its agents kept a watchful eye on them. For example, they monitored foreign-language publications and were on the lookout for editors who violated the Espionage and Sedition acts. The committee's dual role of bringing immigrants into the national effort and simultaneously monitoring their activities symbolized how, during the Great War, patriotic zeal and repression went hand in hand.

Germans

100 Percent Americanism and Immigrants

While the government did its part to try to suppress dissent, going to war unleashed fierce hostilities toward the foreign born. Many Americans found it unsettling to be at war with countries that were the birthplaces of such a large segment of America's civilian population. Based on one contemporary survey, approximately 4,662,000 people living in the United States in 1917 came from territories governed by the Central powers, and nearly 2.5 million of these foreign-born inhabitants were German. In the highly charged atmosphere of 100 percentism, Americans already fidgety about alleged divided loyalties became ever more intolerant of the foreign born.

"Are you 100% American," ca. 1918.

Germans were among the first victims of the wave of intolerance that spread over wartime America. Before the United States went to war, anti-German sentiment was already affecting the lives of both foreign- and native-born Germans. Germany's invasion of Belgium in the summer of 1914, which the international community denounced as the "rape of Belgium," stirred anti-Germanism. Subsequent reports of German soldiers allegedly raping women and bayoneting babies intensified already negative feelings. German submarine warfare, which led to the loss of American lives, further inflamed passions against Germans. More and more, in the minds of many Americans, Germany became a barbarous nation and "Germans" became vicious "Huns." When Germany became America's archenemy, existing negative sentiments blossomed into a full-blown anti-German fury.

"The Hun—His Mark," J. Allen St. John poster, 1917.

America's entry into the war immediately generated a rage that turned a once esteemed nationality and its culture into objects of hatred. With mindless intensity, Americans set out to erase all traces of German culture. Restaurants removed German foods from their menus. Traditionally German dishes were given new names. Sauerkraut was renamed "liberty cabbage"; the hamburger was transformed into the "liberty sandwich"; cream-filled Bismarcks became known as "American beauties." An overly zealous doctor in Massachusetts reflected the extreme nature of the attack on anything German. Apparently trying to ensure that his sick patients would not be tagged with an onerous label, he diagnosed them with "liberty" measles instead of the traditional German kind. The attack on all things German generated a stampede of other types of name changing. Throughout the country, towns, streets, schools, parks, and businesses were given American-sounding names. Among countless examples were Berlin, Iowa, which became Lincoln; the German-American Bank in Buffalo turned into Liberty Bank; and Germania Life Insurance Company was renamed Guardian Life. German music also came under fire. Philadelphia's symphony excluded all German pieces from its programs. Performing Beethoven's compositions was forbidden in Pittsburgh. Elsewhere, German works were banned and performances by German musicians were cancelled. German theaters shut down.

The most strident attacks on German culture were directed toward the German language. The furor to rid the country of the "Hun" language led dozens of school boards to order German removed from the curriculum. By the end of the academic year 1918, nearly half of the states had taken steps either to limit or completely do away with the teaching of German. In some communities, abolishing the German language took a particularly nasty turn when local zealots burned German textbooks or literary materials as part of a "patriotic" ceremony. By one count, this happened 19 times in Ohio, while an unrecorded number of instances occurred in the region stretching from the East Coast into the Great Plains.

During the war, thousands of first- and second-generation Germans changed their names. Many Americanized them by adopting the English translation or spelling of their surnames. A person formally known as Koch often became Cook, and Schwartz became Black; by lopping off several letters Lunkenheimer became Lunken. Parents often decided, as one did, to alter their name because they wanted to protect their children from "hostility" and remove what might prove "an unnecessary burden" in the future.[3] This trend to change names, which began within months of the U.S. declaration of war, was indicative of how extensively the anti-German uproar touched the personal lives of individual people.

Beyond making wrenching decisions about their names, life in wartime America meant German immigrants had to live with fears for their personal safety, especially as suspicions about divided loyalties persisted. In an atmosphere of distrust, allegations about German conspiracies and plans for sabotage were rampant. Besides groundless rumors about plots, tales abounded of German Americans supposedly putting ground glass in bandages and food the Red Cross shipped to soldiers. People easily accepted wild claims about Germans poisoning water supplies or purposely spreading deadly germs. In this environment of suspicion, many became victims of vigilantism as 100 percenters took it upon themselves to keep an eye on Germans in their communities. On numerous occasions, Germans suffered physical abuse or humiliation at the hands of local "patriotic" groups or vigilantes. There were instances of Germans being forced publicly to kiss the American flag or sing patriotic songs. Many unfortunate victims of these patriotic excesses were made to do both—

kiss the flag and sing songs—as they were paraded through the streets. To intensify the humiliation, some fanatics forced their prey to make loud public declarations denouncing Germany and its leader, the kaiser.

The precise number cannot be determined, but there were frequent cases of Germans being beaten, publicly whipped, or tarred and feathered. Preachers who conducted foreign-language services received warnings or threatening visits by local "patriotic" societies, but on several occasions ministers were flogged or run out of town for preaching in German. In some places, Germans were hung from trees and had water sprayed on them or were cut down just before they strangled. Robert Prager, a German immigrant in Collinsville, Illinois, was not so fortunate. The victim of hysteria following unfounded rumors about a plot to blow up a local mine, Prager was the only recorded death resulting from anti-German vigilantism during the war. In April 1918, with no evidence of wrongdoing, this rather physically unappealing single male with one eye became the target of a militant crowd looking for alleged plotters. After a two-day ordeal, which included seeking refuge against determined mobs, being stripped to the waist, draped with the American flag, paraded barefoot through the streets, and forced to kiss the flag, Prager was lynched.

German Reaction

Although some German immigrants harbored sympathies for their motherland and most wished that war had not come, the vast majority supported the United States. They accepted, as did other ethnic groups, their obligations to their adopted country. During the war, however, the at least 8 million first- and second-generation Germans in the United States remained under a cloud of suspicion. Germans, who in their hearts knew that they were loyal Americans, were bewildered by the hatred and suspicion that affected their daily existence. One German immigrant expressed the sorrow tinged with outrage that many felt when he declared "in view of my record as a citizen I did expect from neighbors and fellow citizens a fair estimate and appreciation of my honesty and trustworthiness. It had all vanished."[4]

Not all Americans got caught up in the anti-German frenzy. Some courageous souls spoke out against the attack on German culture and the persecution of Germans; moreover, many Germans in the United States did not personally experience the heavy hand of overly zealous 100 percenters or the wrath of vigilantes. Some German Americans even formed their own superpatriotic associations or participated in the rampage against anything German and in the militant nationalism that swept the country. Still, for Germans the reality was that they lived in a society where their loyalty was questioned and their culture hated. A naturalized citizen, who had resided in the United States for a quarter century, again offered an immigrant's perspective on what it was like to be German in wartime America. From the time the United States went to war, he painfully revealed, "I was made to feel the pinpricks of an invisible but . . . hurtful and pernicious ostracism as a traitor to my adopted country."[5] Although not physically abused, this man felt the sting of hostile sideways glances and the subtle as well as open harassment that were elements of ordinary life for so many immigrants during these years.

Wartime Americanization

While Germans became targets of a hysteria directed toward a single nationality, "foreigners" in general became objects of an increasingly aggressive Americanization campaign. After April 1917, the movement expanded by leaps and bounds. This happened, in part, because people from all walks of life saw getting involved in programs to Americanize immigrants as a way of doing their part to help win the war. It became their contribution to the national campaign to promote 100 percent Americanism. Despite differences among its foot soldiers, the growing army of Americanizers shared the belief that learning English and becoming a citizen were evidence of an immigrant's loyalty.

The mounting enthusiasm for Americanizing immigrants led numerous agencies to build up their existing programs, and others to tread into what was for them new territory. School districts expanded the number of adult classes or began offering them for the first time. By war's end, the number of places providing adult language and civics training had reached 504, which represented a 37 percent increase over the 1914 total. A 1920 study revealed, however, that adult classes were typically less common in towns with sizable foreign-born populations than in cities. Throughout the land, churches, patriotic organizations, fraternal orders, women's clubs, civic groups, charities, chambers of commerce, and other local bodies developed some type of Americanization program. They published pamphlets, organized classes, sponsored lectures, held rallies, and sent volunteers into the foreign districts to visit immigrants in their homes. Generally, Americanizers who descended upon the foreign neighborhoods went there to proselytize Americanism and to recruit immigrants for language or citizenship classes—and often both. In the interests of Americanization and getting immigrants to cast off their Old World cultures, some of these unexpected visitors attempted to show residents, especially women, how to make their quarters, and thus their lifestyles, more "American."

The range of activities carried out in communities throughout the country suggests that immigrants could hardly avoid encountering an Americanization agency of one kind or another. On the streets or outside churches, meeting halls, theaters, saloons, or ethnic shops, immigrants might run into an Americanizer with a message or a brochure. Answering a knock at the door could possibly bring a homemaker face to face with someone trying to convince her to find time to learn English but who was also likely interested in giving her unsolicited advice on how to cook, keep house, or live in a more American style. Glancing around during even a short walk

A Department of Labor naturalization class, post-1911. Courtesy of Library of Congress.

in their neighborhoods, individuals undoubtedly saw notices in their own language for classes, meetings, or lectures. When they opened their foreign-language newspapers, immigrants found announcements about such activities scheduled for the towns or cities where they lived.

Despite the increasingly aggressive nature of wartime Americanization, programs targeting immigrants in their communities were based on appeal, not coercion. Immigrants could decide whether to attend or shun adult night schools. They could get rid of unwelcome strangers who came to their homes and tried to sell an Americanization message. As they strolled through their neighborhoods, immigrants could ignore the street notices and published advertisements for classes, lectures, and meetings. When they went to work, however, immigrants did not necessarily enjoy the same freedom of choice. As the 100 percent mentality gained vigor, immigrants had to contend with its force in the workplace, where employers wielded power.

After the United States became a combatant, company officials added to the militancy that characterized wartime Americanization. Besides implementing discriminatory hiring, promotion, or wage policies based on English-language skills or citizenship, plant managers collaborated with school systems to institute night courses and then monitored their employees' progress. They were also more inclined to capitulate to inten-sified pressure to set up factory classes. Lobbying by the Cleveland Ameri-canization Committee resulted in on-site classes being established at 22 local plants; other businesses in this northern Ohio region reportedly followed suit. In other ways, industrialists added to the 100 percent mentality that intruded on immigrants' lives. Some employers adopted the strategy of "Americanization through the pay envelope." This practice involved putting "simple lessons in citizenship" in workers' pay packets. Along with wages, the envelopes might contain notices about English and citizenship classes. Americanization posters with information in different languages advertised adult education classes. In addition to these striking posters on the walls, ads also appeared on bulletin boards. Although sincerity moved many immigrants to become U.S. citizens, campaigns at one South Chicago steelworks demonstrated the potential effect of workplace programs. A management-backed Americanization drive, which included shuttle service to the Federal Building during working hours, saw citizenship applications from the plant skyrocket from a paltry 58 in the final months of 1917 to 1,047 the following year.

Parades

A zeal for public expressions of national unity and 100 percent Americanism generated a rash of multiethnic "patriotic" parades. In 1918, the Committee on Public Information orchestrated a spectacular event designed to draw immigrants nationwide into a simultaneous show of patriotism.

Manifesting 100 Percent Patriotism

Reminiscent of Americanization Day three years earlier, this extravaganza was envisioned "as a day for the foreign born to manifest, by special celebrations, . . . loyalty to this country and to the cause for which we fight." After President Wilson expressed approval for the undertaking, a slew of state and local governments issued proclamations declaring Loyalty Days. Following several weeks of busy preparations, America finally went on parade to celebrate the Fourth of July 1918. Columns of ethnic groups filed through the streets of communities all over the country. In New York, reportedly more than forty nationalities and 70,000 to 75,000 persons joined in what the *New York Times* described as a "kaleidoscopic pageant" and a "wonderful demonstration of loyalty." Representatives of several nationalities traveled to the nation's capital, where they held pageants at various government buildings. Wearing folk costumes and waving the Stars and Stripes, they participated in a parade reviewed by Woodrow Wilson. Ironically, for ethnic groups: marching in segregated divisions, wearing ancestral costumes, and waving the American flag became public statements of their patriotism.

Liberty Loan Drives

Although immigrants faced subtle as well as heavy-handed pressure to manifest 100 percent Americanism, nowhere was the force applied more heavily than in the Liberty Loan campaigns. Although these massive drives to raise money to finance the war were aimed at all Americans, the foreign born received special attention. From coast to coast, eye-catching posters and pithy slogans reminded immigrants what America had done

"Cleveland Many Peoples, One Language," issued by Cleveland Americanization Committee, ca. 1917.

for them and, therefore, the debt they owed their "adopted country." A Second Liberty Loan poster depicting immigrant men, women, and children on a ship passing the Statue of Liberty conjured up memories of arriving in the land of freedom. It told immigrants to "Remember Your First Thrill of AMERICAN LIBERTY" and thus "YOUR DUTY— Buy United States Government Bonds." As an ad in one immigrant newspaper tellingly put it: "Your loyalty to our adopted country will be

"Remember Your First Thrill of American Liberty," anonymous, 1917.

measured by the number of Liberty Bonds you buy." The Committee on Public Information, which directed bond campaigns among the foreign born, announced the total purchases of each nationality. Bond drives, therefore, provided a way for immigrant groups to join in the national effort to win the war and, moreover, to receive public recognition for their support.

Immigrants felt pressure to participate in the bond campaigns, particularly in places where superpatriotic societies were exceptionally active. There were occasions when 100 percenters paid a visit to people's homes or publicly accosted neighbors who failed to purchase war bonds. Generally, though, strategists seeking subscriptions in immigrant communities relied on patriotic, emotional, and ethnically based appeals rather than on coercive methods. But, once again, when immigrants passed through the factory gates and entered their workplaces, they likely encountered strong-arm tactics. Managers or foremen who volunteered as solicitors for war bond drives counted on employees' support. Employers also expected workers to fork over part of their wages in plant-sponsored drives. A few small companies openly touted the slogan "A Bond or Your Job." During a bond campaign in the fall of 1918, the superintendent of one Pennsylvania mill advised employees that investing 25 days' pay was in their "best interest." People subsequently reported that individuals who ignored such "friendly advice" were fired or tarred and feathered. A mixture of this type of coercion, together with a sincere desire by employees to contribute to America's mobilization, meant that plants consistently met and often surpassed their quotas. A steel mill in Lackawanna, Pennsylvania, which exceeded its goal by more than $850,000 and collected more than $1.2 million, was only one of many plants in heavily immigrant-populated areas to experience enormous success.

It is impossible to determine how much immigrants contributed in the war bond campaigns during World War I. Companies generally did not distinguish between native- and foreign-born purchasers. Nevertheless, immigrants regularly made up a significant portion—sometimes half or more—of the workforce in factories that boasted 100 percent employee participation or surpassed projected sales during a drive. In their communities, immigrants responded to appeals to buy bonds in ethnically based campaigns. During one drive, Italians in New York City reportedly subscribed to $20 million worth of Liberty Bonds. Other ethnic groups claimed comparable successes. Immigrant organizations also invested millions of dollars from their treasuries and promoted bond sales among their members.

WARTIME AMERICA: THE VIEW FROM WITHIN IMMIGRANT COLONIES

Response to 100 Percentism

Coping with hostility as well as the country's 100 percent mentality was part of the immigrant experience in wartime America. A view of the times from the immigrants' perspective, however, reveals that the foreign born did not merely knuckle under to the pressure of 100 percentism. The vast majority of immigrants willingly participated in the country's national drive to win the war. For immigrants, however, patriotism during World War I was a complicated matter. Throughout the war, immigrants often combined "patriotic" activities to help their adopted country with efforts to assist their native lands.

Newspapers and Organizations

People of all nationalities worried that they might be subjected to the same hateful treatment German Americans were enduring. So, from the onset of American involvement in the war, immigrants took steps to demonstrate their loyalty to the United States. Realizing that their actions reflected upon the entire ethnic group, editors and organizations producing foreign-language publications exuded patriotism. Immediately after the U.S. declaration of war, many nationality newspapers, whose graphics did not already include the American flag, reproduced this hallowed emblem on their mastheads or editorial pages. Advising persons to demonstrate their loyalty to the United States became the admonition of the day. Aliens were urged to declare their intention to become U.S. citizens so, as one immigrant put it, they would "be considered a friend and supporter of this country." When announcing Loyalty Day 1918, more than one immigrant paper called on countrymen and countrywomen to take part in this "public expression" of patriotism. Throughout the war, newspapers carried appeals pleading with their foreign-born readers to buy Liberty Bonds. By purchasing just one bond, a typical editorialist told readers, they could show that people of their nationality were "loyal not only in words but in their hearts." To prove that their organizations were made up of "loyal" and "grateful citizens," officers begged members of ethnic societies to invest in Liberty Bonds.

Local Communities

While journalists and organization officials strove to call attention to their ethnic groups' allegiance to America, immigrants went to great lengths to do the same wherever they lived. An "All-Slav" event held in Pittsburgh during the summer of 1917 was representative of what was happening in local communities. Within just a few months of the U.S. declaration of war, people were feverishly trying to recruit 20,000 marchers for what organizers were advertising as a "patriotic manifestation." Slavic nationalities in Youngstown, Ohio, organized a multiethnic bazaar. Raving about the function, one English-language newspaper headlined it as "Slavs manifest true allegiance to adopted country." Individual nationalities also arranged their own separate activities. Immigrants touted these affairs, such as one planned for Mount Carmel, Pennsylvania, in the summer of 1917, as opportunities for them to "show Americans especially President Wilson" that they were "always at his service." Suspicion, intolerance, and vigilantism aimed toward immigrants might not have controlled their lives, but these were realities that nevertheless had to be reckoned with.

Homelands and "Patriotic" Displays

As they badgered fellow immigrants to manifest allegiance to their adopted country, ethnic activists still kept a close watch on developments affecting their native lands. Woodrow Wilson's expressed sympathy for oppressed nationalities and his principle of self-determination had the unexpected effect of inspiring immigrants to continue working for their homelands. In the eyes of ethnic nationalists, the American president became the champion of subject minorities everywhere. And the desire to influence Wilson's policies regarding postwar Europe kept the flurry of activities in America's ethnic colonies alive. Ethnic groups continued bombarding the president, government officials, and congressional representatives with telegrams, memoranda, and resolutions. Immigrant newspapers stepped up editorials in favor of liberating their homelands. To further their causes, they organized public rallies.

Ironically, marching in parades designed to manifest their loyalty to America became opportunities for ethnic groups to make political statements. Indeed, despite all the patriotic bravado, Loyalty Day 1918 was one of many instances when immigrants used a "patriotic" event to lobby for their homelands. Floats, together with national flags carried alongside the U.S. flag, symbolized the immigrants' dual interests. In New York, Capartho-Rusyns sported a banner appealing for "American Assistance to Russia." A placard carried by the Romanian unit proclaimed "Rumania's ideal—to be united." Albanian marchers probably had their tiny nation in mind when they lettered a sign affirming support for Wilson, "the protector of small nationalities." A Lithuanian banner boldly proclaimed: "Allied victory and independent Lithuania." Thus, while many Americans reveled in the nationwide display of patriotism on Loyalty Day, from many an immigrant's viewpoint, participating in this massive "patriotic" demonstration offered a chance to advance homeland causes.

Relief Efforts

Community Activities
Throughout the course of the Great War, immigrant communities were abuzz with activity. National organizations and newspapers set up funds to raise money to assist relief efforts, bankroll political activities, and subsidize military units fighting on behalf of independence movements. Although these campaigns supposedly relied on voluntary contributions, ethnic organizations imposed five- or ten-cent assessments that forced their members to fork over cash. Immigrant communities nationwide organized fund-raising events with proceeds earmarked for one or more of their groups' nationalist campaigns. Czechs in Omaha, Nebraska, who arranged a bazaar that netted more than $65,000 and a fellow Czech community in Texas that reaped profits exceeding $50,000 from a similar affair illustrated the pattern. People who attended church, lodge, or other community socials could expect to be approached by someone passing the hat for some type of nationalist organization or homeland-related cause.

Even immigrants who might have been politically indifferent could not ignore the needs of men, women, and children in their homelands who had become victims of a brutal war. During the era of U.S. neutrality, President Wilson actually encouraged the foreign born to engage in activities designed to relieve the suffering of people overseas. In 1916, for instance, the president proclaimed Lithuanian, Armenian, and Syrian days. On these occasions, Americans everywhere were asked to give generously to volunteers soliciting contributions or selling tags to collect money for aid programs in their respective fatherlands. Immigrants also conducted drives, went door to door, or held fund-raisers to garner money to aid refugees, widows, children, or exiles who had signed on as soldiers in ethnic legions of the Allied powers.

In addition to out-and-out fund-raising, ethnic communities initiated their own relief activities. By gathering together in sewing bees to knit socks and sweaters or make other garments, immigrant women used well-honed skills to assist people in their native lands. Czechs and Slovaks, for instance, sent clothes and "comfort kits" containing assorted basic necessities to soldiers fighting in the French army's Czechoslovak Legion. Getting involved in relief activities—and later in the U.S. war effort—provided opportunities for immigrant women, whose days had traditionally been spent in the vicinity of their homes, to venture farther out into neighborhoods and outside the foreign districts. Indeed, females typically took the lead in organizing clothing and blanket drives. On nationality "tag days," in particular, women fanned out into their communities and beyond to solicit contributions for homeland assistance. These volunteers reaped substantial contributions from devoting an entire day to asking people for donations in return for a small tag they could pin onto their outer garments. On a single day in just one Connecticut city, 600 Italian women reportedly found 35,000 people willing to give money.

Immigrants made relief activities for homelands part of their contribution to the American war effort. Once the United States entered the international conflict, nationalities in cities and towns nationwide formed branches of the American Red Cross. In many areas, various ethnic sewing bees and groups that had already been conducting fund-raising, blanket, and clothing drives became auxiliaries of this international relief agency. Associating with the Red Cross facilitated immigrants' ability to continue assisting people in their native lands. The garments that women in the ethnic auxiliaries knitted, the clothes they made, and the bandages they rolled were sent in Red Cross shipments to the Old Country. Italian women in one Connecticut location reportedly inserted notes in garments so the Italian soldier, refugee, or family would know that it came from a countrywoman in America. Immigrants also conducted activities independent of national relief agencies. Fraternal organizations initiated their own assistance programs. Jewish societies cooperated to raise dollars for those suffering in Europe as well as to set up religious and other services to meet the special needs of Jewish servicemen in the U.S. military.

Financial Sacrifices

Doing their part to help the United States win the war, while at the same time advancing homeland causes, strained immigrants' financial resources and, perhaps at times, their patience. At nearly every turn there lurked the possibility they would encounter an appeal of one kind or another. Whether couched in the subtle phrasing of friendly advice or expressed in more intimidating ways, immigrants routinely came face to face with requests for money. On payday, compatriots selling war bonds, soliciting funds for homeland relief, or seeking contributions for one nationalist program or another met workers at factory gates. While they relaxed in saloons or attended lodge meetings, religious services, or socials, people were approached by solicitors. On the streets, ladies selling tags asked for a few more cents. At school, youngsters were prevailed upon to put their pennies toward the purchase of War Saving Stamps. By conducting contests that pitted groups or grades against one another, schools got youngsters to part with money they had either earned themselves or begged out of their parents.

There were always the special fund-raising occasions, where people were bombarded with nationalist speeches, patriotic appeals, and pleas for donations. An affair organized by Slovaks in one Indiana town typified what was probably happening in immigrant communities throughout the United States. On this single occasion in 1917, Whiting's Slovaks heard speakers call on them to assist the movement to free their homeland from Hungarian control. A spokesperson for the Red Cross told revelers that contributing to that organization was the best way to show their loyalty to America. During the course of the day, people bumped into individuals soliciting financial support on behalf of the Old Country and American-sponsored relief efforts. When the money collected was divvied up at the end of the day, the people in charge saw to it that neither the Old Country nor the American effort was slighted. Slightly more than half of the revenues went to a Slovak organization's "million-dollar" campaign for the homeland, and the remainder was given to the American Red Cross.

Participating in "patriotic" demonstrations added to the bustle of life during wartime in the country's foreign districts. People busied themselves designing and constructing floats for local or nationally coordinated events. Committees worked feverishly to recruit marchers for ethnic columns in parades; they pressed countrymen, countrywomen, and children to don native costumes for the events. Take, for instance, the case of Gary, Indiana, where several ethnic colonies spent April 1917 getting ready for what turned out to be an impressive parade of more than 26,000 people of "all nationalities." Planning for their own rallies, bazaars, and other patriotic demonstrations added to the steady flutter in immigrant communities.

Supporting the American Effort

A blend of fear and sincere sentiments fueled a continuous blaze of "patriotic" activities in the foreign colonies. In many ways, though, daily life in immigrant communities was the same as elsewhere in the country. Immigrants made sacrifices and joined in conservation programs to ensure there was enough fuel and staples for America's military forces. When representatives of the Food Administration, which was the federal agency charged with managing the nation's foodstuffs, asked immigrant women to join in grassroots efforts to increase the country's supply, they agreed. Women signed pledge cards—often translated into their own languages—promising to conserve food and to remain on the lookout for waste in their communities. Immigrant households observed designated "meatless" and "wheatless" days as well as cut back on their use of butter and sugar. They curbed their energy usage. In many households, though, cutting back was an accustomed style of living rather than a new experience. Struggling to survive on meager wages and irregular income had made adjusting to scarcity a way of life for most immigrants. In this time of war, however, immigrants likely took these steps more in the spirit of doing their bit than out of a sense of forced deprivation.

Quality of Life

On the face of it, life for working-class immigrants seemingly improved. During the war, wages rose in many industries that employed large numbers of foreign workers. In going from $711 in 1914 to $1,324 in 1918, the annual income for laborers in steel mills, foundries, and machine shops increased by nearly 86 percent. Steelworkers at some mills took home nearly double their prewar earnings. Coal miners did better yet. By war's end, yearly earnings had jumped 123 percent over prewar levels. Overall, during the short time span between 1914 and 1918, the annual take-home pay of unskilled industrial laborers showed an increase of nearly 87 percent. The rise in incomes stemmed, in part, from workers putting in more hours on the job. Labor shortages, due both to the decline in immigration and to young men going into the military, sparked a return to the seven-day week and longer days in industries that had accepted reductions.

Just as annual incomes went up so, too, did the cost of living. By some estimates, when inflation was factored in, real wages for industrial labors climbed by only 19 percent to 25 percent during World War I. Thus, despite some striking increases in yearly incomes, because their purchasing power did not improve substantially, many immigrant families continued to live at near-subsistence levels. A constant stream of appeals for money to support the American war effort, to assist relief activities, and to back homeland causes further nibbled away at immigrants' incomes.

Eligibility and Enemy Aliens

While immigrants coped with life on the home front, able-bodied immigrant males did their part in the Great War by serving in the U.S. military. The Selective Service Act of 1917 made naturalized citizens and "declarants"—individuals

Immigrant Soldiers

who had filed their first papers—eligible for the draft. Aliens who had not declared their intention to become citizens could voluntarily waive their exemption and, hence, be added to the conscription pool. Men classified as "enemy aliens," however, could neither enlist nor be drafted into the U.S. armed services.

Throughout the war, issues involving immigrant eligibility for military service raised thorny questions. Nonnaturalized Germans already in the army in April 1917 posed the first problem because, as soon as the United States declared war, noncitizen Germans became enemy aliens ineligible for military duty. The adjutant general of the army directed that these Germans be permitted to remain in service if their division commanders deemed them loyal to the United States. Germans unwilling to risk fighting relatives and friends on the battlefields of Europe were discharged. Former inhabitants of the Austro-Hungarian Empire created a trickier issue. Declarants and aliens who gave up their exempt status qualified for the draft until December 1917, when the United States declared war on Austria-Hungary. With this declaration, they became enemy aliens ineligible to serve in the military. Many of the empire's onetime subjects resented this designation and the accompanying restriction on military service. Because they despised the Austro-Hungarian government and viewed the war as possibly ending with the liberation of their homelands, some former nationals wanted to join in America's fight.

Uncertainty over how to enforce the rules regarding noncitizens, together with the resolve of some individuals to skirt the rules, resulted in a significant number of enemy aliens joining the U.S. military. Given all the confusion and mix-ups, the army finally dealt with the issue by following the same policy it had laid down for Germans already in uniform in April 1917. Enemy aliens were allowed to stay in the service if their commanding officers determined they were "loyal" to the United States. During the 19 months the United States was at war, this policy resulted in 5,637 enemy aliens being discharged from the army; at the same time, thousands more served.

Language and Training Problems

Between 1917 and 1918, slightly more than 487,000 foreign-born individuals were drafted into military service and a few thousand more enlisted. All told, these recruits represented at least 46 separate nationalities. Immigrants posed a particularly difficult problem for a military rushing to ready troops for quick deployment overseas. A large portion of the foreign-born draftees could not read, write, or converse in English. Commanders at some training camps estimated that perhaps half to three-fourths of the immigrants reporting for duty at their facilities did not grasp English well enough to function effectively as soldiers. Both to solve the communication problems created by poor English-language skills and to boost morale among foreign-born recruits, the War Department endorsed a plan developed at Camp Gordon, Georgia. Under this system, during basic training men who could not speak English or had only minimal language skills were assigned to ethnic units. Bilingual first- or second-generation immigrants of their own nationality commanded them. Immigrant draftees who were sufficiently proficient in English joined the general recruits. In their special ethnic units, immigrants received military training in their native tongues, but, under the Camp Gordon Plan, they also attended English-language classes. Once the initial training period ended, if possible these immigrants were kept in small ethnic platoons attached to larger companies. Each day, immigrant soldiers in the ethnic units conversed in their own language but had opportunities to interact with English-speaking servicemen. When immigrants went into battle, fellow countrymen fought together but alongside other nationalities and native-born Americans.

Treatment

The young immigrants who marched off to basic training and subsequent deployment overseas endured the same horrendous experience as native-born soldiers. By most accounts, the antiforeign sentiment and negative stereotypes that had shaped popular conceptions, especially of the new immigrants, for more than two decades were, in the main, set aside. Jews still felt the sting of prejudice, but for many anti-Semitism was not the major problem. It was difficult and, at times impossible, for Jews to uphold dietary laws and observe Jewish holidays; moreover, by the end of the war, there were only six rabbis to tend to the 100,000 Jews in the U.S. military. The extremely small number of rabbis meant that Jewish soldiers' basic religious needs went unmet, but it also had a ripple effect on communities in America. Out of ignorance rather than prejudice, some burial details put crosses on the graves of Jewish soldiers killed in battle. The pain that grieving Jewish families back home felt was made all the worse when they received a picture and saw a cross on their beloved's final resting place.

Service and Naturalization

Being in the military, which gave immigrants the opportunity to serve their adopted country, ultimately eased the way for them to become U.S. citizens. By eliminating both the first papers and residency requirements, legislation passed in May 1918 made all foreign-born soldiers eligible for immediate citizenship. In line with the emphasis on patriotism that characterized wartime America, servicemen had to present "evidence of loyalty." Applicants were required to provide a witness who would personally vouch for them. The law further stipulated that, before an application could go forward, commanding officers had to be convinced of the petitioner's loyalty. A significant number of the applicants survived the scrutiny. Between the summers of 1917 and 1920, as a result of their military service, 244,300 aliens became U.S. citizens; they represented about 45 percent of the immigrants naturalized during those three years.

In every immigrant community, signs of military service and sacrifice were plainly evident. Service flags were prominently displayed in the windows of tenements and simple abodes. These small white banners, trimmed in red, contained a blue star for each male in the household currently serving in the military. The red-trimmed banners with one or more gold stars signified that a grieving family resided within; each gold star represented a soldier killed while in the service. Passersby also witnessed men of foreign and native birth heading off to register at the local office of the U.S. Selective Service Board. Parents, siblings, and spouses could be seen saying their tearful good-byes to young men going off to basic training. People likely saw Old World traditions at sway as some soon-to-be soldiers tucked away or were handed a treasured religious article or charm that they, or their loved ones, believed would protect them.

Foreign Legions

In some communities, people passed recruitment offices for ethnic divisions of foreign armies or, perhaps, glimpsed young men engaged in conversation with a recruiter for these units. During the war, the U.S. government permitted people representing three foreign divisions to recruit aliens not subject to the U.S. draft. These foreign legions included: the Polish Army of France; the Czechoslovak Legion, which was attached to the French army; and the Jewish Legion of Palestine, which was part of the British army. Enthusiasts viewed immigrant communities as fertile recruiting ground for the foreign military divisions because many of the residents were temporary migrants whose futures lay in their homelands.

Rousing support for the foreign legions added yet more zest to wartime activities in some immigrant communities. Besides opening centers in areas with large concentrations of Czech, Slovak, Polish, and Jewish immigrants, recruiters plastered posters throughout the neighborhoods. Local groups sponsored special events to stir enthusiasm as well as raise money for the foreign divisions. People attending any type of event might expect to hear speakers appealing both for volunteers and financial donations while someone collecting money passed through the crowd. Despite the fervor for independence and the fact that many migrants planned to return to their homelands after the war, only a relatively small number of foreign-born men responded to these recruiting efforts. Available records on recruits from the United States indicate that only about 3,000 Czechs and Slovaks joined the Czechoslovak Legion. The Jewish Legion managed to draw only 5,000 enlistments. By attracting about 20,000 volunteers from America's alien population, the campaign for the Polish Army of France fared much better.

"Czechoslovaks! Join Our Free Colors!," Vojtech Preissig poster issued by the Czechoslovakia Recruiting Office, Tribune Building, New York, ca. 1917.

IMMIGRANTS IN POSTWAR AMERICA

For many immigrants, getting involved in the war effort was the first time since they had set foot on American soil that they participated in life beyond their ethnic colonies. Even as communities organized their own activities, doing their bit to help win the war provided foreign-born men and women with unprecedented opportunities to share in the country's sense of dedication to a national purpose. But, while native- and foreign-born inhabitants were drawn together by common aims, many Americans still could not shake their suspicions or disdain for the "foreigners" in their midst. When the Great War came to an end on November 11, 1918, the intolerance toward the foreign born and foreign ways that had characterized the war years did more than flow easily into peacetime; it became a torrent of hostility.

Americanization and Immigrant Reaction In an ongoing atmosphere of intolerance, Americanizers pushed forward with programs to transform aliens into English-speaking citizens. During the war, some particularly zealous public officials had taken strong measures to try to wipe out foreign languages. The governor of Iowa, for instance, issued an order prohibiting the use of any language except English in schools, religious services, public conversations, and telephone communications. Following the war, an English-only tidal wave swept over much of the nation. Reflecting the same attitude evident in Iowa's wartime dictate, Nebraska required that meetings, except for religious services and lodge gatherings, be held in English. Determined to do away with foreign tongues, 15 states ordered that English be the sole language of instruction in every public and private elementary school. Several states enacted new regulations requiring that public school teachers be U.S. citizens.

Industrial jobs could still be linked to language competency or citizenship status. Stories in the immigrant press revealed that some employers were continuing the practice of discriminating against both aliens and naturalized citizens. In 1920, one immigrant organization informed its members that a Newark, New Jersey, firm had advertised that it would employ only persons who "can talk the English language." Workers who did not lose their jobs might still face pressure to attend Americanization classes. Factory schools sponsored by companies remained popular as Americanizers emphasized their potential for reaching larger numbers of immigrants. The Department of Interior's Board of Education reported that in 1919 more than 800 Americanization committees were hard at work in industrial plants. Antiforeign sentiment became extreme when companies adopted measures similar to those at a Baltimore establishment that announced it planned gradually to "discharge all foreigners, even if naturalized" and to replace them with "genuine Americans." While some employers openly targeted immigrant laborers, some state legislatures passed laws permitting discrimination against foreign-born professionals.

The continuing stress on Americanism and English-language proficiency was part of the popular climate affecting the real-life existence of ordinary immigrants, but, despite such relentless emphasis, immigrants did not simply cave in to aggressive Americanization. Some fought back. English-language editorials in immigrant newspapers lambasted proposed legislation that would make studying English obligatory for every non-English-speaking person between the ages of 21 and 45. One editorialist typified the attack on compulsory Americanization by pointing out that the idea was "inhumane" and "stupid," especially for laborers who worked 10 to 12 hours every day or for women who would have to leave children and household duties to attend school. There was, he admitted, no quibbling with the premise that "every resident of this country" should be encouraged to study English "as a matter of expediency." Like so many immigrants, he did not question the necessity of knowing English or challenge its proper standing as the country's premier language; rather, he rejected heavy-handed measures aimed at wiping out all other languages. He and the many immigrants whose views he articulated called, instead, for encouraging bilingualism. While some foreign-born journalists and organization officers railed against forced Americanization, ordinary immigrants who opposed the idea reacted by refusing to enroll in programs. Even in the weighty climate of 100 percentism, into the 1920s advocates of Americanization continued to complain about the poor and irregular attendance at the adult classes.

Besides being the objects of intense campaigns to Americanize them, immigrants also became targets of a hyste- **The Red Scare** ria that gripped the nation in 1919 and 1920. Only a few months after the guns of war fell silent in Europe, America experienced the early stages of what came to be known as the "Red Scare." Lasting for nearly a year and a half, this was a period when many Americans believed that radicals were hatching plots to overthrow the government. Because, in the popular mind, immigrants were associated with radicalism, much of the paranoia that characterized the Red Scare focused on them.

Radicals and Unrest

A combination of international and domestic events stoked popular fears that foreign radicals in America were allegedly conspiring against the United States. The Russian Revolution, which occurred in November 1917, stirred apprehension, especially as the victorious Bolsheviks called for working classes around the world to rise up in revolution. In 1919 and 1920, turmoil shook industries far and wide in the United States. The Russian Bolsheviks did not instigate them; nevertheless, approximately 3,600 work stoppages involving perhaps 4 million workers put the country's nerves on edge. Three strikes in particular grabbed national attention. A citywide strike, which paralyzed Seattle for a short period in January 1919, followed in September by Boston policemen walking off the job led many to accept the idea that radical conspiracies were afoot. Then, as the Boston police were on the picket lines, 365,000 steelworkers went on strike. In the public's mind, a massive nationwide strike in an industry with an enormous immigrant workforce reinforced notions that radicalism flourished among the foreign born. Although workers were striking for fewer hours and better wages, popular opinion blamed unrest in so many industries on foreign radicals who wanted to ignite a class revolution.

At the same time that a rash of labor strikes rocked postwar America, a series of bombings and failed attempts deepened the national panic. In the spring and early summer of 1919, mail bombs were addressed to judges, government officials, legislators, and business tycoons. In June, a bomb exploded at the home of Attorney General A. Mitchell Palmer. Evidence at the scene suggested that the bomber, who inadvertently blew himself up, was an Italian immigrant. No one ever claimed responsibility for any of the bombings or botched tries, and neither local nor federal law enforcement officers ever uncovered evidence of conspiracies or arrested anyone. Nevertheless, in an environment shaped by panic and stereotypes, the unrest in the nation was blamed on "foreign agitators."

Raids and Deportation

Legislators and authorities at the federal level helped inflame the public temper. By amending legislation governing deportation, the U.S. Congress made it easier to expel radicals. Accepting guilt by association, in October 1918 it changed the rules so that—regardless of how long they had lived in the United States—aliens could be deported solely on the grounds of membership in an organization that advocated revolution or sabotage. Armed with this law, Attorney General Palmer launched his own crusade to crush the "Reds." In the fall of 1919, when strikes, bombs, and disturbances had already frazzled the nation's nerves, Palmer helped further whip up the frenzy. Claiming that foreigners made up 90 percent of the country's radicals, he undertook to banish the extremists from America. Under his leadership, Justice Department agents began rounding up immigrants suspected of being radicals. The dramatic end to these first actions came on December 21, 1919, when 249 people were put aboard the *Buford*, which was dubbed the "Soviet Ark," and deported to Russia. Subsequent investigations revealed that the majority of the immigrants forced to set sail on the ship had never engaged in violence and did not have criminal records. Forty-three were anarchists already slated for deportation and another 199 were expelled because of their membership in the Union of Russian Workers, which was deemed a radical organization. The other seven individuals fell into the "public charge" and "criminal" categories.

A few weeks after the *Buford* chugged out of New York Harbor, the Red Scare reached a climax. On January 2, Justice Department agents, assisted by local police, conducted simultaneous raids in 33 cities in 23 states. During this nationally coordinated operation, agents barged into people's homes and burst into meeting halls, pool rooms, and anywhere else immigrants gathered. As a rule, everyone on the premises was arrested and taken to detention centers or police stations. An estimated 4,000 individuals were carted off to jail that day. Some persons were let go immediately, but many remained in cramped cells for weeks while awaiting a preliminary hearing. In some instances, persons who visited the detainees were arrested. All told, of the estimated 5,000 to 6,000 people netted in raids carried out in December and January, only 591 persons were finally deported. A careful study by the Department of Labor, which had jurisdiction over deportation proceedings, revealed that the vast majority of immigrants snagged by the Justice Department and its accomplices were guilty of no wrongdoing.

The End

Palmer continued to fan public fears and keep the panic over the so-called foreign threat alive. His predictions that a plot to overthrow the government would get under way on May 1, 1920, finally helped bring the public delirium to an end. When May Day came and neither the predicted wave of bombings nor the massive general strike took place, Palmer's credibility with the public died and the national hysteria waned. Although Americans remained ever wary of foreigners in their midst, by the fall of 1920 the Red Scare was over.

The Immigrants' Perspective

Despite its spectacular nature, the Red Scare that seized the nation was also local. It brought immigrants in contact with government agents and their civilian accomplices. At the community level, authorities and volunteer groups hounded foreigners. It was not unusual for the police to arrest individuals whom they judged suspicious looking and to hold them overnight. Russian immigrants, in particular, could expect this treatment. The sympathy that Russian Jews displayed for a revolution that overthrew the czarist government, which had historically sanctioned anti-Semitic violence and discrimination, reinforced the misguided tendency to link them to radicalism. Instances of immigrants being physically abused or tarred and feathered also occurred.

After the Red Scare subsided, superpatriots still stalked communities. Hundred percenters continued to take aim at new immigrants, especially as the hatred of Germans gave way to a resurfacing disdain for peoples from southern and eastern Europe. One foreign-born commentator portrayed what ordinary immigrants were coping with when he proclaimed, "We are living in an age of confused slogans" and "are still living in the atmosphere of the war." Another immigrant gave voice to the cynicism and resentment that many surely felt. "If you haven't yet found your place in your community, just pick on the foreigners," he sneered in the spring of 1920. Immigrants lived in a hostile society, and they knew it.

Language and Citizenship

During the 10 years spanning 1910 to 1920, language patterns and citizenship trends did change. In 1910, more than 2.6 million immigrants twenty-one or older admitted **Postwar Trends** they could not speak English; by1920, this number had declined to just less than 1.4 million. In 1910, individuals unable to speak English made up slightly over 22 percent of adult immigrants residing in the United States at the time of the census; by 1920, they represented just more than 11 percent. The percentage of immigrants that had become naturalized citizens or, equally important, had taken out their first papers had also risen. With slightly over 1.6 million people filing between 1914 and 1919, the war years experienced a significant spike in declarations of intention. Still, by 1920, nearly one-third of immigrant males were aliens who had taken no steps to acquire U.S. citizenship. Because the citizenship status of married women remained linked to that of their husbands, patterns for females cannot be determined.

Migration

Following the armistice in November 1918, migration trends also changed. The immediate postwar era witnessed a dramatic reversal of patterns that had historically characterized the movement to and from the United States. For roughly two years after the war ended, more people departed than entered the country. Individuals hurrying to reconnect with family and friends in Europe probably made up the majority of the nearly 427,000 U.S. citizens who left. Although these citizens likely planned to return to America, the intentions of the nearly 300,000 aliens who exited are unclear. Regardless of intent, from 1918 to 1920 twice as many people went out of the United States as came into it. In 1920, the trend began to shift as departures nearly equaled arrivals, and by 1921 migration seemingly had reverted to prewar patterns. That year, officials reported that approximately 398,000 aliens went out of the country while slightly double that number—837,013 aliens—entered. Migrants from North America accounted for some of this coming and going. The record of arrivals and departures indicated, however, that people booking transatlantic voyages were responsible for what appeared to be a reemergence of the earlier two-way migratory streams.

Nativism

Fears about "undesirable" immigrants pouring into the United States added a sense of alarm to the already rapidly resurfacing of nativist sentiments. In 1920 and 1921, for example, readers of the popular *Saturday Evening Post* came across dire predictions about an impending deluge of "undesirables." In a series of articles, Kenneth L. Roberts, a longtime critic of the new immigrants, embellished self-proclaimed "emergency" warnings by adding his own firsthand descriptions of ports in Europe. According to him, thousands were supposedly waiting to set sail. He was putting the country on alert: An ignorant humanity, infested with contagious diseases, was going to swarm into the United States and sink into the country's slums. These were not oppressed human beings in search of asylum. Instead, Roberts claimed, they were economic refugees who would become "parasites on the community." Roberts's diatribes did not represent an exception. Anti-immigrant materials regularly appeared in the media.

News reports occasionally added to popular fears. In late September 1920, the *New York Times* reported that a "near riot" at Ellis Island forced the commissioner of immigration to halt temporarily the landing of passengers so the "congestion" at the receiving depot could be relieved. According to the report, "so many immigrants" had arrived that they could not be quickly processed. Weary of waiting for their relatives or friends, people outside stormed the gate. Although only a small portion of the country's newspaper readership likely saw the story, the event nevertheless pricked fears lurking in the popular mind. Even longtime sympathizers of the foreign born were pondering whether, perhaps, the time had come either to reduce or temporarily suspend immigration. This was certainly the view of a majority in the U.S. Congress when it passed the Quota Act in May 1921 and thus imposed measures that were designed to reduce immigration at least for the short term.

As it turned out, 1920 was a landmark in the history of American immigration. It was the last year that there **1920: Taking** were no numerical limits on immigration into the country. **Measure** Despite growing restrictions on who was admissible, up to June 1921 anyone who met the eligibility requirements could enter the United States. Quotas were unprecedented, and total numbers were irrelevant. It was the historical policy of no numerical limitations that had allowed millions and millions to migrate to America. Newly enacted restrictions in 1921 did more than reduce the number of immigrants who could enter the nation; they had a personal impact on the foreign born already in the country. Those planning for loved ones to join them not only had to comply with new regulations and procedures, in all likelihood they also had to wait a considerable length of time before relatives could come. It was no longer simply a matter of sending prepaid passage to someone and then hoping he or she would pass inspection at the receiving stations. And previously undecided migrants had to make up their minds whether they wanted to stay in America. Quotas imposed on countries outside the Western Hemisphere meant that aliens who left the United States could no longer simply return. Limiting the number of arrivals and putting an end to the back-and-forth movement that had characterized overseas migration for over a quarter century also had an affect on immigrant communities. Although people still moved around and single individuals still lived with their families, ethnic communities no longer contained large contingents of temporary migrants and recent arrivals from the Old Country. By and large, they were made up of permanent immigrants who believed their future lay in America.

In 1920, as Americans and policy makers fretted over the impact that immigration was having on the country, the foreign born carried on with their lives. Most were still striving to secure the goals that had prompted them to migrate. Despite all the folklore about immigrants imagining America as a country where wealth was to be had, most people had come with reasonable expectations. Although migrants' aspirations were characteristically modest, they certainly were not the same. In the main, immigrants arrived with their own views about what constituted success and, moreover, typically defined it within the context of their own cultural values. Some understood success as owning a home and providing a decent living for their families. Others considered becoming independent tradespeople or business owners as constituting success. Achieving such independence and, perhaps, a higher social status also allowed them to provide for their families. There were those who defined success in terms of their children's futures. In this case, immigrants struggled so their children could acquire the education or have a stable business to achieve a secure future. Even though ethnic groups had their own standards for measuring success, there were always those individuals who did not match any pattern. They went after goals that bore no similarity to others in their nationality group. The fact that they seemed out of sync only demonstrated that, while cultural values and backgrounds influenced them, immigrants were not captive to any set cast of mind. Additionally, immigrants did not remain unaffected by American culture. They blended American values they liked with those they wanted to preserve from their premigration past.

However they measured success, most immigrants who came in the half century preceding 1920 had not yet achieved it. Except for successful entrepreneurs and those who had taken up farming and had effectively persevered, the vast majority of immigrants probably did not yet enjoy what they considered "the good life." In 1920, day after day, foreign-born men and women still worked long hours. The greater part of them still did unskilled labor, nearly all were still scraping by while looking to the future, and most still lived in run-down housing and tenements. In 1920, immigrants also still resided in distinctive districts, and many would remain there for the foreseeable future. Probably only a fraction of the millions dreamed of moving up America's social ladder, and few actually had. Nevertheless, immigrants who remained locked in the lower ranks of America's socioeconomic scale discovered that their own communities provided a unique avenue of mobility. Through fraternal, church, and sundry organizational activities, people who had not been prominent in their native lands gained recognition and even power within the parameters of their own ethnic communities. It was true that success took many forms. And it was also true that in 1920 most immigrants were still striving to realize the promise they believed America offered.

With newly imposed restrictions in the early 1920s, the massive second wave that had dominated American immigration for three decades came to a rather abrupt end. Migration into the United States, however, did not stop. In 1922, Felipe Orozco was but one of many who migrated from Mexico. And his story was similar to Mexicans who had come before him and those who would soon follow. He spent two years on a section gang in Le Grand, California, where he laid rails for $2.46 a day, before heading off to Los Angeles to get a job with a construction company. Even with stricter procedures ostensibly in place as of 1921, Orozco apparently had had no trouble crossing the border. Except for keeping a close watch to ensure that Chinese did not get by them, U.S. officials along the Mexican border had traditionally not rigorously enforced laws requiring inspections of all incoming migrants. After 1917, El Paso, Texas, represented the dramatic exception. Migrants who arrived at the Santa Fe Street Bridge, which was the primary crossing area into El Paso, endured a terrible ordeal. Individuals were required to bathe, undergo delousing, and have their clothes and baggage fumigated. In the nude, they were inspected and deloused with gasoline or harsh chemicals. Immigrants who spoke of the dreaded "Ellis Island" experience could hardly have imagined such a horror.

As the European waves subsided to a mere trickle after 1920, increasingly Mexicans, Canadians, and other peoples from the Western Hemisphere filled the migratory currents streaming into United States. Some

International bridge connecting Juarez, Mexico and El Paso, Texas, ca. 1909. Courtesy of Library of Congress.

of these migrants were part of ongoing chains while others were the pioneers of new ones. Some were immigrants intending to stay permanently while others were migrant laborers planning to return to their homelands. Regardless of their intentions, like those who came before them, these newcomers were willing to struggle with the challenges of daily life in the United States in order to try to make real what they believed was the promise of America.

NOTES

Immigrant life story derived from Manuel Gamio, ed., *The Life Story of the Mexican Immigrant* (1931; repr., New York: Dover, 1971). Immigrant quotations and translations from the original documents were also derived from June Granatir Alexander, *Ethnic Pride, American Patriotism: Slovaks and Other New Immigrants in the Interwar Era* (Philadelphia: Temple University Press, 2004). Life stories and quotations derived from other secondary sources are cited separately.

1. As quoted in Peter Roberts, *The New Immigration: A Study of the Industrial and Social Life of Southeastern Europeans in America* (New York: Macmillan, 1912), 282; John F. McClymer, "The Americanization Movement and the Education of the Foreign-Born Adult, 1914–25," in *American Education and the European Immigrant: 1840–1940,* ed. Bernard Weiss (Urbana: University of Illinois Press, 1982), 106.

2. As quoted in Gerd Korman, *Industrialization, Immigrants, and Americanizers: The View from Milwaukee, 1866–1921* (Madison: State Historical Society of Wisconsin, 1967), 144–46.

3. As quoted in, Frederick C. Luebke, *Bonds of Loyalty: German Americans and World War I* (De Kalb: Northern Illinois University Press, 1974), 282.

4. As quoted in, ibid., 227–28.

5. As quoted in, ibid.

Glossary

alien—Foreign-born, nonnaturalized individual. *See also* naturalized citizen.

Allied powers—The empire and nations united against the Central powers during World War I. The major Allied powers were the British Empire, France, and the Russian Empire. When the United States entered the war in 1917, it joined forces with these powers. *See also* Central powers.

anarchist—One who rejects all forms of authority and who believes in or advocates violent measures to overthrow established government.

binder—A machine or attachment on a reaper that bundles and ties cut grain. *See also* reaper.

birds of passage—Disdainful term for temporary immigrants or foreign-born workers who traveled repeatedly between the United States and their homeland. *See also* sojourner.

blacklist—To put on a list that excludes an individual or group from particular activities or benefits. This tactic was used to thwart union activity; employers refused to hire individuals whose names appeared on blacklists.

Bolshevik—A member of the radical wing of the Russian Social Democratic Labor Party that seized control of the government in Russia in 1917. *See also* Russian Revolution

Central powers—The empires and nations united against the Allied powers during World War I. The major Central powers were the German

Empire, the Austro-Hungarian Empire, and the Ottoman Empire. The Ottoman Empire was often simply referred to as Turkey.

conjunctivitis—Inflammation of the inner surface of the eyelid.

Dillingham Commission—A joint Senate-House body appointed in 1907 to investigate every facet of "the subject of immigration." Officially the Immigration Commission, it is commonly identified with its chairman, Senator William P. Dillingham of Vermont. Following three years of investigation and tabulating data, it published a forty-two-volume report in 1911. Although the commission operated under the biased assumption that new immigrants were "undesirables" and detrimental to the United States, its published reports contained important raw data on immigration and contemporary immigrant life.

enemy alien—Noncitizen immigrant born in a country at war with the United States.

extended family—The family unit that, in addition to parents and their children, includes relatives. *See also* nuclear family.

festa—(pl. *feste*). Annual festival organized by Italian villagers to celebrate their village's patron saint. A popular tradition upheld by Italian immigrant communities in the United States.

first-generation immigrants—Also known as the first generation; includes all foreign-born individuals regardless of their age at the time of arrival.

folk—Refers to the culture, traditions, and lifestyles of common people.

harrow—An agricultural implement consisting of a wood or metal frame with attached spikes or disks and used to break up clods of dirt and to level plowed ground.

hyphenism—Term employed by Americans of the World War I era to describe the alleged conflicted loyalties of immigrants; immigrants were accused of putting homeland interests before those of the United States.

Immigration Commission—(U.S.) *See* Dillingham Commission.

lutfisk—Swedish spelling for dried fish cured in lye and traditionally served at Christmastime. The Norwegian spelling for this popular Scandinavian dish is lutefisk.

nationality church—Served a particular ethnic group and was based on language or ethnicity instead of territorial boundaries.

nativism—A fierce hostility toward immigrants rooted in the belief that they are detrimental to the country or to the "American" way of life.

naturalization—The process through which a foreign-born individual becomes a citizen.

naturalized citizen—Foreign-born individual who legally becomes a citizen of a country. *See* naturalization.

nuclear family—The family unit made up of a father, a mother, and their children. *See also* extended family.

100 percenters—Individuals, groups, or agencies who aggressively promoted unqualified patriotism during World War I and afterward often by relying on intimidation or resorting to vigilante-style measures.

Orthodox churches—In the United States included the Russian Orthodox, Greek Orthodox, Serbian Orthodox, and Syrian Orthodox churches. Similar in doctrine, these four bodies were independent of one another but were collectively known as the Eastern Orthodox churches.

Pinkerton detectives—Employees of the Pinkerton National Detective Agency founded in 1850 by Scottish immigrant Allan Pinkerton. Specializing in antiunion activities, these agency employees functioned as industrial spies and served as private security forces during strikes. Their aggressive activities to break strikes earned them the reputation of being thugs. Industrial workers both despised and feared the Pinkertons.

pogrom—Organized attack on or massacre of Jews in czarist Russia. Beginning in 1881, these government-condoned assaults, which included killings, beatings, and looting, took place sporadically over a thirty-year period.

polygamist—A person who has two or more spouses at the same time.

privy—An outdoor toilet. Usually a shed or small building with interior benches with holes cut out to accommodate users. These toilets did not have flush capabilities.

privy vault—The cavity underneath privies where excreted human fluid and solid waste were deposited. *See also* privy.

reaper—Agricultural machine used for harvesting (cutting and gathering) grains.

public charge—A person requiring any form of financial aid or charitable assistance.

remittance—Money sent in the form of cash or a financial draft to an individual or agency

Russian Revolution—A series of events in 1917 that began with the overthrow of the czarist regime in February and culminated with the Bolshevik Party, led by Vladimir Lenin, seizing control of the government in October. According to the Gregorian calendar, the Bolshevik takeover occurred in early November; however, according to the Julian calendar, which was used in Russia at the time, it occurred in late October. *See also* Bolshevik.

second-generation immigrants—Also known as the second generation; includes American-born children with either one or two foreign-born parents.

section gang—Crews responsible for the maintenance of specific segments of railroad tracks.

sojourner—Temporary immigrant.

trachoma—A contagious disease of the inner eyelid characterized by inflammatory granulations.

transient—Immigrant who remained temporarily in a location in the United States. *See also* sojourner.

undesirables—Disdainful term commonly used by Americans to refer to southern and eastern European immigrants. It was grounded in the belief that these peoples were biologically and culturally inferior and would not assimilate but, instead, would debase American society.

viticulture—The cultivation of grapes, often for use in wine making.

Selected Bibliography

This volume is indebted to a rich variety of primary and secondary sources. The bibliography is by no means a complete listing of the sources that informed it. In addition to decennial censuses and a wide variety of materials generated by immigrants, the author drew on contemporary investigative studies. Many of these late nineteenth- and early twentieth-century investigations were commissioned by federal, state, and local bodies or undertaken by reform-oriented organizations or individuals. Conducted by critics as well as sympathetic advocates, the findings and narrative often reflected prejudices or hostile attitudes toward immigrants, especially the new immigrants from Europe and peoples from Asia. Despite flawed assumptions and biases, contemporary studies still contain raw data that, when treated carefully, shed light on immigrant daily life.

The author relied heavily on the scholarly literature on immigrants and immigration. This scholarship is not only vast but, since the 1960s, has grown immensely. The massiveness and cumulative nature of the scholarly literature preclude listing every secondary source that influenced the author's ideas or shaped the narrative. Besides acknowledging works that were particularly influential, the bibliography is designed to serve as a guide to readers who wish to pursue particular topics. While classics and standard works are listed, more recent publications are emphasized. The author also attempted to cite reprint editions. These later editions are often prefaced with informative introductions or contain bibliographic material that will direct interested readers to older or other relevant materials. Selected Web sites dealing with immigration and immigrant topics are also listed. These sites provide access to online documents, records, and data as well as information on related Web sites. The bibliography closes with a short list of documentary films on immigrants and immigration.

GENERAL HISTORIES AND REFERENCE WORKS

Barkan, Elliott R., ed. *A Nation of Peoples: A Sourcebook on America's Multicultural Heritage.* Westport, CT: Greenwood Press, 1999.

Bodnar, John. *The Transplanted: A History of Immigrants in Urban America.* Bloomington: Indiana University Press, 1985.

Daniels, Roger. *Coming to America: A History of Immigration and Ethnicity in American Life.* 2nd ed. New York: Perennial, 2002.

Dinnerstein, Leonard, and David M. Reimers. *Ethnic Americans: A History of Immigration.* 4th ed. New York: Columbia University Press, 1999.

Gale Encyclopedia of Multicultural America. 2nd ed. 2 vols. Detroit: Gale, 2000.

Handlin, Oscar. *A Pictorial History of Immigration.* New York: Crown, 1972.

Jones, Maldwyn A. *American Immigration.* 2nd ed. Chicago: University of Chicago Press, 1992.

———. *Destination America.* New York: Holt, Rinehart, and Winston, 1975.

Kraut, Alan M. *The Huddled Masses: The Immigrant in American Society, 1880–1921.* 2nd ed. Wheeling, IL: Harlan Davidson, 2001.

Nugent, Walter. *Crossings: The Great Transatlantic Migrations, 1870–1914.* Bloomington: Indiana University Press, 1992.

Schoener, Allon. *Portal to America: The Lower East Side, 1870–1925.* New York: Holt, Rinehart, and Winston, 1967.

Seller, Maxine. *To Seek America: A History of Ethnic Life in the United States.* Rev. ed. Englewood, NJ: Ozer, 1988.

Stolarik, M. Mark, ed. *Forgotten Doors: The Other Ports of Entry to the United States.* Philadelphia: Balch Institute Press, 1988.

Takaki, Ronald. *A Different Mirror: A History of Multicultural America.* Boston: Little, Brown, 1993.

———. *Strangers from Different Shores.* Boston: Little, Brown, 1989.

Taylor, Philip. *The Distant Magnet: European Emigration to the U.S.A.* New York: Harper and Row, 1971.

Thernstrom, Stephan, ed. *Harvard Encyclopedia of American Ethnic Groups.* Cambridge, MA: Harvard University Press, 1980.

Thistlethwaite, Frank. "Migration from Europe Overseas in the Nineteenth and Twentieth Centuries," XIe Congrès International des Sciences Historiques, *Rapports,* 5:32–60. Uppsala, Sweden, 1960. Reprinted in *A Century of European Migrations, 1830–1930,* ed. Rudolph J. Vecoli and Suzanne M. Sinke, 17–49. Urbana: University of Illinois Press, 1991.

IMMIGRATION AND NATURALIZATION POLICY

Bennett, Marion T. *American Immigration Policies: A History.* Washington, DC: Public Affairs Press, 1963.

Gardner, Martha. *Qualities of a Citizen: Women, Immigration, and Citizenship, 1870–1965.* Princeton, NJ: Princeton University Press, 2005.

Gavit, John Palmer. *Americans by Choice.* 1922. Reprint, Montclair, NJ: Patterson Smith, 1971.

Gyory, Andrew. *Closing the Gate: Race, Politics, and the Chinese Exclusion Act.* Chapel Hill: University of North Carolina Press, 1998.

Hutchinson, E. P. *Legislative History of American Immigration Policy, 1798–1965.* Philadelphia: University of Pennsylvania Press, 1981.

Konvitz, Milton R. *Civil Rights in Immigration.* Ithaca, NY: Cornell University Press, 1953.

LeMay, Michael, and Elliott Robert Barkan, eds. *U.S. Immigration and Naturalization Laws and Issues: A Documentary History.* Westport, CT: Greenwood Press, 1999.

Pitkin, Thomas. *Keepers of the Gate: A History of Ellis Island.* New York: New York University Press, 1975.

Preston, William Jr. *Aliens and Dissenters: Federal Suppression of Radicalism, 1903–1933.* 2nd ed. Urbana: University of Illinois Press, 1994.

Salyer, Lucy E. *Laws Harsh as Tigers: Chinese Immigrants and the Shaping of Modern Immigration Law.* Chapel Hill: University of North Carolina Press, 1995.

Ueda, Reed. "Naturalization and Citizenship." In *Harvard Encyclopedia of American Ethnic Groups,* ed. Stephan Thernstrom, 734–48. Cambridge, MA: Harvard University Press, 1980.

Vecoli, Rudolph J. "Immigration, Naturalization and the Constitution." *News for Teachers of Political Science* 50 (Summer 1985): 9–16.

LETTERS, INTERVIEWS, AND AUTOBIOGRAPHIES

Adamic, Louis. *Laughing in the Jungle: The Autobiography of an Immigrant in America.* 1932. Reprint, New York: Arno, 1969.

Antin, Mary. *The Promised Land.* 1912. Reprinted with forward by Oscar Handlin. Boston: Houghton Mifflin, 1969.

Barton, H. Arnold, ed. *Letters from the Promised Land: Swedes in America, 1840–1914.* Minneapolis: University of Minnesota Press, 1975.

Blegen, Theodore C., ed. *Land of Their Choice: The Immigrants Write Home.* Minneapolis: University of Minnesota Press, 1955.

Bodnar, John, ed. *Workers' World: Kinship, Community, and Protest in an Industrial Society, 1900–1940.* Baltimore: Johns Hopkins University Press, 1982.

Bok, Edward. *The Americanization of Edward Bok.* New York: Charles Scribner's Sons, 1922.

Coan, Peter M. *Ellis Island Interviews: In Their Own Words.* New York: Facts on File, 1997.

Conway, Alan, ed. *The Welsh in America: Letters from the Immigrants.* Minneapolis: University of Minnesota Press, 1961.

Dublin, Thomas, ed. *Immigrant Voices: New Lives in America, 1773–1986.* Urbana: University of Illinois Press, 1993.

Erickson, Charlotte. *Invisible Immigrants: The Adaptation of English and Scottish Immigrants in Nineteenth-Century America.* Coral Gables, FL: University of Miami Press, 1972.

Ets, Marie Hall. *Rosa: The Life of an Italian Immigrant.* With forward by Rudolph J. Vecoli. Minneapolis: University of Minnesota Press, 1970.

Gamio, Manuel, ed. *The Life Story of the Mexican Immigrant.* 1931. Reprint, New York: Dover, 1971.

Gjerde, Jon, ed. *Major Problems in American Immigration and Ethnic History.* Boston: Houghton Mifflin, 1998.

Hareven, Tamara K., and Randolph Langenbach, eds. *Amoskeag: Life and Work in an American Factory City.* New York: Pantheon, 1978.

Holt, Hamilton, ed. *The Life Stories of Undistinguished Americans as Told by Themselves.* 2nd ed. With new introduction by Werner Sollors. 1906. New York: Routledge, 1990.

Kamphoefner, Walter D., Wolfgang Helbich, and Ulrike Sommer, eds. *News from the Land of Freedom: German Immigrants Write Home.* Trans. Susan Carter Vogel. Ithaca, NY: Cornell University Press, 1991.

Morrison, Joan, and Charlotte Fox Zabusky, eds. *American Mosaic: The Immigrant Experience in the Words of Those Who Lived It.* 1980. Reprint, Pittsburgh: University of Pittsburgh Press, 1993.

Namias, June. *First Generation: In the Words of Twentieth-Century American Immigrants.* Rev. ed. Urbana: University of Illinois Press, 1992.

Nee, Victor G., and Brett de Bary Nee. *Longtime Californ': A Documentary Study of an American Chinatown.* New York: Pantheon, 1972.

Panuzio, Constantine E. *The Soul of an Immigrant.* New York: Macmillan, 1921.

Pupin, Michael. *From Immigrant to Inventor.* New York: Charles Scribner's Sons, 1926.

Ravage, Marcus E. *An American in the Making: The Life Story of an Immigrant.* 1917. Reprint, New York: Dover, 1971.

Rønning. N. N. *Fifty Years in America.* Minneapolis: Friends, 1938.

Saloutos, Theodore. *They Remember America: The Story of the Repatriated Greek-Americans.* Berkeley and Los Angeles: University of California Press, 1956.

Stave, Bruce M., and John F. Sutherland, eds. *From the Old Country: An Oral History of European Migration to America.* With Aldo Salerno. New York: Twayne, 1994.

Steiner, Edward A. *From Alien to Citizen: The Story of My Life in America.* New York: Revell, 1914.

———. *On the Trail of the Immigrant.* New York: Revell, 1906.

Thomas, William I., and Florian Znaniecki. *The Polish Peasant in Europe and America.* 2 vols. New York: Knopf, 1927.

Virtanen, Keijo. *The Finns in the United States: The Project on Finnish Immigration of the Michigan Historical Collections.* Michigan Historical Collections, Bentley Historical Library. Bulletin no. 26. Ann Arbor: University of Michigan, 1976.

Vlček, František. *The Story of My Life.* Trans. ed. by Winston Chrislock. Kent, OH: Kent State University Press, 2004.

Zempel, Solveig, ed. and trans. *In Their Own Words: Letters from Norwegian Immigrants.* Minneapolis: University of Minnesota Press, 1991.

BIOGRAPHIES AND NOVELS

Bell, Thomas. *Out of This Furnace.* 1941. Reprint, Pittsburgh: University of Pittsburgh Press, 1976.

Bojer, Johan. *The Emigrants.* Trans. A. G. Jayne. New York: Century, 1925.

Cahan, Abraham. *The Rise of David Levinsky.* New York: Harper, 1917.

Cather, Willa. *My Antonia.* Boston: Houghton Mifflin, 1918.

———. *O Pioneers!* Boston: Houghton Mifflin, 1913.

Di Donato, Pietro. *Christ in Concrete.* Indianapolis: Bobbs-Merrill, 1937.

Jorgenson, Theodore, and Nora O. Solum. *Ole Edvart Rölvaag: A Biography.* New York: Harper, 1939.

Oakes, Vanya. *Footprints of the Dragon: A Story of the Chinese and the Pacific Railways.* Philadelphia: Winston, 1949.

Rockswold, E. Palmer. *Per: Immigrant and Pioneer.* Staples, MN: Adventure, 1981.

Rölvaag. O. E. *Giants in the Earth.* New York: Harper, 1927.

Yezierska, Anzia. *Bread Givers.* 1925. Reprinted with forward by Alice Kessler-Harris. New York: Persea Books, 1999.

INDIVIDUAL IMMIGRANT GROUPS, GENERAL HISTORIES, AND CONTEMPORARY STUDIES

Addams, Jane. *Twenty Years at Hull-House.* New York: Macmillan, 1911.

Alexander, June Granatir. *Ethnic Pride American Patriotism: Slovaks and Other New Immigrants in the Interwar Era.* Philadelphia: Temple University Press, 2004.

———. *The Immigrant Church and Community: Pittsburgh's Slovak Catholics and Lutherans, 1880–1915.* Pittsburgh: University of Pittsburgh Press, 1987.

Anderson, Philip J., and Dag Blanck, eds. *Swedes in the Twin Cities: Immigrant Life and Minnesota's Urban Frontier.* Saint Paul: Minnesota Historical Society, 2001.

Azuma, Eiichiro. *Between Two Empires: Race, History, and Transnationalism in Japanese America.* New York: Oxford University Press, 2005.

Balch, Emily Greene. *Our Slavic Fellow Citizens.* 1910. Reprint, New York: Arno, 1969.

Barrett, James R. *Work and Community in the Jungle: Chicago's Packinghouse Workers, 1894–1922.* Urbana: University of Illinois Press, 1987.

Barton, Josef J. *Peasants and Strangers: Italians, Rumanians, and Slovaks in an American City, 1890–1950.* Cambridge, MA: Harvard University Press, 1975.

Bodnar, John. *Immigration and Industrialization: Ethnicity in an American Mill Town, 1870–1940.* Pittsburgh: University of Pittsburgh Press, 1977.

Bodnar, John, Roger Simon, and Michael P. Weber. *Lives of Their Own: Blacks, Italians, and Poles in Pittsburgh, 1900–1960.* Urbana: University of Illinois Press, 1982.

Boris, Eileen, and Cynthia R. Daniels, eds. *Homework: Historical and Contemporary Perspectives on Paid Labor at Home.* Urbana: University of Illinois Press, 1989.

Brault, Gerald J. *The French-Canadian Heritage in New England.* Hanover, NH: University Press of New England, 1986.

Breckinridge, Sophonisba P. *New Homes for Old.* 1921. Reprint, Montclair, NJ: Patterson Smith, 1971.

Briggs, John W. *An Italian Passage: Immigrants to Three American Cities, 1890–1930.* New Haven, CT: Yale University Press, 1978.

Brody, David. *Steelworkers in America: The Nonunion Era.* 1960. Reprint, New York: Harper and Row, 1969.

Brøndal, Jørn. *Ethnic Leadership and Midwestern Politics: Scandinavian-Americans and the Progressive Movement in Wisconsin, 1890–1914.* Northfield, MN: Norwegian-American Historical Association, 2004.

Bukowczyk, John J. *And My Children Did Not Know Me: A History of the Polish-Americans.* Bloomington: Indiana University Press, 1987.

———. "Mary the Messiah: Polish Immigrant Heresy and the Malleable Ideology of the Roman Catholic Church, 1880–1930." *Journal of American Ethnic History* 4, no. 2 (Spring 1985): 5–32.

Butler, Elizabeth Beardsley. *Women and the Trades: Pittsburgh, 1907–1908.* 1909. Reprint, New York: Arno, 1969.

Byington, Margaret. *Homestead: The Households of a Mill Town.* 1910. Reprint, Pittsburgh: University Center for International Studies, University of Pittsburgh, 1974.

Camarillo, Albert. *Chicanos in a Changing Society: From Mexican Pueblos to American Barrios in Santa Barbara and Southern California, 1848–1930.* 1979. Reprinted with new foreword by John Chávez and afterword by the author. Dallas: Southern Methodist University Press, 2005.

Caroli, Betty Boyd. *Italian Repatriation from the United States, 1900–1914.* New York: Center for Migration Studies, 1973.

Caroli, Betty Boyd, and Thomas Kessner. "New Immigrant Women at Work: Italians and Jews in New York City, 1880–1905." *Journal of Ethnic Studies* 5, no. 4 (Winter 1978): 19–31.

Chan, Sucheng. *Asian Americans: An Interpretive History.* Boston: Twayne, 1991.

———. *This Bittersweet Soil: The Chinese in California Agriculture, 1860–1910.* Berkeley and Los Angeles: University of California Press, 1986.

Chudacoff, Howard P. *Mobile Americans: Residential and Social Mobility in Omaha, 1880–1920.* New York: Oxford University Press, 1972.

Cinel, Dino. *From Italy to San Francisco: The Immigrant Experience.* Stanford, CA: Stanford University Press, 1982.

Cole, David. *Immigrant City: Lawrence, Massachusetts, 1845–1921.* Chapel Hill: University of North Carolina Press, 1963.

Daniels, John. *America via the Neighborhood.* 1920. Reprint, Montclair, NJ: Patterson Smith, 1971.

Daniels, Roger. *Asian Americans: Chinese and Japanese in the United States since 1850.* Seattle: University of Washington Press, 1988.

David, Jerome. *The Russian Immigrant.* New York: Macmillan, 1922.

Davis, Michael M. Jr. *Immigrant Health and Community.* 1921. Reprint, Montclair, NJ: Patterson Smith, 1971.

Dolan, Jay. *The American Catholic Experience: A History from Colonial Times to the Present.* Garden City, NY: Doubleday, 1985.

———. "Immigrants and Their Gods: A New Perspective in American Religious History." *Church History* 57, no. 1 (March 1988): 61–72.

Early, Frances H. "The French-Canadian Family Economy and Standard of Living in Lowell, Massachusetts, 1870." *Journal of Family History* 7, no. 2 (Summer 1982): 180–99.

Eastman, Crystal. *Work Accidents and the Law.* 1910. Reprint, New York: Arno, 1969.

Echeverria, Jeronima. *Home Away from Home: A History of Basque Boardinghouses.* Reno: University of Nevada Press, 1999.

Ehrlich, Richard D., ed. *Immigrants in Industrial America, 1850–1920.* Charlottesville: University Press of Virginia, 1977.

Emmons, David. *The Butte Irish: Class and Ethnicity in an American Mining Town, 1875–1925.* Urbana: University of Illinois Press, 1989.

Erickson, Charlotte. *American Industry and the European Immigrant, 1860–1885.* New York: Russel and Russel, 1967.

Ewen, Elizabeth. "City Lights: Immigrant Women and the Rise of the Movies." *Signs* 5, no. 3 (Spring 1980): S45–S66.

———. *Immigrant Women in the Land of Dollars: Life and Culture on the Lower East Side, 1890–1925.* New York: Monthly Review Press, 1985.

Fitch, John A. *The Steel Workers.* 1911. Reprint, New York: Arno, 1969.

Foerster, Robert F. *The Italian Emigration of Our Times.* Cambridge, MA: Harvard University Press, 1924.

Ford, Nancy Gentile. *Americans All! Foreign-born Soldiers in World War I.* College Station: Texas A&M University, 2001.

Frisch, Michael H., and Daniel J. Walkowitz, eds. *Working-Class America: Essays on Labor, Community, and American Society.* Urbana: University of Illinois Press, 1983.

Gabaccia, Donna R. *From the Other Side: Women, Gender, and Immigrant Life in the U.S., 1820–1990.* Bloomington: Indiana University Press, 1994.

———. *From Sicily to Elizabeth Street: Housing and Social Change Among Italian Immigrants, 1880–1930.* Albany: State University of New York Press, 1984.

García, Mario T. *Desert Immigrants: The Mexicans of El Paso, 1880–1920.* New Haven, CT: Yale University Press, 1981.

Gerson, Louis L. *The Hyphenate in Recent American Politics and Diplomacy.* Lawrence: University of Kansas Press, 1964.

Gjerde, Jon. *From Peasants to Farmers: The Migration from Balestrand, Norway, to the Upper Middle West.* New York: Cambridge University Press, 1985.

———. *The Minds of the West: Ethnocultural Evolution in the Rural Middle West, 1830–1917.* Chapel Hill: University of North Carolina Press, 1997.

Golab, Caroline. *Immigrant Destinations.* Philadelphia: Temple University Press, 1977.

Greene, Victor R. *For God and Country: The Rise of Polish and Lithuanian Ethnic Consciousness in America.* Madison: State Historical Society of Wisconsin, 1975.

———. *A Singing Ambivalence: American Immigrants between Old World and New, 1830–1930.* Kent, OH: Kent State University Press, 2004.

———. *The Slavic Community on Strike: Immigrant Labor in Pennsylvania Anthracite.* Notre Dame, IN: University of Notre Dame Press, 1968.

Guerin-Gonzales, Camille. *Mexican Workers and American Dreams: Immigration, Repatriation, and California Farm Labor, 1900–1939.* New Brunswick, NJ: Rutgers University Press, 1994.

Gurock, Jeffrey S. *When Harlem was Jewish, 1870–1930.* New York: Columbia University Press, 1979.

Halter, Marilyn. *Between Race and Ethnicity: Cape Verdean American Immigrants, 1860–1965.* Urbana: University of Illinois Press, 1993.

Hansen, Marcus. *The Mingling of the Canadian and American Peoples.* 1940. Reprint, New York: Arno, 1970.

Harney, Robert F. "Boarding and Belonging: Thoughts on Sojourner Institutions." *Urban History Review* no. 2, (October 1978): 8–38.

Hartman, Gary. *The Immigrant as Diplomat: Ethnicity, Nationalism, and the Shaping of Foreign Policy in the Lithuanian-American Community, 1870–1922.* Chicago: Lithuanian Research and Studies Center, 2002.

Hartmann, Edward George. *The Movement to Americanize the Immigrant.* 1948. Reprint, New York: AMS Press, 1967.

Helbich, Wolfgang, and Walter D. Kamphoefner. *German-American Immigration and Ethnicity in Comparative Perspective.* Madison: University of Wisconsin Press, 2004.

Higham, John. *Strangers in the Land: Patterns of American Nativism, 1860–1925.* 2nd ed. New Brunswick, NJ: Rutgers University Press, 1988.

Hoglund, A. William. *Finnish Immigrants in America, 1880–1920.* Madison: University of Wisconsin Press, 1960.

Holmquist, June Drenning, ed. *They Chose Minnesota: A Survey of the State's Ethnic Groups.* Saint Paul: Minnesota Historical Society, 1981.

Hudson, John C. "Migration to an American Frontier." *Annals of the Association of American Geographers* 66, no. 2 (June 1976): 242–65.

Hunter, Robert. *Poverty.* New York: Macmillan, 1904. Reprinted with an introduction by Peter d'A. Jones as *Poverty: Social Conscience in the Progressive Era.* New York: Harper and Row, 1965.

Hvidt, Kristian. *Danes Go West: A Book about the Emigration to America.* Copenhagen, Denmark: Rebild National Park Society, 1976.

Ichioka, Yuji. *The Issei: The World of the First Generation Japanese Immigrants, 1885–1924.* New York: Free Press, 1988.

Jablonsky, Thomas J. *Pride in the Jungle: Community and Everyday Life in Back of the Yards Chicago.* Baltimore: Johns Hopkins University Press, 1993.

Jordan, Terry G. *German Seed in Texas Soil: Immigrant Farmers in Nineteenth-Century Texas.* Austin: University of Texas Press, 1966.

Katzman, David M. *Seven Days a Week: Women and Domestic Service in Industrializing America.* New York: Oxford University Press, 1978.

Kellogg, Paul Underwood, ed. *The Pittsburgh District Civic Frontage.* 1914. Reprint, New York: Arno, 1974.

———, ed. *Wage-Earning Pittsburgh.* 1914. Reprint, New York: Arno, 1974.

Kleinberg, S. J. *The Shadow of the Mills: Working-Class Families in Pittsburgh, 1870–1907.* Pittsburgh: University of Pittsburgh Press, 1989.

Korman, Gerd. *Industrialization, Immigrants, and Americanizers: The View from Milwaukee, 1866–1921.* Madison: State Historical Society of Wisconsin, 1967.

Kraut, Alan M. *Silent Travelers: Germs, Genes, and the "Immigrant Menace."* Baltimore: Johns Hopkins University Press, 1994.

Lee, J. J., and Marion R. Casey, eds. *Making the Irish American: History and Heritage of the Irish in the United States.* New York: New York University Press, 2006.

Linkh, Richard M. *American Catholics and European Immigrants (1900–1924).* New York: Center for Migration Studies, 1975.

Loewen, Royden. *Hidden Worlds: Revisiting the Mennonite Migrants of the 1870s.* Winnipeg: University of Manitoba Press, 2001.

Lovoll, Odd S. *A Century of Urban Life: The Norwegians in Chicago before 1930.* N.p.: Norwegian-American Historical Association, 1988.

Luebke, Frederick C. *Bonds of Loyalty: German Americans and World War I.* De Kalb: Northern Illinois University Press, 1974

———, ed. *Ethnicity on the Great Plains.* Lincoln: University of Nebraska Press, 1980.

————, ed. *European Immigrants in the American West: Community Histories.* Albuquerque: University of New Mexico, Press 1998.

Manning, Caroline. *The Immigrant Woman and Her Job.* 1930. Reprint, New York: Arno, 1970.

McBee, Randy D. *Dance Hall Days: Intimacy and Leisure among Working-Class Immigrants in the United States.* New York: New York University Press, 2000.

McBride, Paul. *Culture Clash: Immigrants and Reformers, 1880–1920.* San Francisco: R and E Research Associates, 1975.

McClymer, John F. *War and Welfare: Social Engineering in America, 1890–1925.* Westport, CT: Greenwood Press, 1980.

McQuillan, D. Aidan. "The Mobility of Immigrants and Americans: A Comparison of Farmers on the Kansas Frontiers." *Agricultural History* 53 (July 1979): 576–96.

McWilliams, Carey. *Factories in the Field: The Story of Migratory Farm Labor in California.* Boston: Little, Brown, 1939.

Mesrobian, Arpena S. *"Like One Family"—The Armenians of Syracuse.* Ann Arbor, MI: Gomidas Institute, 2000.

Meyer, Stephen III. *The Five Dollar Day: Labor Management and Social Control in the Ford Motor Company, 1908–1921.* Albany: State University of New York Press, 1981.

Miller, Kerby. *Emigrants and Exiles: Ireland and the Irish Exodus to North America.* New York: Oxford University Press, 1985.

Miller, Randall M., and Thomas D. Marzik, eds. *Immigrants and Religion in Urban America.* Philadelphia: Temple University Press, 1977.

Miller, Sally M., ed. *The Ethnic Press in the United States: A Historical Analysis and Handbook.* Westport, CT: Greenwood Press, 1987.

Mirak, Robert. *Torn Between Two Lands: Armenians in America 1890 to World War I.* Cambridge, MA: Harvard University Press, 1983.

Mohl, Raymond. "Black Immigrants: Bahamians in Early Twentieth-Century Miami." *Florida Historical Quarterly* 65 (January 1987): 271–97.

Morawska, Ewa. *For Bread with Butter: Life-worlds of East Central Europeans in Johnstown, Pennsylvania, 1890–1940.* New York: Cambridge University Press, 1985.

Mormino, Gary R., and George E. Pozzetta. *The Immigrant World of Ybor City: Italians and Their Latin Neighbors in Tampa, 1885–1985.* Urbana: University of Illinois Press, 1987.

Murray, Robert K. *Red Scare: A Study of National Hysteria, 1919–1920.* 1955. Reprint, New York: McGraw-Hill, 1964.

Naff, Alixa. *Becoming American: The Early Arab Immigrant Experience.* Carbondale: Southern Illinois University Press, 1985.

————. "Belief in the Evil Eye among the Christian Syrian-Lebanese in America." *Journal of American Folklore* 78, no. 307 (January–March 1965): 46–51.

Nelli, Humbert S. *The Italians in Chicago, 1880–1930: A Study in Ethnic Mobility.* New York: Oxford University Press, 1970.

O'Grady, Joseph P., ed. *The Immigrants' Influence on Wilson's Peace Policies.* Lexington: University of Kentucky Press, 1967.

Orsi, Robert. *The Madonna of 115th Street: Faith and Community in Italian Harlem, 1880–1950.* New Haven, CT: Yale University Press, 1985.

Ostergren, Robert C. *A Community Transplanted: The Trans-Atlantic Experience of a Swedish Immigrant Settlement in the Upper Middle West, 1835–1915.* Madison: University of Wisconsin Press, 1988.

———. "Land and Family in Rural Immigrant Communities." *Annals of the Association of American Geographers* 71, no. 3 (September 1981): 400–11.

Pacyga, Dominic. *Polish Immigrants and Industrial Chicago: Workers on the South Side, 1880–1922.* 1991. Reprinted with new introduction. Chicago: University of Chicago Press, 2003.

Papanikolas, Helen. *An Amulet of Greek Earth: Generations of Immigrant Folk Culture.* Athens, OH: Swallow Press, 2002.

Park, Robert E. *The Immigrant Press and Its Control.* 1922. Reprint, Westport, CT: Greenwood Press, 1970.

Peffer, George Anthony. *If They Don't Bring Their Women Here: Chinese Female Immigration Before Exclusion.* Champaign: University of Illinois Press, 1999.

Philpott, Thomas Lee. *The Slum and the Ghetto: Neighborhood Deterioration and Middle-Class Reform, Chicago, 1880–1930.* New York: Oxford University Press, 1978.

Reid, Ira. *The Negro Immigrant: His Background, Characteristics and Social Adjustment, 1899–1937.* New York: Columbia University Press, 1939.

Rice, John G. "The Role of Culture and Community in Frontier Prairie Farming." *Journal of Historical Geography* 3, no. 2 (April 1977): 155–75.

Riis, Jacob. *How the Other Half Lives.* 1890. Reprinted with a new preface by Charles A. Madison and 100 photographs from the Jacob A. Riis Collection, Museum of the City of New York. New York: Dover, 1971.

Rischin, Moses. *The Promised City: New York's Jews, 1870–1914.* Cambridge, MA: Harvard University Press, 1962.

Roberts, Peter. *Anthracite Coal Communities: A Study of the Demography, the Social, Educational and Moral Life of the Anthracite Regions.* 1904. Reprint, New York: Arno, 1970.

———. *The New Immigration: A Study of the Industrial and Social Life of Southeastern Europeans in America.* New York: Macmillan, 1912.

Rolle, Andrew F. *The Immigrant Upraised: Italian Adventurers and Colonists in an Expanding America.* Norman: University of Oklahoma Press, 1968.

Saloutos, Theodore. *The Greeks in the United States.* Cambridge, MA: Harvard University Press, 1964.

———. "The Immigrant Contribution to American Agriculture." *Agricultural History* 50 (January 1976): 45–67.

———. "The Immigrant in Pacific Coast Agriculture." *Agricultural History* 49 (January 1975): 182–201.

Sánchez, George J. *Becoming Mexican American: Ethnicity, Culture and Identity in Chicano Los Angeles, 1900–1945.* New York: Oxford University Press, 1993.

Seller, Maxine, ed. *Ethnic Theatre in the United States.* Westport, CT: Greenwood Press, 1983.

Soyer, Daniel. *Jewish Immigrant Associations and American Identity in New York, 1880–1939.* Cambridge, MA: Harvard University Press, 1997.

Speek, Peter A. *A Stake in the Land.* 1921. Reprint, Montclair, NJ: Patterson Smith, 1971.

Stein, Leon. *The Triangle Fire.* Philadelphia: Lippincott, 1962.

Sterba, Christopher M. *Good Americans: Italian and Jewish Immigrants during the First World War.* New York: Oxford University Press, 2003.

Street, Richard Steven. *Beasts of the Field: A Narrative History of California Farmworkers, 1769–1913.* Stanford, CA: Stanford University Press, 2004.

Swierenga, Robert P. *Faith and Family: Dutch Immigration and Settlement in the United States, 1820–1920.* New York: Holmes and Meier, 2000.

Taylor, Robert M., and Connie A. McBirney, eds. *Peopling of Indiana: The Ethnic Experience.* Indianapolis: Indiana Historical Society, 1996.

Thompson, Frank V. *Schooling of the Immigrant.* 1920. Reprint, Montclair, NJ: Patterson Smith, 1971.

Vázonsyi, Andrew. "The Cicisebo and the Magnificent Cuckold: Boardinghouse Life and Lore in Immigrant Communities." *Journal of American Folklore* 91, no. 360 (April–June 1978): 641–56.

Vecchio, Diane C. *Merchants, Midwives, and Laboring Women: Italian Migrants in Urban America.* Urbana: University of Illinois Press, 2006.

Vecoli, Rudolph J., ed. *Italian Immigrants in Rural and Small Town America.* New York: American Italian Historical Association, 1987.

———. "Peasants and Prelates: Italian Immigrants and the Catholic Church." *Journal of Social History* 2 (Spring 1969): 215–68.

Wald, Lillian D. *The House on Henry Street.* 1915. Reprint, New York: Dover, 1971.

Ward, David. *Cities and Immigrants: A Geography of Change in Nineteenth-Century America.* New York: Oxford University Press, 1971.

———. *Poverty, Ethnicity, and the American City, 1840–1925: Changing Conceptions of the Slum and the Ghetto.* New York: Cambridge University Press, 1989.

Weiss, Bernard, ed. *American Education and the European Immigrant: 1840–1940.* Urbana: University of Illinois Press, 1982.

Wong, Marie Rose. *Sweet Cakes, Long Journey: The Chinatowns of Portland, Oregon.* Seattle: University of Washington Press, 2004.

Worrall, Janet, Carol Bonomo Albright, and Elvira G. Di Fabio, eds. *Italian Immigrants Go West: The Impact of Locale on Ethnicity.* Cambridge, MA: American Italian Historical Association, 2003.

Wyman, Mark. *Round-Trip America: The Immigrants Return to Europe, 1880–1930.* Ithaca, NY: Cornell University Press, 1993.

Yans-McLaughlin, Virginia. *Family and Community: Italian Immigrants in Buffalo, 1880–1930.* Ithaca, NY: Cornell University Press, 1977.

WEB SITES

General Immigration History

Digital History. "Recommended Websites Ordered by Time Period." http://www.digitalhistory.uh.edu/historyonline/annot_links_list.cfm

University of Minnesota. History Department. U.S. History Internet Sources. "Immigration & Ethnicity." http://www.hist.umn.edu/~hist20c/internet/immigration.htm

Library of Congress. American Memory: The Learning Page. "Immigration." http://lcweb2.loc.gov/ammem/ndlpedu/features/immig/introduction.html

National Park Service. "Ellis Island." http://www.nps.gov/elis/

Angel Island Immigration Station Foundation. "Immigration Station History." http://www.aiisf.org/history

Documents and Databases

Gibson, Campbell J., and Emily Lennon. "Historical Census Statistics on the Foreign-Born Population of the United States: 1850–1990." http://www. census.gov/population/www/documentation/twps0029/twps0029.html

National Archives. "Immigration Records (Ship Passenger Arrival Records)" http://www.archives.gov/genealogy/immigration/

National Archives. "Naturalization Records" http://www.archives.gov/ genealogy/naturalization/

Statue of Liberty—Ellis Island Foundation, Inc. http://www.ellisis land.org/

University of Minnesota. Immigration History Research Center. http:// www.ihrc.umn.edu/

Online Exhibits and Educational Sites

History Channel. "Ellis Island/" http://www.history.com/minisites/ellisis land/

Kheel Center, Catherwood Library, ILR School at Cornell University. "Triangle Factory Fire." http://www.ilr.cornell.edu/trianglefire/

Lower East Side Tenement Museum. http://www.tenement.org/

DOCUMENTARY FILMS

Carved in Silence (1987, Felicia Lowe Productions).
Chinatown (1996, Neighborhoods—Hidden Cities of San Francisco series).
Free Voice of Labor: The Jewish Anarchists (1980, Pacific Street Film Project).
Heaven Will Protect the Working Girl (1993, American Social History Film Project).
Italians in America (1998, History Channel).
Journey to America (1989, Charles Guggenheim Productions).

Index

About the Author

JUNE GRANATIR ALEXANDER is on the faculty of the Russian and East European Studies Program at the University of Cincinnati. She is the author of *Ethnic Pride, American Patriotism: Slovaks and Other New Immigrants in the Interwar Era* (2004) and *The Immigrant Church and Community: Pittsburgh's Slovak Catholics and Lutherans, 1880-1915.*

DATE DUE

FOLLETT